The Sixth Form
and its Alternatives

Judy Dean
Kath Bradley
Bruce Choppin
Denis Vincent

NFER Publishing Company

Published by the NFER Publishing Company Ltd.,
Darville House, 2 Oxford Road East,
Windsor, Berks. SL4 1DF
Registered Office: The Mere, Upton Park, Slough, Berks SL1 2DQ
First published 1979
© NFER 1979
ISBN 0 85633 182 1

Typeset in 11 on 12pt Baskerville by
Jubal Multiwrite Ltd, 66 Loampit Vale, London SE13 7SN
Printed and bound in Great Britain by Staples Printers Rochester Limited at
The Stanhope Press

Contents

Preface

This book forms the final report of a study of different forms of educational provision for students over the age of 16. It is the result of an NFER-funded research project carried out between 1974 and 1978.

The issues raised in the report are the subject of considerable current debate. The authors hope that the evidence presented here will be of assistance and interest to those involved at all levels in the education of 16—19-year-olds.

This report would not have been possible without the active co-operation of a great many people. We would like to take this opportunity to thank the staff of the schools and colleges which took part in the project for allowing us into their premises and for giving up their time to talk to us. We are very conscious of the pressure under which teachers and lecturers work and of the added burden imposed by participation in a research project. Nevertheless, our many requests for information were met with unfailing willingness and courtesy. We are also very grateful to the students whose progress through the sixth form or college we followed, and whose lively and often entertaining accounts of their experiences illuminate the following pages.

We would also like to acknowledge the contribution made by Lea Orr to the early stages of the project, particularly her part in its planning and initiation.

Finally, our thanks go to Dianne Horton and Lorna Ormond for their help in so many different aspects of the project's activities, not least the production of the final typescript.

Chapter 1

Background

a. Types of provision made for students in 16—19 education

Until comparatively recently the pattern of full-time education for pupils over the school-leaving age was clearly defined, both in terms of the institutions providing for it and in the courses available. Just as the 1944 Education Act embodied the view that pupils in secondary education fell into distinct groups which could be catered for in very different types of school, so this differentiation was reflected in the provision made for those over the school-leaving age. Under the selective system, the major part of post-compulsory education was undertaken by the grammar school sixth forms and the colleges of further education, the former concentrating on the provision of A-level courses primarily for pupils aiming at higher education, and the latter, on technical and vocational courses.

The traditional sixth form was held in high esteem as the setting in which love of academic learning and a sense of responsibility towards oneself and others would be nurtured and skills of leadership would be developed. In the sixth form, pupils would begin to take some part in the running of the school, and its discipline and morale would be to some extent in their hands. At the same time they would be free to arrange their own work schedules and a large proportion of their timetable devoted to private study in which they would develop the skills required in higher education. It is indicative of the grammar school sixth form's highly selective and academic nature that pupils not passing the required number of O-levels deemed necessary for A-level work were, and still are in many cases, excluded from it.

The colleges of further education, on the other hand, were in most areas the only providers of vocational and technical education, from craft courses in the skilled trades, through technician-level courses to those leading to membership of professional bodies. While the emphasis in some colleges on certain subjects reflected the needs of industry in their area, the majority offered a wide range of courses at a variety of levels.

For pupils wishing to further their education beyond the school-leaving age, the progression was therefore either from grammar schools via the sixth form to higher education or from secondary modern or technical schools to colleges of further education. The majority of pupils had embarked on the academic or the vocational path by the age of 11. A few individuals were able to make the transition from one path to the other; for example, very able secondary modern pupils sometimes entered the sixth form of the local grammar school at 16, and some grammar school pupils who were not entirely committed to higher education became aware of opportunities provided by further education and moved accordingly; but such transfers were always the exception.

A number of factors in the 'sixties and early 'seventies which led to an expansion and diversification of post-compulsory education resulted in the blurring and, in some areas, complete removal of this demarcation between the schools and further education sectors. Not only was there a rise in the birth rate, reaching a peak in 1964, but there was also a steady increase in the proportion of young people wishing to stay on beyond the school-leaving age. A general rise in the standard of living meant that their children's continued education entailed less financial sacrifice for most families. The demands of an increasingly complex industrialized society and the recognition by school leavers of the value of educational qualifications in the job market played their part in this expansion. The widescale introduction of the Certificate of Secondary Education also contributed to an increase in the demand for continued education on the part of less academic pupils.

Figure 1.1 shows that from 1960 to 1973 there was a steady increase in the proportion of 17-year-olds in maintained schools and this has only recently levelled off at approximately 18 per cent of the age group.

A further development which has caused local authorities to review their provision for 16+ students is the growing tendency for young people to question the authoritarian aspects of school life. A Schools Council study published in 1970[1] found that pupils in all types of school considered 'too many restrictions, regulations, not enough freedom, privileges' to be the least satisfactory aspect of their sixth-form experience. Evidence of this dissatisfaction was shown in the growing number of students during the late 1960s transferring to courses in colleges of further education which were in many cases available in their own schools, particularly A-level courses. Further education has always been sensitive to the needs of its clientele, and, as demand arises for a particular course, responds accordingly. Such was the case with GCE A-level for which there were already a number of potential candidates not adequately catered for by the secondary school system. Many of the colleges' intake on these courses was from schools which did not have sixth forms or schools where the sixth form was not able to offer unusual choices of subjects or combinations of subjects. Others were mature students for whom a return to school was not possible. But a significant proportion, particularly from grammar and independent schools, made this transition because they found the school atmosphere frustrating.

The changeover to non-selective secondary education meant that most local education authorities had cause to review their provision for sixth-form and further education in the light of these developments. Difficult decisions had to be made. If every comprehensive school created by reorganization were to develop its own sixth form, either the resulting sixth forms would be small and find it hard to offer a suitable range of options or the schools would need an intake sufficiently large to support a viable sixth form. Although the pattern of large all-through schools was introduced in many

The Sixth Form and its alternatives

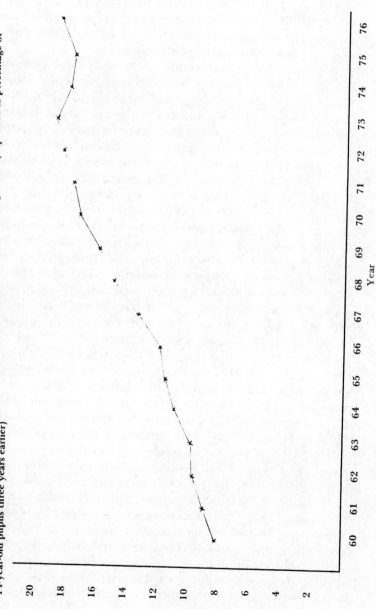

Figure 1.1 Percentage of pupils in maintained schools remaining at school until the age of 17 (expressed as percentage of 14-year-old pupils three years earlier)

Source: DES Statistics of Education 1976 1 Table 10

of the early comprehensive schemes, more recent plans have tended to consider alternative solutions. Many authorities regarded the formation of very large schools as undesirable — not only because they foresaw possible educational and administrative problems, but existing school buildings seldom fitted in with a scheme of amalgamation.

The pattern of comprehensive reorganization implemented was therefore very much affected by considerations concerning the provision of sixth-form education. Policy makers had to take into account the availability and best use of existing resources, the likely demand for post-compulsory education following the rise and subsequent fall in the birth rate, the effect on pupils and teachers of systems of reorganization entailing a change of institution and the increasing demand on the part of sixth formers for an 'adult environment'. It is one of the unique features of the British educational system that local authorities are at liberty to introduce whatever system best suits the needs of their locality, and it is this autonomy which has resulted in the diversity of secondary and post-secondary establishments now in existence. Figures 1.2—1.6 illustrate in diagrammatic form the post-compulsory options available both in the schools and further education sectors within the different systems, and there follows a brief account of each of these. Readers with an interest in the history of developments in this area, particularly the growth of separate institutions for the 16—19 age group, are referred to *Educational Provision 16—19*[2], a critical review of the relevant literature. Detailed descriptions of individual examples of the different types of institution catering for this age group are contained in King's *School and College: Studies of Post-Sixteen Education*.[3]

i. *Selective secondary system*

The pattern of post-compulsory education under a selective secondary system has already been outlined. Although the number of grammar schools is slowly declining as more authorities become comprehensive, schools of this type will no doubt continue to play a significant role in the education of the 16—19 age group for several years. In 1977 more than half of the 108 local education authorities in England and

Figure 1.2 Selective secondary system

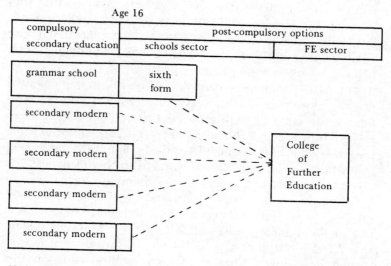

Note: *Under the selective system, some secondary modern schools may develop their own small sixth forms*

Figure 1.3 All-through comprehensive system

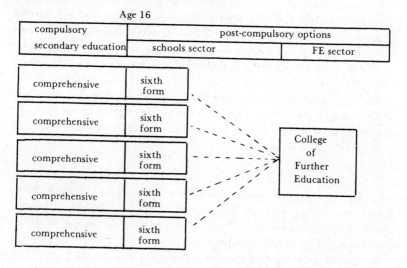

Figure 1.4 Sixth form centre

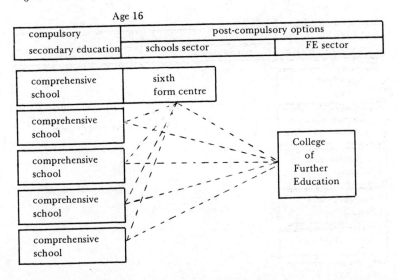

Figure 1.5 Sixth form college

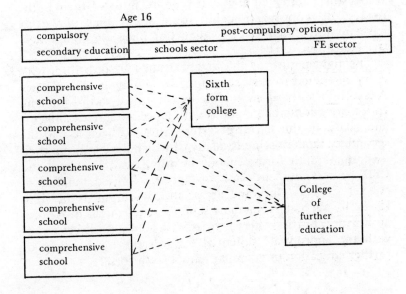

Figure 1.6 Tertiary College

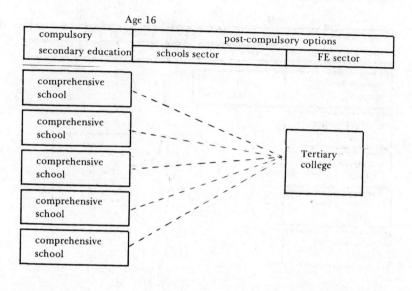

Wales still maintained grammar schools, most of them in the process of reorganization, but some at the time of writing have no firm intentions of submitting plans for comprehensive education.

The rigid nature of the highly academic sixth form with entry restricted to very able students aiming at two or three A-levels does not allow for the expansion of sixth-form education to accommodate pupils with more modest attainments and goals. In the selective system, this has been left to the secondary modern schools, many of which have built up their own small sixth forms, mainly in order to offer O-level and CSE courses but in some instances a limited number of A-level subjects. In some areas, the development of sixth forms by secondary modern schools is encouraged by local authorities, but in others it is official policy to direct pupils with the appropriate potential towards the local college of further education or grammar school sixth form.

ii. *All-through comprehensive schools and consortia*

This category covers schemes in which each comprehensive secondary school in a given area has its own integral sixth form. For the purpose of this report it applies both to systems in which pupils transfer at the age of 11 or 12 and to those where middle schools exist and transfer takes place at age 13 or 14. These schemes were the kind most commonly introduced in the early days of comprehensive education, and might have become the standard pattern had not the educational and economic factors previously mentioned grown in importance. It is clear that some authorities which originally introduced a comprehensive system of this kind are now, because of the falling birthrate and financial stringencies, considering a *second* phase of reorganization, and seeking to rationalize their sixth-form provision in some way.

There is strong opposition in some areas to the separation of the sixth form from lower forms and the concentration of 16—19 year old students in a college. Schemes have been suggested, and in some cases implemented, which make economies in sixth-form education without the loss of sixth forms on the part of the schools. Some groups of schools have attempted to co-ordinate their A-level provision in order to avoid very small teaching groups in minority subjects and, rather than each school offering an A-level subject for which there is relatively little demand, have agreed that only one school in the group should offer it.

Sixth-formers in schools which are members of a consortium of this type travel to another school in order to attend classes in an A-level subject not available in their own sixth form. The geographical distribution of the schools involved is therefore crucial, and it is likely that such schemes can only work effectively in urban areas. The consortium approach also requires the member schools to co-ordinate their timetables. Reluctance to do so on the part of some heads may also prove a stumbling block in introducing a scheme of this nature.

Other authorities who support the principle of the all-through school but wish to avoid very small A-level groups have set up centres which pupils and teachers attend for part of the week for sixth-form courses in subjects for which their school is unable to form a viable class. Such a centre is in operation in the Tower Hamlets division of the ILEA. Its co-ordinator of studies sets out the case for this solution to the problems caused by small sixth-form groups[4].

> A Centre, unlike a sixth form college, allows the school to retain sixth-form pupils on the school roll. It enables the school to continue the pastoral care developed during the first five years of the secondary school including careers guidance. Many young people prefer to stay in the school that they know and venture out of it for other courses for part of the time. This enables them to meet other students for intellectual stimulus and broadening of interests while retaining links with their own school which can be of benefit to both pupils and the school.
>
> A centre does not have any permanent teaching staff. It depends upon the willingness of teachers in the contributory schools to teach their subject to A-level for part of the week at the centre and to complete their teaching time in their own school.

Yet another type of rationalization which has been suggested is that schools should develop specialist sixth forms. All schools in a group would offer the most popular subjects but one school would specialize in modern languages, another in craft subjects and so on. Pupils at 16 would then enter the sixth form which offered subjects most appropriate to their requirements. In this way, minority subjects would be kept alive, classes would be of an economic size, yet no school would lose its sixth form.[5]

iii. *Sixth-form centres*

A number of local authorities which, for one reason· or another, decided against the introduction of 11—18 comprehensive schools have implemented instead systems in which only a minority of schools have sixth forms. The remainder cater for pupils up to the age of 16 and those wishing to continue their education transfer to a school with a sixth form attached, the latter thereby fulfilling the function of a 'sixth-form centre'.

In most centres the students are housed in buildings separate from the lower school, sometimes in purpose-built sixth-form blocks with appropriate facilities. The sixth-form centre differs from the sixth-form college in that it is attached to a lower school, the headmaster is also responsible for younger pupils and the staff teach both in the centre and in the lower forms of the school. The situation for one group of pupils is therefore akin to that of an all-through school in that they will have the same teachers in the sixth form and, although they may be taught in a different building, it is probably adjacent to the lower school. Pupils from feeder schools in the group may be more likely to see transfer to the centre as moving to another school.

Under the selective system a number of grammar schools perform a similar function to that of a sixth-form centre by taking in pupils at 16 from surrounding secondary modern schools, and certainly, in many areas, the centres have developed from grammar schools, and secondary-modern schools have become the 11–16 feeders. Figures 1.2 and 1.4 show the similarity between this system and the selective system. No figures are available on the number of schools in the country involved in schemes of this type although it is recognized that they now play a significant role in the provision of sixth-form education. Authorities in which this type of provision now exists include Croydon, Wiltshire, Oxfordshire, Cambridgeshire, Doncaster, Surrey and Lancashire.

A system which has something in common with the sixth-form centre is that of the school–college co-operative ventures operating in different parts of Oxfordshire. Here the colleges of further education and local comprehensive-school sixth forms join together to form Centres of Advanced Studies, co-ordinating their timetables and the courses they offer. Booklets are distributed to fifth-year pupils which describe the courses available in all the institutions involved. In this way, unnecessary duplication of courses is avoided and pupils can make an informed choice. A number of authorities other than Oxfordshire have instituted similar schemes. However, the principal of a college of FE has recently described how the Centre of which his college forms a part has developed and lost sight of its original objectives, and he now has serious doubts about the success of the scheme[6].

iv. *Sixth-form colleges*

Where sixth-form colleges exist, secondary comprehensive schools cater for pupils up to the age of 16 (see Figure 1.5). A sixth-form college then provides full-time courses, mainly at A-level but also O-level and CSE, for students aged 16–19. The college is self-contained, it has its own principal and administrative staff and teachers are exclusively engaged in sixth-form work.

The sixth-form college has attracted an increasing amount of attention since the introduction of the first institutions of this type in the mid-'60s. There are now about 90 in England and Wales, and their numbers increase annually.

With very few exceptions, the sixth-form colleges are 'open-entry' and do not insist that applicants reach a certain level of examination attainment before being admitted. They are therefore willing to cater for students who wish to continue their education but who are not qualified for A-level work, and a significant proportion of the students in colleges of this sort are studying for O-level and CSE examinations. However, because they are run under school regulations, the sixth-form colleges are prevented from offering a number of vocational courses, such as those leading to Ordinary National Diploma and Certificates and certain of the examinations of the City and Guilds of London Institute; these remain the province of further education.

v. *Tertiary colleges*

In all the systems so far considered, sixth-form provision co-exists, sometimes in close proximity, with a college of further education. While the latter provides all the part-time, vocational and technical education in the area, it may also have developed its own full-time A-level courses, in which case a student of 16 may be faced with a choice of two or more institutions all of which offer the A-level subjects he or she wishes to take.

This situation reflects the existence of the two sectors of

the education system — schools and FE. Although some authorities have attempted to co-ordinate and rationalize their provision and to consider post-compulsory education as a whole, in many cases the two sectors are in direct competition for students. This is not in the best interests of students, and often results in their making a wrong choice at 16 because of lack of information about the opportunities available.

The tertiary college overcomes these difficulties by concentrating all post-compulsory education in one institution run under FE regulations (Figure 1.6). All secondary education ends at 16 and students wishing to continue their education, whether on a full-time or part-time course, transfer to the college. There is no division between institutions offering academic and technical qualifications, and all are catered for under the same roof. At the time of writing there are 15 tertiary colleges in existence, and their numbers are likely to increase in the future.

b. **Current issues**

There is then a variety of patterns of educational provision for the 16—19 age group, much of it still on an experimental basis. We conclude this chapter by listing the issues raised by the range of current experiments, and examining some of the more detailed questions they contain.

i. *Continuity of educational experience*

A major question concerns the extent to which young people in the 16—19 age range require educational facilities which are distinct and separate from the rest of the secondary school. Several of the innovative patterns described earlier involve a break at age 16+ and a transfer between educational institutions for all or most of the students. Advantages for this transfer and the consequent 'fresh start' are claimed by some, although others feel it creates additional problems. Issues to be resolved concern the effects of a break in educational continuity on both older and younger pupils, and the implications of alternative organizational patterns for the teaching staff.

ii. *Freedom of choice and educational efficiency*

Students may choose not only which courses to take but also where to enrol. In many parts of the country school sixth forms operate in parallel with colleges of further education. The local education authority allows the 16—19 student to choose whether to stay within the school sector or to transfer to the college. Although each will offer some subjects that the other will not, both school and college run GCE courses in the major areas of interest. Elsewhere, although 16—19 provision is still divided between school and college, the local authority has intervened to prevent duplication. If the school offers, for example, A-level biology, the college does not, and vice versa. Under this system, by choosing the subjects he wishes to study or the type of course he wishes to follow the young person has essentially settled the question of which institution he is to attend. In other areas all 16—19 provision has been co-ordinated under the single roof of a tertiary college, and the youngster has virtually no choice at all as regards which institution he is to attend. To what extent is choice of institution a good thing? Is the wider range of courses offered by a tertiary college more advantageous than the opportunity to continue one's education within familiar school surroundings? To what extent do different students need a variety of learning environments? How expensive is the duplication of courses?

iii. *Sixth-form organization*

Here there are a number of issues. It has been argued that FE regulations offer a more appropriate structure than do school regulations for shaping the learning environment of the post-compulsory student. This may or may not be true, and it may or may not be important. Much recent discussion has centred on the need to avoid having very small sixth forms spread across the country. Within such sixth forms, offering a wide choice of subjects is seen to be uneconomic. On the other hand it is said that some sixth-form colleges are just too large, and that some students suffer from an inability to adjust to this. Must breadth of curriculum and overall size be so closely related? Again school sixth forms and many sixth-form colleges tend to cater for a relatively homogeneous group of able students, whereas a much greater variation in academic ability is found within the FE sector. Is further education providing the logical extension of the comprehensive principle to post-compulsory education? Is the greater mix of courses in further education socially and educationally desirable? An important task of 16—19 education is the preparation of young people for higher education or more usually for employment. How can this preparation be made effective? Which type of sixth-form structure yields the best results?

Clearly there are more questions than a single research study could hope to answer. These are, however, the issues we have had in mind, and where we have relevant evidence we report it. This is a time of considerable innovation as far as sixth-form education is concerned, and some attempt to explore the alternative patterns of provision in the context of these issues seems imperative.

Chapter 2

The Research Programme

a. The project

In 1973 different factors appeared to reinforce the need for a research programme in the area of 16—19 education. A rapid expansion of numbers of pupils in the sixth form that in a decade had raised the proportion of 17-year-olds remaining in school from 10 to 18 per cent appeared to have reached a plateau. The Robbins Report[7] had predicted a steady increase of only about 0.5 per cent each year but continuing through until about 1990. Up until 1971 the rate of expansion in the sixth form had actually been about three times that predicted, and this was reflected in the greater number of students being entered for the GCE Advanced-level examinations and subsequently qualifying for entry to higher education. Since 1971 there has hardly been a discernible increase in the school sector, although the number of full-time students on A-level courses in colleges of FE has been growing steadily.

There was also evidence to suggest that curricular patterns for the 16—19 age group were changing. The polytechnics, offering a substantial number of places on a wide range of degree courses as well as on courses for the Higher National Diploma, created more opportunities for the sixth-form student to proceed to higher education. Most subjects saw some expansion, but the principal work areas were the applied sciences followed a year or two later by the social sciences. Sixth-formers were becoming aware of these new opportunities and were beginning to plan their sixth-form courses with them in mind.

In addition to this, experiments were going on in various local authorities into different patterns of provision for the 16—19 age group. The main alternative patterns were set out in Chapter 1. Although these were mostly local initiatives some of them were on a fairly substantial scale involving literally thousands of post-16 students. By the beginning of 1974 a not inconsiderable number of 16- and 17-year-olds had been drawn into one or other pattern of provision that could be labelled experimental. Some evaluation of these alternative patterns was clearly needed.

The main aims of the research were therefore as follows:

1. To investigate, analyse and describe the aims behind the various patterns of 16—19 provision, particularly with respect to the educational experiences offered to the students.
2. To report on the methods being adopted to achieve these aims.
3. As far as possible, to arrive at some evaluation of the success of the various schemes.

To make progress toward the attainment of such a broad collection of aims, a number of different research methodologies was needed.

The major portion of the study consisted of following a cohort of young people through a period of post-compulsory education and on into employment or a higher education course. A sample of approximately 4,500 students aged 16+ was chosen from a full range of school sixth forms, colleges of FE, sixth-form colleges and tertiary colleges. A fuller description of the sample may be found in the next chapter, but here it may be noticed that initially all these were full-time students and the majority were beginning what was planned as a two-year course of study leading to a General Certificate of Education at Advanced-level. The data gathered and collated from these individuals during the course of the study came from questionnaires and interviews put to both the students and teaching staff, from group discussions, and from formal records such as examination results.

While the main part of the study concentrated on students enrolled on two-year GCE A-level courses, several related investigations were also carried out. One of these was a special examination of the provision made by the various institutions for 16-year-old students who wished to enrol for only one 'post-compulsory' year. The existence of this type of student for which the not very satisfactory phrase 'new sixth-former' was coined[8] is to some extent a reflection of changing attitudes to post-compulsory education in society at large, although it must be said that the recent shortage of opportunities in the job market for 16-year-olds was also a contributing factor. A report on this investigation of 'new sixth-formers' has already been published[9], and a further investigation which looks specifically at the content and level of the courses on offer to this group has been mounted by the NFER.

An examination of recent publications on post-compulsory education[2] concludes that the organizational pattern is the single most crucial issue. Whether to introduce a break at 16 or not is the major question to be answered, and it is clearly a major theme of the present study. But in order to set it in its proper context, another supplementary investigation was carried out, this time into 11—16 schools which had no sixth-form provision. Relevant data were gathered from a representative sample of fifth-form pupils and their teachers, and the results are discussed at some length in Chapter 10 of the present report.

The project's main activities were therefore as follows:

Preliminary phase
1973　　A national survey of local authority provision for 16—19 education in England and Wales[10]

Phase I
1974　　1. Questionnaire survey (S1) of 4,448 16-plus students commencing full-time courses in different types of school and college.
　　　　2. Questionnaire and background survey (I)

of the 45 institutions involved.

Phase II

1975   1. Critical review of literature on 16–19 education[2].

2. Follow-up of examination attainment and further destinations of 802 one-year students[9]

1976   1. Questionnaire survey of principals/head teachers/senior teachers dealing with aims and values of 16–19 education.

2. Second questionnaire survey (S2) of two-year students and one-year students who stayed on to do further courses.

3. Follow-up of examination attainment and further destinations of two-year students.

1977   1. Questionnaire survey (P5) of fifth-form pupils in all-through schools and 11–16 schools.

2. Questionnaire survey (T5) of heads and senior staff in 11–16 comprehensive schools and secondary modern schools.

3. Questionnaire survey (S3) of a sub-sample of two-year students during their first year of employment/higher education.

The source of data shown in the tables in this report is indicated by use of the questionnaire code given in brackets above, e.g. S1, S2, P5 etc.

b. **The criteria for evaluation**

During the early part of the project a considerable amount of time was devoted to trying to establish some criteria by which alternative sixth-form provisions could be judged. Through discussion with numerous individuals, and at a special one-day conference held at the NFER's premises in Slough in February 1974, we attempted to arrive at a consensus position regarding what would be evidence of successful and unsuccessful educational arrangements. We did not reach consensus. The range of experts consulted (educational philosopher; university lecturer; principal of tertiary college; principal of FE college; principal and career teacher from sixth-form college; head, deputy head, and sixth-form tutor from a grammar school and from a comprehensive school) could not be brought to agreement on a list of suitable criteria however short or long that list might be.

We felt nevertheless that it was essential to define at the outset the variables which would be used in our evaluation. The list we have worked with is given below. It represents at least a majority viewpoint expressed during our consultations.

i. *The quality of educational experiences offered*

There is no very direct way to measure this variable. We have attacked it through questionnaire, interview and discussion. In many cases students responding to questionnaires were able only to describe their own experiences, and had no basis for comparison with what occurred at other institutions. However some of our discussions which have brought together students from different types of provision have revealed startling differences in the way in which institutions approached their educational task. These matters are taken up in Chapter 6.

ii. *Academic success*

This is measured in a conventional way by means of passes achieved and grades awarded on public examinations. Direct comparison is a little difficult because different institutions adopt different policies with regard to the entering of students. Nevertheless we feel we have made sufficient sense of the data to report some conclusions, and they are to be found in Chapter 7.

iii. *The attraction of pupils to post-compulsory education*

Here we have tried to assess the proportion of young people staying on within the educational system after passing the age of 16. It should be noted that although some of the experts we consulted felt that more students should be encouraged to stay on and extend their secondary education, a substantial minority felt that already too many young people were staying within the educational system — many enrolled in irrelevant or inappropriate courses. Direct comparisons are in any case rather difficult because of local variations with regard to a tradition of post-compulsory education. Local employment difficulties also distort the picture, and some young people return to school just to give them a base from which to look for a job. Data related to this and to staying on rates in general are presented in Chapter 4.

iv. *The effects on younger pupils*

This is of course related to iii above, but different types of provision also have a more direct impact on the education of younger children in that they alter the atmosphere and particularly the staffing of schools. In schools with sixth forms the senior pupils frequently play an active part in organizing and running the day-to-day life of a school (through the prefect system), and are supposed to set an example of responsible young adulthood towards which younger pupils can aspire. Schools which finish at 16 cannot offer this, and the role played by the teaching staff of necessity changes. Further it has been argued that many academically able people are attracted into school teaching by the prospect of being able to do some work with the sixth form. Such people might not want to teach in schools whose responsibility for pupils ends with the statutory school-leaving age. We have looked into these matters in some detail and our findings are reported in Chapter 10.

v. *Preparation for entry of students to further or higher education and preparation for employment*

Many of the students who enrolled for a new course at age 16, whether within school or college, saw it as a step to more advanced study, possibly at university or polytechnic, while others planned to progress from the educational system to the world of work. Much criticism has been expressed and is still being expressed about the adequacy of the careers guidance offered to pupils within secondary education, although great strides have clearly been made in recent years. Criticism has also been expressed at the failure of the curriculum explicitly to prepare students to earn their own

living in the world outside. The extent to which the students
in our sample were appropriately prepared and counselled is
discussed in Chapter 8.

vi. *The inculcation of good study methods and habits*
   This is seen as an issue of increasing importance in the
sixth form. In the past students had been thrown abruptly
into a new and different learning environment with little or
no advice being offered as to effective ways of coping with it.
More institutions, both schools and colleges, are making some
formal commitment to the training of their entering sixth-
form students in appropriate study skills. Our preliminary
findings in this area are reported in Chapter 9 but it has
already been decided to make this topic the focus of a new
NFER research project beginning in 1979.

vii. *Organizational efficiency and use of resources*
   This was a difficult criterion to pin down, especially since
we had decided at the outset to eschew economic issues
(which will be fully reported on by Professor Gareth
Williams' team at Lancaster University). To the extent that
we were able to draw conclusions from the information provided by head teachers and principals, these are summarized
in Chapter 3.

c. **Aims of 16–19 education**
   In order to evaluate different types of 16–19 education
it was necessary to know that the criteria to be employed
accorded with the stated aims and values of the institutions
involved. It was also necessary to establish how far, if at all,
different types of institutions varied in their aims. It would
not be unreasonable, for example, to find the concerns of
staff teaching pupils in a single-sex, grammar school sixth
form were, in some respects, different from those teaching
a range of students and courses in a large FE college. The
study therefore included an examination of the aims of
16–19 education, as perceived by senior staff in the institutions in the research sample.
   This exercise involved completion of a short questionnaire
by the heads of schools or principals of colleges in the

research sample. Full details of this sample are provided in Chapter 3. It will suffice here to say that 45 institutions were approached, and that completed questionnaires were received from all but eight of these. A total of 39 replies was received as two institutions returned, on their own initiative, separate versions completed by different members of staff to represent different departmental interests. In the case of some of the FE colleges the questionnaires were, in fact, completed by a vice-principal or head of department with a particular responsibility for the 16—19 students.

The questionnaire contained three main sections. First, the respondents were asked to state what they regarded as the three most important general aims of 16—19 education in their school or college. Secondly, they were asked to name the most valuable educational experience offered to the 16—19 age group in their institution. In addition, they were asked to complete a more structured section. This presented the respondent with 20 statements of possible aims for 16—19 education (see Figure 2.3). These had to be rated on a five-point scale for the value attached to them (ranging from 'essential' to 'undesirable') and four-point scales for the estimated success in achieving them ('little or none' to 'considerable') and the amount of provision made for them ('little or none' to 'substantial'). The 20 statements of aims were those selected from a much larger pool of aims statements which were drawn partly from previous research into the aims of sixth-form education, and from suggestions made by staff who were attending an LEA in-service course on 16—19 education. The final selection was made, on the basis of the research team's intuitions, to provide a comprehensive coverage with the minimum of overlap of ideas.

The answers given to the first open-ended section were classified under 12 headings (Figure 2.1). The classification scheme was derived by inspection of typewritten transcriptions of the answers without knowledge of, or reference to, the identity of the respondents. Subsequently a frequency count was made of the number of times each category of aim was mentioned by respondents from schools and by those from 16—19 colleges. This revealed that most categories of aim were mentioned by both groups. In other words, at their

Figure 2.1: Stated aims of 16—19 education

	Schools N = 22	Colleges N = 17
Development of social responsibility and awareness	14	8
Development of mental, intellectual or academic capacities	11	7
Preparation or qualification for careers, vocational roles	9	9
Development of personal qualities, particularly maturity and confidence	6	8
Provision of academic opportunities and choices	5	2
Preparation or qualification for higher education	6	3
Provision (or continuation) of a broad or general education	3	5
Development of a capacity for independent study and individual responsibility for work	6	1
Encouragement of students to continue education after 16 years	1	2
Change or improvement of attitudes towards learning and knowledge	1	2
Inculcation of Christian values	3	0
Development of capacity for effective use of leisure	1	0

most general level the stated aims of 16—19 education appeared to be roughly the same, regardless of type of institution. It could thus not be said that one set of aims obtains for schools and another set for colleges.

At the same time, minor differences were apparent. For example, no colleges respondent mentioned religious aims, while three school heads did so. The fostering of mental, intellectual or academic development was more often, and more clearly, stated as an aim by school heads, as was the importance of the development of social responsibility and awareness.

It is evident from Figure 2.1 that the respondents were most readily inclined to mention aims that dealt with the personal development of the individual, and that the acquisition of examination credits or entry into higher education enjoyed only secondary prominence.

It is also noteworthy that the responses given did not lend themselves to any direct or immediate means of evaluation. For example, the most popular category, dealing with the student's social responsibility, often related to behaviours that could only be observed later: ' . . . preparing them for the responsibilities of living in the larger community of society'; '. . . to prepare the student for voting and citizenship'; '. . . to produce well-balanced individuals, able to play a responsible part in the community . . .'; '. . . to produce future citizens who are confident, responsible and courteous'. The last of the above examples raises a point which deserves some brief mention. The statement is one which was equally appropriate to the first and fourth category. There were certainly other cases of answers where a dual categorization would have been possible, and the final allocation was, in effect, arbitrary.

This shortcoming does not, however, detract from the strength of the main conclusions to be drawn from the exercise, that schools and colleges do not differ in their perceptions of the aims of 16–19 education and that these aims deal very largely with the development of individual qualities that cannot be directly measured, but which might usefully be studied through the opinions and introspections of the students themselves.

The second question, which asked the respondents to describe the most valuable educational experiences offered by their institutions, elicited a much greater diversity of responses and an evident difference of emphasis between schools and colleges. Again, a classifying scheme was devised after inspection of the answers, although in this case the exer-

Figure 2.2: Most valuable educational experiences provided for 16—19 students

	Number of times mentioned	
	Schools N = 22	*Colleges* N = 17
Opportunities for acquisition of personal autonomy	11	6
Benefits of contact with younger pupils and leadership opportunities	15	0
Provision of adult (or near-adult) environment	3	12
Mental, intellectual and academic stimulation	10	2
Opportunities for independent study	7	4
Closer relationships with staff	8	2
Opportunities for mixing with a wide range of students	1	7
Experience of community life	5	2
Quality of teaching staff	1	5
Work experience schemes	4	1
Opportunity for personal insight, greater self-knowledge	2	2
Stimuli of working to an objective	1	3
Chance to acquire qualifications	1	1
Small classes	2	0
Breadth of subject choice	0	1
A caring community	1	0

cise proved less easy. The categories employed are presented in Figure 2.2 together with the number of responses given.

It was evident from these results that most of the colleges regarded the provision of an adult environment or the opportunity for adult treatment as valuable ('adult environment'; 'working in an adult atmosphere with few regulations'; 'one of the most valuable experiences offered to the 16–19 age group is that of working in an adult, mature and multi-racial environment'; 'an adult environment where individuals are nevertheless cared for').

This was rarely claimed by schools, who frequently mentioned the benefits of contact with younger pupils, particularly the leadership opportunities ('the chances offered through a House System for Leadership and Responsibility'; 'contact with younger pupils through the medium of a form-prefect structure'; 'wider outlook because of their role in lower school as helper and guide'; 'by having responsibility for younger pupils they learn that if a society is to run smoothly its members must be actively interdependent').

Schools were also more inclined to mention the improved relationships with staff — often in connection with smaller teaching groups — which a sixth form made possible ('the opportunity to work closely, in small groups, with skilled and talented teachers'; 'close, friendly association with members of staff'; working in small groups, closer contact with teachers'; 'depth — both in relation to studies and relations with staff'; 'improved relationships with teachers').

They also placed greater emphasis upon the opportunities provided for mental, intellectual and academic stimulation ('study in depth'; 'for some a chance to widen their mental horizons'; 'learning, by means of a subject or subjects, to think for themselves'; 'the opportunity of "sharpening their minds" on those able to extend them intellectually').

In a close subsequent reading of the answers the impression was formed that many of these views of school heads were based on an implicit contrasting of life in the sixth form and in the lower school. Opportunities for independent study, personal autonomy and freedom, close relationships with staff and work experience, for example, represent a development and improvement from the fifth form, as well as worthwhile experiences in their own right. College staff were not placed to make such fine internal comparisons. Instead they tended to make more global comparisons with schools, often explicitly: 'the opportunity to develop self-discipline while still at home and subject to a ... system designed for young adults rather than children'; 'being taught in certain disciplines by men and women with much wider experience of working life than is normally found among those teaching in schools'; 'a chance to develop ... without having to compromise with the demands of the sort discipline makes on lower age groups'.

In their efforts to make such broad comparisons, the college respondents may have overlooked or taken for granted some items of value which they might otherwise have emphasized. It is also possible that, had the school heads been ready to make explicit comparisons with college provision, the very continuity of education which lay behind so many of the answers would have received greater attention. These reservations apart, the items listed in Figure 2.2 can be said to represent a fairly accurate rehearsal of the contrast in values between the school sixth form approach and college-based approach to 16-plus education.

The results from the two open-ended sections confirmed that the selection of content for the third and more structured part of the questionnaire was generally valid and relevant. The analysis of responses to this section also provided some further insight into the way school and college heads viewed the aims of 16—19 education. In the first place, it was found that a high value was placed by all the respondents upon all the possible aims presented. Nearly all the ratings were in the 'desirable-important-essential' range, and the average ratings of each statement by the 17 college respondents and 22 school respondents were very close, with a correlation of .82. The school heads tended to attach significantly less importance to the various aims overall, notably in the case of Nos. 10, 12, 13 and 15. Of these, three deal essentially with the role of education in preparing students for employment, a function which the FE sector in particular has always emphasized.

The ratings for the degree of provision and of success

associated with each aim can be taken as no more than an indication of the general impression of the respondent. All the ratings tended to be high. Little use was made of categories below the 'moderate' level. The responses from the college group were somewhat higher than those from school heads, but the nature of the exercise does not allow any firm interpretation to be placed on this apparent optimism. It is sufficient to conclude that, on the evidence of this study, an independent investigation into any, or all, of the 20 areas listed in the questionnaires would cover ground where the institutions themselves all claimed a fair degree of success.

It is clear, from the above evidence, that a substantial consensus about the aims for educating this age group exists amongst senior staff in both the college and school-based approaches to 16–19 education. It follows that criteria derived from the aims listed in Figures 2.1 and 2.3 (and to a lesser extent Figure 2.2) could, some with qualifications, be applied to all five types of institution (i.e. comprehensive and grammar schools, sixth-form colleges and tertiary and FE colleges). The qualifications are necessary because, as the answers to the second question showed, there are some variations in what senior staff perceive as valuable educational experiences. Furthermore, consensus does not imply complete unanimity. Sixteen-plus students are by no means a uniform group. A few respondents stressed this in completing their questionnaires, suggesting different aims for one-year as opposed to two-year students, and for students on vocational as opposed to academic courses. There are also certain differences in emphases to which this small-scale study did not do full justice. For example, the emphasis upon religious aims and values in some schools might have been amplified by a larger survey, as might the concern with vocational preparation in the FE colleges. The results, however, do answer the questions posed at the beginning of this section, by providing a serviceable inventory of the educational aims upon which the evaluative criteria can be based, and by demonstrating that there is sufficient common ground for many such criteria to be applied to all forms of 16-plus education.

Figure 2.3: Possible aims of 16—19 education

1. To offer a wide range of academic courses.

2. To equip students with study skills, work habits and general attitudes necessary for success in higher education.

3. To equip students not destined for higher education with the personal qualities necessary for success in employment.

4. To develop aesthetic values and interests.

5. To develop social awareness.

6. To develop an understanding of the nature, possibilities and limitations of science and technology.

7. To help students discover and pursue leisure interests.

8. To enable students to communicate and express themselves effectively.

9. To provide effective careers guidance.

10. To provide students with skills and qualifications which meet the requirements of local commerce and industry.

11. To provide courses which will interest students while meeting their need for particular qualifications.

12. To educate students to be adaptable in the face of social and industrial change.

13. To provide opportunities and amenities for the students' social life during a sixth-form or college course.

14. To foster a rational, critical and questioning approach to problems by students.

15. To offer a wide range of practical courses.

16. To give a general education beyond that provided by examination work.

17. To discover and foster talents the student may have.

18. To provide opportunities for development of relationships with staff beyond the level possible in a fifth-form.

19. To ensure that students generally enjoy their time at school or college.

20. To further the student's self-knowledge, and increase awareness of personal potential and limits.

Chapter 3

The Students and their Schools and Colleges

As the purpose of the study was to survey and evaluate the different forms of full-time educational provision for 16—19 year-olds, the five main types of institution offering full-time courses for this age-group were included — maintained comprehensive and grammar schools, sixth-form colleges, tertiary colleges and colleges of further education other than tertiary. The sample of schools and colleges was designed to provide sufficiently large numbers of students in each of these five types to enable comparisons between them to be made.

a. The sample

i. *Institutions*

Prior to the selection of the sample of schools, it was decided to restrict it to schools which had a first-year sixth-form group of at least 25. It was anticipated that schools with a group smaller than this were most likely to be comprehensive schools in the process of building up their sixth forms, and to have compared their provision with that of ✻ long-established grammar schools or well-endowed sixth-form colleges would have served little purpose. Similarly, as not all colleges of further education could be expected to contain a group of full-time A-level students, it was decided to restrict the sample to those containing such a group. The presence of an A-level group in every institution in the

sample was essential for viable comparisons to be made both
between individual institutions and between types. Tertiary
colleges by definition contain groups of A-level students.

As far as possible, institutions were selected from both
rural and urban areas. Some limitations were placed on the
areas of the country which could be covered by the study
because of the geographical distribution of the tertiary
colleges and, to a lesser extent, the sixth-form colleges. Seven
areas in England and Wales were chosen — Greater London,
the Birmingham area, the Manchester area, Cumbria/North
Lancashire, East Anglia, the West Country and North Wales.
The balance of areas in this 'cluster sample' was considered to
be similar to that which would have been obtained by more
elaborate systems of sample design. Within these areas
institutions were selected at random, any institution failing
to meet the relevant requirements being replaced with
another of the same type.

The final sample comprised 45 different institutions
which would, it was anticipated, provide the required number
of students from each of the five types. Fifteen of these
institutions were comprehensive schools, 12 were grammar
schools, six were sixth-form colleges, three were tertiary
colleges and nine were colleges of further education. Eight
of the grammar schools and three of the comprehensives
were single-sex institutions; all the remaining institutions
were co-educational.

ii. *Students*

All first-year sixth-formers in the schools and sixth-form
colleges were included in the sample, but in each tertiary
college and college of further education approximately 150
students were selected from the much larger total number
of students. This selection was based on the type and nature
of the course being followed. Only full-time students were
considered, thereby excluding part-time, day and block
release students, and only 'non-advanced'* courses were

---

* The term 'non-advanced' is used here according to the DES definition, i.e.
GCE A-level, Ordinary National Diploma or Certificate, the Intermediate
examination of most professional associations and all courses at or below the
standard of instruction required for these examinations.

considered. In addition to A-level students, students who were on the following courses in these two types of institution were included in the sample: art, business studies, catering, hairdressing, nursery nursing, pre-nursing, secretarial and technology. These courses had been found to be common to several institutions, and the inclusion of students on them provided further opportunities for inter-institutional comparisons. The courses generally led to such qualifications as the Ordinary National Diploma, City and Guilds certificates, Royal Society of Arts and Pitman Certificates and other externally- or internally-awarded certificates and diplomas.

A small number of the students in all five types of institution was found to be outside the intended age-range of the study. Those younger than 16 were retained, but those over the age of 19 — mainly in the two types of further education colleges — were excluded as was the small number of overseas students in some of the further education colleges.

All the students in the sample could therefore be described as being aged less than 20 at the time of their initial involvement in the project (September 1974) and embarking at that time on a full-time non-advanced course of post-compulsory education.

No claims are made that this sample of students was representative as a whole of all students in full-time non-advanced post-compulsory education in 1974 for this was not the purpose of its design. There were, for example, proportionally many more students in the sample in sixth-form and tertiary colleges than there were nationally at the time.[10] The sample was, however, separately representative of each of the five types of provision, and as such any generalizations made about one particular type of institution, have reasonable claim to be generalizable to the total population of such institutions, with the possible exception of tertiary colleges of which there were, and still are, too few for the notion of a 'national' picture to have much meaning.[11]

b. General characteristics of the sample

i. *Students*

The complete sample of students numbered 4,448. Approximately a quarter was in colleges of further education, one fifth each were in comprehensive schools, grammar schools and sixth-form colleges and the remaining 12 per cent were in tertiary colleges. All the college students (sixth-form college, tertiary and further education) were in co-educational institutions, whereas 22 per cent of the comprehensive school students and 63 per cent of those in grammar schools were in single-sex institutions (Table 3.1).

Overall, there were slightly more girls than boys in the sample, 52 and 48 per cent respectively. The proportion of girls to boys in the tertiary college sample was identical to this, while the comprehensive school sample and the sixth-form college sample contained nearly equal proportions. The greatest discrepancy in terms of the balance of boys and girls existed in the FE sample, where 61 per cent were girls. This imbalance can largely be attributed to the predominance of girls on many of the courses which were included in the sample, such as secretarial courses, those leading to careers in the health service and, to some extent, catering courses. By contrast many of the courses excluded from the sample, particularly those involving day and block release have a predominance of boys. A further contributory factor to this predominance of girls in the FE sample was that A-level students, of which there were generally more boys than girls, accounted for a smaller proportion than in the other four component samples. This majority of boys over girls on A-level courses was reflected in the grammar school sample, where 57 per cent were boys (Table 3.2).

The majority of the students was aged 16 at the beginning of the academic year 1974/75. Of the very small percentage which was aged 15, the largest proportions were in the grammar schools and the sixth-form colleges; they were presumed to be able students who had taken O-level at an earlier age than normal. A similarly small percentage of the students was aged 18 and over, almost all being in the tertiary and FE colleges. These older students comprised ten

Table 3.1: The survey sample: institutions and students

Type of Institution	No of Institutions in Sample	No. of Students in Sample	%
Mixed comprehensive schools	12	761	17
Boys comprehensive schools	1	75	2
Girls comprehensive schools	2	145	3
All comprehensive schools	15	981	22
Mixed grammar schools	4	317	7
Boys grammar schools	4	328	7
Girls grammar schools	4	221	5
All grammar schools	12	866	19
Sixth-form colleges	6	946	21
Tertiary colleges	3	530	12
FE colleges	9	1125	25
Total	45	4448	100

Table 3.2 (S1)*: Distribution of student by sex

	Boys	%	Girls	%	Total = 100%
Comprehensive schools	492	50	489	50	981
Grammar schools	491	57	375	43	866
Sixth-form colleges	465	49	481	51	946
Tertiary colleges	253	48	277	52	530
FE colleges	437	39	688	61	1125
Total	2138	48	2310	52	4448

* For an explanation of the source of data in tables, see page 27

Table 3.3 (S1): **Distribution of students by age**

					Age on 1st September 1974				
	15	%	16	%	17	%	18+	%	Total = 100%
Comprehensive schools	23	2	913	94	38	4	1		975
Grammar schools	33	4	789	92	37	4	1		860
Sixth-form colleges	35	4	851	90	47	5	9	1	942
Tertiary colleges	7	1	456	86	53	10	12	2	528
FE colleges	11	1	703	63	286	26	115	10	1115
Total	109	2	3712	84	461	10	138	3	4420

per cent of the total FE sample. Table 3.3 shows the distribution of the students by age and by type of institution. The figures are based on a total of 4,420 as 28 students omitted to give their date of birth.

ii. *Courses*

The information which follows is based on the students' responses in the first questionnaire to the question 'What is the main qualification or examination to which your present course leads?' Nine possible courses were presented, and the question allowed for an 'other qualification' category.

Most of the students in the schools and sixth-form colleges were on A-level courses, but only half of the tertiary-college students and a third of the FE students were on such courses. Not surprisingly, the grammar school sample was almost entirely made up of A-level students (95 per cent), although the sixth-form college sample also contained a very large proportion (81 per cent). Seventy per cent of the comprehensive school students were on A-level courses.

The grammar school and sixth-form college students who were not primarily on A-level courses were either on O-level courses or secretarial courses. The five per cent of non-A-level grammar school students were fairly evenly divided between these two types of courses. Of the 19 per cent of non-A-level students in the sixth-form colleges, three quarters were on O-level courses.

The non-A-level comprehensive school students, who comprised a comparatively larger proportion of their sample, were also mostly doing O-levels, but a small number — one per cent of the total comprehensive school sample — was primarily working for CSE. The remaining six per cent were on secretarial courses. Although no students were mainly on CEE courses, these were available in six of the comprehensive schools (and one grammar).

Most of the students in the tertiary and FE college samples who were not primarily studying for GCE A-level were on OND, City and Guilds or secretarial courses. In both groups there were also small groups of students who were mainly studying O-levels — slightly more in the tertiary colleges — and others whose course culminated in the award of a college certificate or diploma. The FE sample also included students who were studying for other externally awarded qualifications (Table 3.4).

Most of the OND students were following a business studies course, the remainder being either on technology or catering courses. Slightly more than half the City and Guilds students were on catering courses. Most of the others were on hairdressing or fashion and clothing courses, and a small number was on computing courses. The students who were following courses leading to some form of internal college assessment (although this does not necessarily preclude the taking of external examinations) included those who were on art foundation courses, pre-nursing courses, pre-business studies courses and other courses leading to careers in the National Health Service. The other externally awarded qualifications for which some of the FE students were studying included those of the National Nursery Examinations Board (NNEB), the diploma of the Institute of Travel Agents, the National Council for Home Economics Education Cooks' Professional Certificate and the Preliminary Certificate in Residential Care (Table 3.5).

Many of the students on these vocational courses were studying GCE courses as a subsidiary part of their course, as were many of the secretarial students in the schools and sixth-form colleges. In all, 60 per cent of all the vocational

Table 3.4: (S1): Distribution of students by course and by type of institution (percentages)

	Compre-hensive	Grammar School	Sixth-form College	Tertiary College	FE	All Students N	All Students %
A-level	70	95	81	49	34	2913	66
O-level	23	2	14	5	2	439	10
CSE	1					10	
OND				19	20	322	7
City and Guilds				12	15	232	5
Secretarial	6	3	5	10	14	337	8
Other external					6	71	2
College diploma or certificate				5	9	124	3
Total = 100%	981	866	946	530	1125	4448	100

Table 3.5 (S1): Subject areas of the vocational courses followed by students in the tertiary and FE college samples (percentages)

Subject	OND	City and Guilds	Secretarial	Other External	College Diploma or Certificate	All Students
	%	%	%	%	%	%
Art and design					35	5
Business studies	58				4	20
Catering	14	55				18
Hairdressing						
Fashion and clothing		37				9
Nursery nursing				55		4
Pre-nursing/health care				11	58	8
Secretarial			100			22
Technology/computer science	28	8				11
Other				34	3	3
Total = 100%	322	232	206	71	124	955

course students were studying for some GCE examinations, slightly over half of them intending to take O-level examinations. Over 80 per cent of the secretarial course students was studying GCE subject(s) as opposed to only a fifth of the City and Guilds students. This is no doubt accounted for by the greater 'totality' of City and Guilds courses (Table 3.6).

In response to the question 'What is the normal length of your present course?' 18 per cent of all the students indicated that they were on a course of one year's duration. Almost all the remainder were on two-year courses, although a small number − less than one per cent − indicated they were intending to stay on their present course for three years. Of the initially identified one-year students a number subsequently stayed on for a further year. These one-year students have been the subject of a separate ancillary study which has already been reported[9]. The highest numbers of one-year students were in the comprehensive schools and the FE colleges, where they comprised 27 per cent and 25 per cent respectively of each sample. Corresponding figures for the grammar school, sixth-form college and tertiary college samples were three per cent, 14 per cent and 17 per cent respectively.

The largest group of one-year students overall comprised those on O-level courses (46 per cent). Three quarters of the one-year students in the comprehensive schools and sixth-form colleges were on GCE O-level courses, whereas this applied to only half those in the grammar schools and a third of those in the tertiary colleges. The FE college sample contained comparatively few one-year O-level students (nine per cent of all the one-year students in this sample). The largest single group of one-year students in the FE sample in fact comprised those taking A-levels. Although there were one-year A-level students in all the other samples except the tertiary college, they represented a relatively small proportion of the total one-year groups in these institutions. The second largest group of one-year students in all five samples was secretarial students although almost half of these students overall were on two-year courses. A number of originally intending one-year secretarial students did in fact stay on for

Table 3.6 (S1): Subsidiary GCE courses studied by all students on vocational courses (percentages)

	Taking A-level as Part of their Course %	Taking O-level as Part of their Course %	Not Taking A- or O-levels %	No. of Students = 100% %
Course				
OND	35	20	45	322
City and Guilds	9	12	79	232
Secretarial	25	61	14	337*
Other courses	34	40	27	195
All students	26	34	39	1086

* includes 131 secretarial course students in the schools and sixth-form colleges

a further year.[9]. All except one of the 10 CSE students in the comprehensive schools stated it was their intention to remain on their course for only one year. Approximately a fifth of the City and Guilds students in the tertiary and FE college samples were on one-year courses, all in the field of catering. Half the students on internally assessed courses in these colleges were also on one-year courses, but all the externally assessed courses in the FE college sample were of two years' duration.

Overall, therefore, the majority of the one-year students were on A-level, O-level, or secretarial courses, the latter contributing to an overall predominance (two thirds) of girls in this group. The vast majority of the two-year students were on A-level courses. Overall A-level students constituted 70 per cent of the entire sample, but separate figures for the five component samples show a range from 35 per cent in the FE colleges to over 90 per cent in the schools and sixth-form colleges. OND students accounted for approximately a quarter of the two-year students in the FE and tertiary college samples (Table 3.7).

All the students were asked in the first questionnaire about their plans for the future on completion of their present course. Approximately a fifth indicated that it was not their intention to remain in education, but, of the remainder, a large proportion stated they would most probably continue in full-time education. The subject of the students' intentions

Table 3.7 (S1): Distribution of students by length and type of course (percentages)

Course	Comprehensive School 1yr %	Comprehensive School 2+yrs %	Grammar School 1yr %	Grammar School 2+yrs %	Sixth-form College 1yr %	Sixth-form College 2+yrs %	Tertiary College 1yr %	Tertiary College 2+yrs %	FE College 1yr %	FE College 2+yrs %	All Students 1yr %	All Students 2+yrs %
A-level	6	93	13	98	6	93		59	32	35	15	77
O-level	74	5	50	1	74	4	33		9		46	2
CSE	3	*									1	*
OND								23		26		9
City and Guilds							24	9	10	17	6	5
Secretarial	16	2	37	1	20	3	32	5	29	9	24	4
Other external										8		2
College diploma or certificate							11	4	20	5	8	11
Total = 100%	265	716	30	836	124	812	88	442	285	840	802	3646

* A single student in the comprehensive school sample was intending to remain on a CSE course for two years.

and their realizations is discussed more fully in a subsequent chapter.

iii. *Institutions*

Background information on the institutions from which the sample of students was drawn was obtained by means of a postal questionnaire sent to each institution during 1974. In each case it was completed by the principal or head-teacher or by a senior member(s) of staff with special responsibility for the 16-plus students. As a further source of background information copies of the questionnaire were also sent to a number of additional schools and colleges which were not providing students for the main sample. Any figures quoted in the following paragraphs refer to the sample institutions; where differences occurred between the sample and the additional institutions, these are mentioned.

Comprehensive schools

Most of the 15 comprehensive schools in the sample contained pupils in the age-range 11—18. In three the age-range was 13—18, and in one it was 12—18. At the time of the background survey eight schools had been functioning as comprehensives for four years or less, while the remainder had been operating as schools of this type for at least six years. Two of the latter had only ever been comprehensives whereas most of the others had been formed by an amalgamation of grammar and secondary modern schools. One school had previously been a single grammar school, and four others had been formed from one or two secondary modern schools. Five schools were operating on split sites.

Only four of the schools were in totally comprehensive areas. Most were in LEA areas where there were also selective schools. It must be remembered, however, that local government reorganization had taken place in April 1974, and a number of schools found themselves in newly defined LEA areas. This small number of schools in wholly comprehensive areas possibly accounts for the fact that no comprehensive school in the sample constituted a very well-developed example of an 'umbrella' sixth form, where all 16-plus courses are concentrated in one school in a district, and are

provided as much for pupils from neighbouring schools as
for pupils from the school's own fifth year. In seven of the
15 schools all the sixth form was in fact recruited from the
schools' own fifth forms. The other eight admitted pupils
from outside, usually from local secondary schools without
sixth forms or from independent schools, but in most cases
this accounted for less than 10 per cent of the total sixth
form.

Only two headteachers described their school's buildings
as purpose-built. Two schools were using buildings dating
from pre-World War I, and six were occupying some premises
built in the 1930s. All the schools had had fairly recent
additions to their buildings. Eight housed their sixth-formers
in a separate block — seven mixed and one boys' school.

The smallest of the 15 schools had 881 pupils on its roll,
and the largest had 1,546. The average number was 1,192.
The average size of the sixth form was 117. Three schools
had more than 150 pupils in the sixth form, and one had
less than 50. All of the schools offered A-level and O-level
GCE courses to their sixth-formers, and almost half also
offered CSE courses. Six were currently offering the experimental CEE, and two thirds were offering secretarial courses.
Three schools were only offering O-level and A-level. When
asked whether there was a central body or guidance committee co-ordinating the 16-plus provision in the area, only
one school replied in the affirmative. Six schools reported
'link' courses between themselves and the local college of
further education, but these appeared just as likely to involve
pupils in forms below the sixth form. Computer studies and
A-level science subjects were examples of sixth-form link
courses. Most schools indicated that their pupils could, if
necessary, take unusual subjects at other schools in the area,
but in practice this appeared a rare occurrence. The average
number of A-levels offered by the schools in the sample was
18. Most offered between 13 and 22. The school with the
smallest sixth form was offering 10 subjects.

Two schools insisted on a specified number of O-level
passes for admission to the sixth form, one requiring four
and the other three. Of the remainder, seven stated that
entry to the sixth form was completely open. The other

six made some sort of qualifying statement, such as students 'might be required to show ability to benefit from the sixth form' or might be admitted 'providing we have an appropriate course for them and viable numbers'. Admission to A-level courses within the sixth form was more restricted; seven schools required a certain number of O-level passes — most commonly four — and seven others indicated that recommendation by the subject teacher was required. Thus although all but two of the schools laid down no formal requirements for admission to the sixth form itself, the majority exercised some restriction over enrolment on A-level courses.

All but one of the comprehensive schools had sixth-formers on one-year courses, in most cases the proportion being between 20 and 30 per cent of all its sixth-formers. The school which had no one-year students was the one with a sixth-form entry requirement of four O-level passes. Two pupils who had stayed on at this school with the main purpose of resitting O-levels were repeating the fifth year.

Eleven of the schools indicated that timetabling difficulties could affect the combinations of subjects taken by students, and six stated that 'unreasonable' combinations were advised against, particularly in view of a student's future higher education or employment plans.

A wide variety in the size of sixth-form teaching groups was reported, groups of one or two not being uncommon. The largest groups reported contained 20 pupils. The 'typical' sizes of groups in the schools ranged from two to 16, and were generally higher for arts subjects than for modern languages or science subjects.

Most of the schools reported that between 60 and 79 per cent of the teaching staff involved in sixth-form work were graduates. Four — including all three single-sex schools — stated the proportion to be higher than this. Nine schools involved more than half their staff in sixth-form work. In most of the schools at least three quarters of the staff were aged 50 or under, and in all at least half were aged 40 or under.

All the schools provided a common room for the use of the sixth-formers. In all but one of these there were facilities for making tea or coffee, and most contained newspapers, magazines and a record-player. Only a minority had a radio (four schools) or a TV set (two schools). Similarly, few schools permitted games to be played in the common room (five schools). A few schools provided a separate dining room for sixth-formers, and just under half provided another room for sixth-formers' general use apart from the common room.

On the subject of facilities for private study — an important feature of post-compulsory education — 11 of the comprehensives stated that the central library was used by sixth-formers for this purpose, although not all of these considered it large enough for the uses to which it was put. Approximately half the schools' heads considered the library sufficiently well stocked. The majority reported that an additional room was available for private study.

Eleven of the comprehensive schools were operating a prefect system, and six also had a pupils' council. Just one of the sample schools had neither. Pupils' councils were generally responsible for organizing school societies and charity efforts, and acted as a liaison between staff and pupils by making recommendations and suggestions for improving the general running of the school.

In response to the question 'Are there any opportunities for sixth-formers to participate in community/volunteer work?' 10 of the schools replied that there were. The type of work involved was fund-raising for charities, work for old and disabled people, visiting hospital geriatric units, work with the mentally and physically handicapped, and the organization of holiday play schemes etc. The proportion of sixth-formers involved in such activities was estimated at 'a very small percentage' to approximately 60 per cent.

All the comprehensives had a school uniform, and seven required their sixth-formers to wear it. They were not asked specifically whether the uniform differed markedly for the older pupils. The schools were asked what their attitudes were towards boys wearing their hair long and towards girls wearing jewellery and make-up. Most of the schools stated that 'mild forms' of these were permitted or that they allowed sixth-formers to dress as they please, although this latter point was often qualified, which suggests that most schools attempted to exert some influence over sixth-formers' appearance. In one school students were encouraged to judge each other in order to develop a sense of what might give offence to others. Two schools stated that they strongly discouraged the types of dress mentioned.

Smoking was banned in 13 of the schools; in the remaining two, sixth-formers were permitted to smoke but only in certain rooms.

All maintained schools in England and Wales are required by the 1944 Education Act to hold a daily act of worship, although provision is made for pupils not to attend on religious or moral grounds. As the schools and sixth-form colleges are bound by school regulations these institutions were asked whether attendance at morning assembly was compulsory for those students who were over the minimum school-leaving age. Although individual cases varied, such as the holding of special sixth-form assemblies or attendance being required on only certain days of the week, the comprehensive schools generally expected their sixth-formers to attend school or house assemblies.

The schools were also asked about their policy with regard to sixth-formers remaining on the premises when not attending lessons. Most of the comprehensives did not permit their students to leave the premises. Three schools made the following exceptions respectively: after 2.30 pm; in the last period of the afternoon; in the afternoons.

Grammar schools
Eleven of the 12 grammar schools in the sample contained pupils in the 11—18 age-range; the remaining one admitted pupils at the age of 12. Not unexpectedly, these schools had generally existed in their present form for much longer than the comprehensives. Two of the schools dated back to the sixteenth and nineteenth centuries respectively, and four had been founded between the two world wars. Of those with more recent origins two had only existed in their present form for three years at the time of the survey, but this reflected a recent amalgamation of these schools with other schools of a similar (if not exactly the same) type. Most of

the grammar schools were anticipating some form of LEA
reorganization in the future, but the nature of this was not
certain in every case. Six had plans to become comprehensive
schools.

As in the case of the comprehensive schools, the majority
of the grammar schools were in LEAs where there were both
selective and comprehensive schools. Two were in totally
selective areas. The sixth form in all but one of the grammar
schools contained students who had transferred at 16 from
other schools. In most cases this proportion was less than
10 per cent, but two schools stated that a quarter of their
sixth form came from elsewhere. Secondary modern schools
provided most of these pupils, but a small proportion were
from independent schools.

All the grammar schools were operating on a single site,
and 11 of the 12 described their buildings as partly or wholly
purpose-built. Two had buildings three or four hundred years
old, and six others had buildings dating prior to World War II.
All the schools had relatively modern additions. Only one (a
boys' school) housed its sixth-formers in a separate block.

The smallest grammar school had 319 pupils, and the
largest had 1,531 (both mixed schools). The average size
was 751. The average size of the sixth form was 147. No
school had a sixth form smaller than 50, the smallest being
63 and the largest 302. Most had between 90 and 150. All
the schools offered O-level courses in addition to A-levels
to their sixth-formers. In most schools these were the only
courses provided. Two of the mixed schools offered secretarial courses, and one girls' school, rather exceptionally,
offered CSE and CEE in addition to secretarial courses.
No other instances of provision such as this were uncovered
in the additional grammar school sample. Two schools
reported the existence of some form of co-ordinating body
in their areas. In one this took the form of meetings between
heads and staff in schools offering 16-plus courses, and in the
other there was a general co-ordination at all levels between
schools in a consortium. In this latter case there was also
a committee responsible for arranging link courses with the
further education sector. Seven other schools reported the
existence of link courses with the local college of FE. This

generally involved less common GCE subjects such as computer studies. The average number of A-level subjects offered by the grammar schools in the sample was 18, the same as the comprehensive schools. The smallest number offered by any grammar school was 13, and the greatest was 22.

Four of the grammar schools required passes in three or four O-level subjects for admission to the sixth form. One school stated that entry was completely open, while the remainder required teachers' recommendations. Five schools required an O-level pass for enrolment on an A-level course. In the others enrolment depended on the recommendation of the subject teacher.

Five of the grammar schools had no one-year sixth-formers but in one of the schools such students comprised 20 per cent of the entire first-year group. This was one of the schools which admitted appreciable numbers to its sixth form from local secondary modern schools. Students who were primarily studying O-levels were only allowed to enter the normal sixth form in five of the schools. In three schools there were special sixth-form units for such pupils. In two, such students had to repeat the fifth year. The remaining two schools appeared to make no provision; one stated that students in this category went to the local FE college.

Ten schools indicated that timetabling restrictions could affect the combination of A-level subjects which could be taken, and eight stated that they advised students against 'unreasonable' combinations of subjects.

Teaching groups in the grammar schools tended to be not as small as in the comprehensive schools. Although classes of one or two pupils were reported, they were not as common. The largest reported grammar school teaching group was 35. Typical sizes reported by the schools ranged from five to 18, the highest number being that estimated for science subjects.

Most of the grammar schools reported that over 80 per cent of the staff involved in sixth-form work were graduates. As in the comprehensives, most of these teachers were aged 50 or under, although there was not such a high proportion in the under-40 age-group. On the whole, greater proportions of the entire school teaching staffs were involved in sixth-form work in the grammar schools. Generally this was well over three quarters, and in half the schools it amounted to over 90 per cent.

Every one of the grammar schools provided a common room for the use of sixth-formers, and all but two of these contained tea- or coffee-making facilities. Most contained a record player, and half contained a radio. Just under half contained newspapers and magazines but none contained a TV set. As in the comprehensives few permitted games in the common rooms. Proportionally more grammar schools than comprehensive schools provided a separate dining room for sixth-formers' use, but this only amounted to a quarter of the sample. Only two schools — both girls' schools — provided an additional general room.

In all but one of the grammar schools, the central library was used by sixth-formers for private study. Two heads regarded their library as sufficiently well stocked, and three rated it large enough for its purposes. In four schools a separate room was available for private study, and temporarily empty classrooms were generally utilized for this purpose.

Nine of the schools were operating a prefect system, and in eight a pupils' council existed. No grammar school was without one or other of these arrangements. The role of the grammar schools' pupils' councils was similar to those in the comprehensive schools.

Six of the grammar schools reported that their sixth-formers took part in community and volunteer work. The nature of this was very similar to that undertaken by the comprehensive school pupils. The estimated percentage involvement of sixth-formers in these six schools ranged from ten per cent to 'most'.

School uniform was 'compulsory' in all the grammar schools, but in four this ruling did not apply to sixth-formers. All the four boys' grammar schools in the sample had a compulsory uniform throughout the school. In two of the girls' schools and in two of the mixed schools, sixth-formers were not obliged to wear a uniform. Most of the grammar schools stated that mild forms of long hair styles for boys and the wearing of make-up and jewellery by girls were permitted. Two of the girls' schools allowed sixth-formers to dress as they wished. One mixed and one girls' school 'strongly discouraged' the forms of dress described.

Smoking was forbidden in all but two of the schools and in those where it was permitted at the sixth-form level it was restricted to certain times and rooms.

Attendance at assembly was required of sixth-formers in all the schools except one — a mixed school — where non-attendance was permitted provided the students made their intentions clear. One school expected attendance on a rota basis.

Almost all required sixth-formers to be on the premises when not attending lessons. One girls' school stated its students were allowed one free afternoon a week. Another school indicated that a request for absence had to be made in writing by a parent.

Sixth-form colleges

One of the colleges selected for the sample was subsequently discovered not exactly to meet the project's definition of a college of this type. This was that the colleges should be operating under school regulations for full-time students between the ages of 16 and 19, and should have a teaching staff exclusively engaged on work at this level. In this particular case one of the college's four 11–16 feeder schools was on the same campus and, although the sixth-form centre was a separate unit with its own director and administrative staff, the teaching staff also taught in the lower school. However, on balance the college had many of the characteristics of a sixth-form college, and it was decided not to reclassify it in any way.

All the six colleges in the sample were fairly new establishments, none having been in existence for more than two years at the time of the survey. On their establishment, five had been formed by an amalgamation of one, two or three existing sixth forms, mostly from grammar schools. The sixth had developed from an amalgamation of seven — mostly secondary modern — sixth forms.

Three of the colleges were in totally comprehensive areas, and three were in partly selective areas. The first three naturally drew almost their entire intake from local 11–16 comprehensive schools. The others admitted students from a wider variety of school backgrounds — comprehensive, grammar, secondary modern and independent. Students from the latter formed more than a quarter of the first-year entrants at two of these colleges.

Two of the colleges were housed in new, purpose-built premises. Two others were in buildings 10 and 15 years old respectively. The remaining two were using older buildings including some dating from the late nineteenth century and the 1920s, but each also had some more recently built accommodation. Apart from one college which had its art department in different premises, all the colleges were operating on a single site.

The largest college in the sample contained 471 students, and the smallest — the sixth-form centre — had 187. The average number on roll worked out at 353, which is lower than more recently quoted figures,[12][13] but this can largely be attributed to the presence in the sample of the smaller sixth-form centre. The average figure for the additional sample of sixth-form colleges was 450.

All the colleges offered A-levels and O-levels, and half of them offered secretarial courses. Two offered CSE and CEE, and one offered an internally assessed course. The average number of A-levels offered was 27, the range being from 22 to 33. This average number is exactly the same as that of the additional sample and that reported in the TES survey (op. cit.).[12]

Access to four of the colleges was completely open; no requirements had to be met in terms of previous examination successes. Entry at the remaining two depended on a specific number of O-level or CSE Grade 1 passes. These two colleges in fact had no one-year students; all their students were engaged entirely on A-level work or on a mixture of A- and O-level work. As with the comprehensive and grammar schools some evidence of ability to benefit from an A-level course was required before enrolment was allowed. Two colleges required relevant O-level passes.

Three colleges mentioned timetabling restrictions as possible factors affecting the choice of A-level subjects which could be taken, and a similar number indicated that students were advised against taking 'unreasonable' combinations.

Two colleges stated that there were no limitations on courses which were relevant to a student's needs.

Two colleges reported that there existed in their areas a body or committee co-ordinating the provision of 16-plus courses. In one this was described as a standing committee of principals and advisers for secondary education. The colleges generally reported a high incidence of co-operation with their local college of further education. Certain GCE courses at both Ordinary- and Advanced-level and vocational courses such as secretarial courses, courses in art and design featured in this co-operation.

An important task for sixth-form colleges and other 16-plus institutions is the publicizing of the courses they have to offer. Consequently all three types of college in the sample were asked about the ways they informed their potential students and their parents of the options which were open to them at the various institutions. A list of eight possible channels plus an 'other' category was presented.

All the sixth-form colleges reported that details were sent to the heads of the feeder schools and that a college prospectus was also distributed. Most colleges also employed some or all of the following additional methods of passing on information: regular meetings between school heads and college principals, visits by college staff to the feeder schools, visits by fifth-formers from the feeder schools, information given by the area careers officers. Two colleges also held 'open' days.

The largest reported sixth-form college teaching group was 28. As with the schools, there were instances of teaching groups as small as one or two students, but there were more reported instances of 'smallest' groups containing nine or 10 students. No 'typical' size smaller than eight was reported.

All but one of the colleges reported that at least 80 per cent of the teaching staff were graduates and, as in the schools, the large majority were aged 50 or under. In four of the colleges the largest single group was aged between 31—40.

A students' common room was provided in every college, and in each were tea- or coffee-making facilities. Half contained newspapers and magazines, and five of the six contained a record-player. Radios were less common — being present in only one college common room — and there were no TV sets. Games were played in a majority of the common rooms in the sixth-form college sample, compared with a minority in the comprehensive and grammar school samples. In the additional sample of sixth-form colleges, however, this occurred in a minority of common rooms, suggesting the six sample colleges were atypical in this respect.

In all the colleges the central library was used for students' private study. Two colleges considered the library large enough, and three considered it sufficiently well-stocked. All but one of the colleges reported that a separate room was also available for private study.

Unlike the schools, the three types of colleges were also asked about their policy for timetabling private study and supervising it. In three of the sixth-form colleges private study was timetabled and supervised. In a fourth it was timetabled but not supervised. Two of these four colleges also expected students to allocate some of their free periods to private study. The two remaining colleges let the students themselves decide when they would do their private studying.

All the sixth-form colleges in the survey had a students' council or union. Allowing for the absence of younger pupils, the aims and functions of these student bodies were similar to those in the schools, namely, to promote good relations between the students and staff, to make representations on the students' behalf when necessary, and to support and encourage extra-curricular activities. The students in these colleges appeared to have greater responsibility for social activities than those in the schools, and a number of colleges also stated that the students administered and allocated a student fund. Another activity which was mentioned by the sixth-form college principals was the support and encouragement of community service.

Five colleges reported that their students participated in voluntary or community work, the nature of this being very similar to that described by the schools. One college reported the participation rate to be over 50 per cent, but most approximated it between 10 and 20 per cent.

Three of the colleges stated that they allowed mild forms of long hair styles for boys and jewellery and make-up for girls, and three said they allowed students to dress as they please. There was less tendency for sixth-form college principals to qualify the latter statement, suggesting that students in these colleges had a somewhat greater freedom than those in the schools.

Unlike the schools, smoking was not forbidden in any of these six colleges, although it was restricted to certain areas and rooms, and was not allowed in classrooms. Smoking was, however, forbidden in three in the additional sample of such colleges.

Four of the colleges held assemblies, although not every day. Attendance was compulsory in three of them although in one this did not apply to the religious part of the service. In another it was possible for students to withdraw.

Most of the colleges required students to remain on the premises when not attending lessons. In one college this did not apply to the final hour of the day, and in another it did not apply to second-year students.

Tertiary colleges

At the end of 1974 ten tertiary colleges were in existence, and three of them were included in the sample. Like most tertiary colleges, these three had in the past been colleges of further education, offering the range of full-time and part-time courses usually associated with such institutions. On reorganization, which had taken place between one and four years previously, their intake had grown to include all those students who would previously have entered the sixth form in a school in the area. Two of the colleges were in LEAs where the secondary school system was a mixture of comprehensive and selective schools. The third college was part of a totally comprehensive system. On their establishment, the colleges had absorbed two or three sixth forms from the local area. The one college in a totally comprehensive area was the only institution in its area offering full-time courses for 16–19-year-olds. Sixteen-plus students in the areas of the other two colleges could continue their education in sixth forms in schools.

The three colleges were very varied in size. One had 360 full-time students, another 820 and the largest, 1,375. Corresponding numbers of part-time students were 2,218, 3,530 and 4,370 respectively. Approximately two-fifths of the full-time students in each college were on A-level courses. Most of these came to the college directly from school, very few having spent time in employment. Each of the colleges reported that a few students who had come to them to take A-levels could have stayed on in their own schools. The three colleges had between four and eight feeder schools.

None of the tertiary colleges in the sample was in premises especially built for its present purpose. All three were operating on split sites, and all were using some fairly old buildings dating from the late nineteenth or early part of this century. They all also had buildings dating from the 1930s or 1940s and some recent additions.

In addition to A-level courses, all the colleges were offering full-time O-level, secretarial, OND and City and Guilds courses. Pre-professional, college diploma or certificate and other courses were also available in at least two of the colleges. Two of the tertiary colleges were also offering advanced courses, but as these were not relevant to the sample of students no further reference will be made to them. The average number of A-levels offered was 30; no college offered less than 26. The average figure compares closely with the 29 reported by the TES in its survey of eight of the 12 colleges operating in 1977.[12]

Requirements for enrolment on courses in the further education sector vary very much according to the course. For example, students are normally required to have four O-level passes in order to enrol on an OND course. Certain City and Guilds courses specify CSE or O-level examination passes but entry to many depends on having 'reached a good average fifth-year standard'. With the wide variety of courses other than A- or O-level available in further education, access to the colleges is therefore generally 'open' but restrictions may apply at entry to courses. Two of the three tertiary colleges required students enrolling on a three-subject A-level course to have four GCE O-level passes; one also specified certain grades. The remaining college stated that offers of a place were conditional on 'an adequate foundation on which to build an A-level course; O-levels, personal circumstances and motivation are considered'. One college stated that time-tabling restrictions could be a factor affecting the choice of A-level subjects but none stated that combinations across departments were discouraged. Again, students tended to be advised against taking 'unreasonable' combinations of subjects.

On the question of informing school pupils of the courses available to them in the tertiary colleges, all three sample institutions indicated that they used many and various mechanisms, including visits by staff to schools, visits by school pupils, meetings between heads and principals, open days, and the distribution of prospectuses.

There was evidence that the tertiary colleges, like the schools and sixth-form colleges, were willing to put on courses irrespective of the number of students requesting them. Groups consisting of one or two students were again reported, although 'typical' numbers for groups were generally much higher, usually at least seven. The largest reported group in the tertiary colleges had 21 students. Again this appeared to be untypical; the largest 'typical' size given being 14.

Information about staffing was not requested of the tertiary and colleges of further education in view of the wide diversity of courses in these institutions and the large numbers of part-time staff.

All three colleges provided a common room for their students' use, and in two of these there were tea- and coffee-making facilities. Record-players existed in all three, but newspapers and magazines were in only one and none had a radio or TV set. Games were played in two.

Only one tertiary college considered the central library large enough to be used both as a library and for private study. All three colleges reported that other rooms and arrangements were available for this purpose. In none of the colleges was private study supervised. In one it was time-tabled; in the other two students were stated to have free periods which they could use for private study, but this was left to the individual.

The student representative body in the tertiary colleges was a students' union and, in two, it was affiliated to the National Union of Students. The unions had representation on various boards and committees in the colleges. In all three colleges the students had representation on the Academic Board and/or subcommittees. Organization of social and sporting activities was a function of the Students' Unions; they also organized community and volunteer work. In two of the colleges membership of the Students' Union was automatic. Details of participation rates in community and volunteer work were not requested of the tertiary and FE colleges.

The tertiary and FE colleges were asked in a more open-ended way than the schools to give details of 'any rules governing students' dress, personal appearance etc.' The three tertiary colleges had no rules as such; any reference to control over students' appearances was made in the context of safety, in certain courses and workshops etc.

The tertiary and FE colleges were also asked about their regulations regarding regular attendance in order to discover to what extent they exercised control over this in the absence of the strict rules and practices operating in the schools sector. From their responses it was apparent that these institutions exercised as tight a control as possible. One of the tertiary college principals pointed out that certain external examination boards, such as that for the OND, made a certain level of attendance a requirement of their courses; the college applied a similar standard to courses which did not have this externally imposed condition. Failure to reach a required minimum attendance could result in a request to leave. Another college stated that expulsion was used as a last resort.

None of the tertiary colleges banned smoking, but it was not permitted in classrooms or in workshops.

A difference between students in the tertiary colleges and those in schools and sixth-form colleges was revealed in the former institutions' attitudes towards 16-plus students remaining on the premises when not attending lessons. None of the tertiary colleges imposed any restrictions on the movement of their students during these non-lesson times.

Colleges of further education

Nine colleges of further education other than tertiary, were included in the sample. They contained an average of 800 full-time and 4,700 part-time students. The average number of full-time A-level students was 210. Overall, 86 per cent of these full-time A-level students had been in full-time education in the previous year. Seven per cent had spent some time in employment, and the remaining seven per cent were overseas students. Two of the colleges in the sample were offering 'advanced' level work although this applied to the majority of FE colleges in the additional sample.

Six of the colleges were in areas where the secondary school system was a mixture of comprehensive and selective schools. Three had a sixth-form college in the area. On average the colleges reported that there were four other institutions in their area offering sixth-form work, the range being from two to five. All but one college stated that some of their full-time A-level students could have stayed on in the sixth form of their school. Their main reasons for not doing so were suggested to be either a dissatisfaction with school in general or an inability to take the subjects or combinations of subjects of their choice at their school. Both maintained and independent schools were mentioned in this context.

Six of the colleges were operating on split sites. Three colleges were entirely housed in post-war buildings. Most of the others were using buildings dating back to the early part of the century in addition to more modern ones; one was using some premises approximately three hundred years old.

The ranges of courses offered by the colleges to full-time non-advanced students was very similar to that offered by the tertiary colleges although, whereas not all the tertiary colleges in the sample were offering pre-professional courses, such courses were on offer in every one of the nine FE colleges.

All the colleges specified a certain number of O-level passes as a necessary requirement for enrolment on a full-time A-level course. Six required four O-level passes and two colleges required three. The ninth college stated the number varied between three and five according to the number of A-level subjects to be studied. Five colleges also said certain grades at O-level were necessary. Students without these qualifications sat an entrance examination in one of the colleges, as did mature students in another. The recommendations of a student's previous head teacher were also generally taken into account. Timetabling restrictions were said to have some effect on the choice of subjects which could be taken at A-level but, as with the tertiary colleges, no restrictions were placed on combining subjects from different departments in the colleges. Six colleges stated that they advised against 'unreasonable' combinations and, as in all types of institution in the sample, this was seen to apply particularly to a student's long-term future plans.

All the colleges reported that they used the services of the area careers officers to pass on information about the courses they offered. They all also sent information to heads of secondary schools, distributed a college prospectus and made arrangements for their staff to visit schools. Proportionally fewer FE colleges than tertiary colleges reported that regular meetings between school heads and college principals took place, and not all FE colleges reported that visits from school fifth-formers took place. Open days were also less frequent than in the tertiary colleges. All the colleges ran link courses with local secondary schools but only two reported the existence of a central body or committee co-ordinating the provision of 16+ courses in their area.

The size of teaching groups in the FE colleges was generally larger than in the other types of institutions. There were no instances of classes smaller than four in the sample colleges, and this was also true of the additional sample. The largest reported teaching group contained 43 students (an arts subject), and another contained 31. 'Typical' sizes ranged from eight to 25.

All nine colleges provided a students' common room. Not all these contained tea- and coffee-making facilities but the majority (seven) did. A majority also contained a record-player, but newspapers and magazines, radios and TV sets, while present in some, were only evident in a minority of institutions. Games, on the other hand, were played in all nine common rooms.

The majority of these colleges considered their library

large enough. Four provided a separate room for private
study, and a small number reported that other arrangements
were made for students' private study, such as facilities in
corridors. In two colleges there were said to be no special
facilities for private study other than the central library. Four
colleges timetabled and supervised private study; four others
timetabled it but carried out no direct supervision. The ninth
college indicated that students had free time and it was left
to them to organize their own private study.

As with the tertiary colleges, there was a students' union
in every FE college in the sample, and the functions were
similar. All but one of the FE students' unions were affiliated
to the NUS, and membership was automatic for full-time
students in all but one college.

Attitudes towards the personal appearance of students
were very similar to those of the tertiary colleges, attention
being paid to certain features according to the course being
followed, for example safety in workshops, hygiene in
courses relating to health and food and general personal
appearance in secretarial courses.

Attitudes towards regular attendance were also similar
to that of the tertiary colleges. More examples were provided
of steps taken to ensure this, as more colleges were involved.
One college reported weekly checks, with letters sent out to
parents in appropriate cases, and another indicated that
written explanations of absence were required. Unlike the
tertiary college sample, some of the FE colleges (five) required students to remain on the premises during non-lesson
times.

Smoking was not banned in any of the FE colleges, but
was again restricted to certain areas, such as common rooms
and refectories.

Table 3.8 (I1): Numbers of A-level subjects offered by the institutions in the sample

	Number of institutions				
	Compre-hensive	Grammar	Sixth-form College	Tertiary	FE
Number of A-levels offered					
10—14	2	2			
15—19	9	6			
20—24	3	4	1		4
25—29	1		4	1	5
30—34			1	2	
Total numbers of institutions	15	12	6	3	9
average number offered	18	18	27	30	25

Table 3.9 (I1): Courses (other than A-levels) available to students in the sample

	Number of institutions				
	Compre-hensive	Grammar	Sixth-form College	Tertiary	FE
Courses	N = 15	N = 12	N = 6	N = 3	N = 9
O-level (or OA level)	15	12	6	3	9
CSE	7	1	2		
CEE	6	1	2		
RSA	10	3	3	3	9
Pitman	6	1	1	3	8
Pre-Professional				2	9
College Certificate/Diploma			1	2	6
OND				3	9
City and Guilds		1	2	2	5

Chapter 4

Staying On

---

a. Educational and social background of students who stay on
Students in the main sample were asked to provide details of
the type of school they had attended in the fifth year and the
examinations they had passed prior to entry to the sixth
form or college.

Table 4.1 shows the type of school attended in the fifth
year by students in the sample. It shows that the 16—19
colleges drew students from both selective and non-selective
backgrounds, although in theory the feeder schools for such
colleges would be entirely comprehensive. This discrepancy
can be explained partly in terms of the relative recency of
comprehensive reorganization in some areas, and by the
admission of students from outside a college's official catchment area. FE colleges do not have designated feeder schools,
but have traditionally provided a 'second chance' for many
secondary modern pupils, and this arrangement is clearly
illustrated in the table. Ten per cent of the grammar school
sample was also made up of pupils transferring from local
secondary modern schools.

It should be noted that while independent schools were
not included in the research, nevertheless the sample included
students from the fifth forms of such schools; indeed these
comprised 12 per cent of the total sample of college students.

The average number of O-level and CSE passes obtained
by students in the different types of institution are shown in
Table 4.2. CSE Grade 1 passes are included in the O-level

Table 4.1: (S1): School backgrounds of students

Previous school attended	Comprehensive School		Grammar School		Sixth-form College		Tertiary College		FE College		Total	
	N	%	N	%	N	%	N	%	N	%	N	%
Secondary Modern	30	3	87	10	106	11	62	12	376	33	661	15
Grammar	70	7	716	83	345	37	108	20	244	22	1482	33
Comprehensive	822	84	9	1	342	36	301	57	299	27	1773	40
Independent	10	1	11	1	117	12	43	8	154	14	335	8
Other	5	6	3	5	10	4	9	3	27	4	54	4
Total = 100%	981		866		946		530		1125		4448	

Table 4.2: (S1): Fifth-year examination attainment of students by type of institution

	Comprehensive School	Grammar School	Sixth-form College	Tertiary College	FE College	Total
Mean no. of O-level passes (including CSE Grade 1s)	4.4	6.5	5.1	4.4	4.2	4.9
Standard Deviation	3.0	2.2	2.9	2.8	2.6	2.8
Mean no. of CSE passes	2.0	0.5	1.6	1.5	2.2	1.6
Standard Deviation	2.2	1.1	2.1	2.0	2.2	2.1
Total	981	866	946	530	1125	4448

figures. The table shows that grammar school sixth-formers, with an average of 6.5 O-levels to their credit, had significantly more passes than those in the other types of institution. The sixth-form college students were also better qualified than those in either comprehensive schools or FE establishments. This may reflect the point made above that some of the colleges were ex-grammar schools and their students part of a selective intake. However, 25 per cent of the sixth-form college students had fewer than three O-level passes, and this suggests that the open-access policy is attracting a significant proportion of students of more modest attainment.

Table 4.3 gives the same information for students on different types of courses. This shows that while students on A-level courses had significantly more O-level passes than other groups, there was considerable variation in the academic attainment of those following vocational courses. Students studying for Ordinary National Diplomas, where four O-levels is normally the entry requirement, had an average of 4.9 O-level passes. The students following secretarial courses were very varied in their educational background, one quarter of this group having five or more O-level passes and a similar proportion, none.

Students with the fewest number of O-level passes to their credit had passed commensurately more CSE subjects, and were concentrated on either City and Guilds or O-level courses.

In order to obtain a measure of social status students were asked to give details of their father's occupation. These were then coded according to the Hall-Jones Scale of Occupational Prestige for Males as follows:

Class 1: Professionally qualified and high administrative
Class 2: Managerial and executive
Class 3: Inspectional, supervisory and other non-manual (higher grade)
Class 4: Inspectional, supervisory and other non-manual (lower grade)
Class 5: Routine grades of non-manual and skilled manual
Class 6: Manual, semi-skilled
Class 7: Manual, routine

Table 4.3 (S1): **Fifth-year examination attainment of students by type of course**

	A-level	O-level	OND	City & Guilds	Sec.	Other
Mean no. of O-level passes (including CSE Grade 1s)	6.1	1.3	4.9	1.5	2.9	2.5
Standard Deviation	2.2	1.5	1.9	1.9	2.4	2.2
Mean no. of CSE passes	0.9	3.8	1.6	3.2	2.5	3.2
Standard Deviation	1.5	2.4	1.8	2.4	2.2	2.3
Total	2913	449	322	232	337	195

Table 4.4 (S1) Social background of students (percentages)

Father's occupation	Comprehensive School %	Grammar School %	Sixth-Form College %	Tertiary College %	FE College %	Total %	GHS 1973* %
1. Professional	11	10	11	9	8	10	4.0
2. Managerial	21	24	18	14	20	20	14.6
3. Inspectional – upper	26	23	23	23	24	24	⎫ 20.0
4. Inspectional – lower	5	7	7	10	7	7	⎭
5. Routine non-manual/ skilled manual	26	28	29	27	25	27	33.4
6. Semi-skilled	2	2	2	4	4	3	19.5
7. Unskilled	1	0	1	2	1	1	6.6
8. Unclassifiable or no information given	9	6	9	11	11	9	(2.0)
Total = 100%	981	866	946	530	1125	4448	

*Socio-economic group of head of household (Great Britain)

Table 4.4 shows the percentages of students in the five different types of institution according to their father's occupational class. Figures are also given showing the percentage of each occupational class in the population according to the General Household Survey of 1973.

The table shows that the sample contained a higher proportion of students with fathers in occupational class 1—4 than in the population as a whole, and a correspondingly lower proportion in classes 5—7. These figures were consistent with the national tendency for young people with fathers in professional, managerial and supervisory occupations to be proportionally over-represented in full-time post-compulsory and higher education. It must be appreciated that the percentages presented certainly underestimate the extent of social discrepancies. The number of children born to parents in the higher occupational classes is smaller than that of children born to parents in the lower occupations. Direct comparisons with the percentages presented for the General Household Survey cannot therefore be made, although the latter might serve as a rough yardstick. An examination of the figures for the different types of institution shows that they contained an approximately equal proportion of students in any one class, and that although classes 1—4 were over-represented in the sample, they were equally over-represented in each institutional type, and classes 5—7 were equally under-represented.

This casts some doubt on the claim that fifth-formers with working-class backgrounds might, for various reasons, be more easily deterred from entry to post-compulsory education if to do so would involve the upheaval of a change of institution at 16-plus, and it appears that the type of institution makes little difference to the overall numbers. The effect of different forms of provision at 16+ on the aspirations of fifth-formers is discussed later in this chapter.

In addition to information about their father's occupations, students were also asked whether their parents had stayed on at school beyond the statutory leaving age, what qualifications, if any, they had obtained and to what extent they were in favour of their children's continued education.

Overall, one quarter of students in the sample came from families where the father had stayed on. This proportion was significantly higher amongst grammar school sixth-formers, 30 per cent of whom fell in this category. However, the proportion of students in other types of institution who did not know whether their father had done so was higher than in grammar schools, and it may be that the latter group were simply better informed about their father's education. There were no significant differences between students in terms of their father's educational qualifications. Over half said their father had no formal qualifications, 19 per cent that he had passed GCE or School Certificate examinations, 13 per cent had fathers with technical qualifications of some sort and an equal proportion, a teaching certificate or degree. Two thirds of the students said that their mother had no formal educational qualifications, and here again there was no difference between students in different institutions in this respect. Although hardly any students reported that parental pressure had been their main reason for staying on in full-time education, it is evident that most did so with their parents' approval and support. Over three quarters of the students said their parents were in favour of their staying on. While 13 per cent said their parents did not mind whether they did so and seven per cent reported a tendency for one parent to be more in favour than the other, only one per cent of the students said that their parents were opposed to their staying on.

b. FE as an option

A college of FE exists as an option for virtually all 16-year-olds planning to continue their education. There are very few areas of the country which are not served by such a college, and nearly all of them offer a sufficient range of full-time courses to present, in theory if not in practice, a viable alternative to either a school sixth form or a sixth-form college. Of the schools completing the institutional background questionnaire (I1) only four said there was no FE college in their immediate catchment area, and these were all in isolated rural areas.

For many young people further education will be the only possibility on their horizon. Those in search of technical qualifications such as Ordinary National Diplomas or basic training in a skilled trade examined by the City and Guilds of London Institute can only take the relevant courses in FE institutions. But as FE continues to develop its academic courses there will be many areas where provision made by school sixth forms is duplicated by the local FE college.

The increase in the number of students voluntarily enrolling in a college in preference to a school sixth form and the recognition of this trend in local authorities' reorganization of their post-compulsory provision has already been outlined in Chapter 1. This section will consider in some detail the characteristics of students in the research sample who chose to enter colleges of further education and, in particular, the group who left schools with sixth forms. Students on A-level courses in tertiary colleges have been omitted from this section of the report as these colleges are the only providers of post-compulsory education in a given area and students can therefore hardly be said to opt for them. The backgrounds and motivations of students on A-level courses in tertiary colleges may therefore be expected to differ somewhat from the corresponding group in traditional colleges of FE. On the other hand, the students on vocational courses such as OND, City and Guilds and secretarial courses in these two types of institution have been considered as a single group as it was found there was very little difference between them.

i. *Dissemination of information about further education*

Before we go on to investigate the characteristics of the different groups of students in further education, it is worth examining the means whereby they were made aware of the opportunities available in the colleges. Students in all three types of college, i.e. sixth-form, tertiary and FE, were asked to indicate which was their first source of information about it. The responses from the three groups were as shown in Table 4.5.

It is apparent from the table that the students in FE had had to rely more on unofficial channels and those external to school for information about courses offered at the college. For example, whereas 30 per cent of the FE group first heard

Table 4.5 (S1): College students' first source of information about institution attended (percentages)

	Sixth-form College Students	Tertiary College Students	FE Students
Member of college staff visited school	26	22	6
I visited the college	10	20	10
School staff informed me	21	17	10
I read college prospectus/advert	13	13	30
Friends told me about it	8	5	13
Parents advised me to apply	2	4	6
Brother or sister attended the college	4	5	6
Careers officer told me	1	2	10
Part of my fifth-form course was taken at the college	5	4	2
Total = 100%	946	530	1125

about the college through reading either the prospectus or an advertisement, this was true of only 13 per cent of the students in sixth-form and tertiary colleges. The major sources of information for the tertiary and sixth-form college students were either a visit to the school by a member of the college staff, teachers at the school or a visit to the college themselves. Where such colleges exist and secondary school education finishes at 16, the channels of information between them and the schools seem therefore to be reasonably satisfactory. However, the colleges of FE are not so well publicized. Only six per cent of FE students said a member of the college staff had visited the school, and 10 per cent that a school teacher had suggested the college to them. It is interesting to note that the careers officer played as important a part in disseminating information about the FE colleges as did school teachers, and also that 13 per cent of FE students had relied on their friends as a source of information.

What are the reasons for poor dissemination of informa-

tion about the colleges of further education on the part of
the schools? Where schools are anxious to build up their own
sixth forms, they may be tempted to persuade fifth-formers
to stay on at school rather than transfer to a college. Many
colleges experience difficulties in making their courses known
within the schools and often report a suspicious and sometimes hostile reaction in situations where they are seen as
rival recruiting agents.

> In some areas youngsters do not have a free informed
> choice. Quite a few are conned into staying in the sixth
> form, then not liking it and leaving in disgust and are
> definitely lost to education. That worries me. I think
> the 11—18 school or the FE college — telling them in
> the fifth form — you have a choice, this is what the
> school offers and this is what the college offers. Some
> authorities do this and I would have thought that if
> they make an informed choice at 16 then they are
> going to get a much better set-up. They will start on
> something they want to see through. Too often in areas
> where FE is disguised and hidden they will start on a
> sixth-form course to which they're unsuited and at the
> end of the first year, will leave education for good.
> (FE lecturer.)

The sources of information used by students entering FE
from different types of feeder schools are shown in Table
4.6. Although reading the college prospectus or seeing an
advertisement had been the most common source of information for all groups of students, those from grammar and
independent schools had been particularly likely to hear of
FE in this way. They were also more likely to have heard
about the college from their friends than students from
secondary modern and comprehensive schools. A quarter of
ex-independent school pupils said their friends had told them
about the college. Students from grammar and independent
schools were less likely to have heard about the opportunities
in FE from school teachers or their careers officer.
    In summary, therefore, it appears that the information
concerning local FE colleges and the courses they offer is

Table 4.6 (S1) Students in FE: First source of information about college of FE by type of school attended in fifth year (percentages)

	Secondary Modern	Grammar School	Comprehensive School	Independent School	Other	All FE Students
Member of college staff visited school	9	6	6	—		6
I visited the college	14	5	8	8		10
School staff informed me	13	9	12	4		10
I read college prospectus/advert	23	39	25	41		30
Friends told me about it	9	16	13	23		13
Parents advised me to apply	6	4	7	5		6
Brother or sister attended the college	3	5	7	9		6
Careers Officer told me	14	9	12	4		10
Part of my fifth-form course was taken at the college	2	—	2			2
Total = 100%	376	244	299	154	(52)	1125

less likely to be disseminated through formal channels via the school, and this is particularly true of schools with a long-established tradition of academic sixth forms, i.e. the grammar and independent schools.

While it is reasonable to argue that students of 16 should be told that there is a number of alternatives available to A-level, in institutions run under schools regulations it appears that all too often it is automatically assumed that any student with the appropriate potential should be encouraged to do an A-level course. Schools recognize that a certain antagonism exists between them and FE, and admit that they are concerned to build up their sixth-form numbers as this exchange between two teachers and an FE lecturer illustrates.

> I don't think the antagonism is based on qualifications. I think that partly it is an inevitable sadness when you see a good student that you have enjoyed taking disappearing into the blue somewhere else. (Comprehensive school teacher.)

> It's not just the sadness either. It's the practical problems of the school where the 11–18 system is operating and one has the problem of building up a viable sixth form. Two very good sixth-formers lost to the FE colleges would make your groups even less viable than they are. So very often, it's a purely practical problem. (Another teacher from the same school.)

> Well, another slight problem is, of course, that the student in school is used to the progression from O- to A-level and if, in fact, he is going to have to diversify slightly because his grades are not good enough or some other reason, he is going to be on slightly uncharted waters. The student presented at sixteen with the choice of A-level and OND, for example, is going to say to you, What is OND? as his first question. That is a very difficult problem — the currency of the alternatives to the O-level, A-level, university system. It is, to some extent, a communication problem which goes on in the vocational part of FE and HE and which doesn't entire-

ly percolate down to the schools. I don't think this is a
criticism of the schools. It is mainly because few people
have actually been through that system themselves.
Relatively few people in school have been through
anything except schools/universities. (FE head of
department.)

Many students sensed, at various stages in their educational
career, that they had been pressurized into taking A-levels
and that there was a lack of information about the alternatives. Some commented on this at the outset of their
course.

I would just like to say in our school we are geared
towards A-levels. Very intelligent people are expected
to go to university. When we had an interview with our
careers teacher, we were automatically asked first what
A-levels we would be taking, rather than what we
wanted to do. This came after. This annoyed me in-
tensely. (Grammar.)

I would like to see the college facilities advertised in
schools. I knew nothing about the opportunities here
till I was forced to come here to take my A-levels.
People aren't aware of the openings here which seems a
shame. (FE.)

Others, sadly, did not realize that they had been ill advised
until it was too late. The following comment is from a
student who obtained A-level passes in biology, chemistry
and physics.

At the end of the fifth year I was virtually unaware of
the possibility of taking ONC in place of A-levels. Consequently, when I went into employment after taking
A-levels I was told by the ———— Technical College
that I could not begin an HNC course in Medical Laboratory Studies without first completing the final year of
the ONC course (despite the fact that I was qualified to
go on to HNC). In their opinion A-levels did not contain

enough practical experience to cope with the HNC course directly and this to a certain extent is true. I am obviously disappointed that I have wasted a year of study and wish that the pros and cons of ONC had at least been made known to me before embarking on an A-level course.

A student now studying for an HND voiced the same reservations about A-level: 'I believe that A-levels are considered by employers to be of a lower standard than ONDs. People who have studied ONDs are in a much better position than those who have A-levels, so why do schools direct pupils to take A levels?'

A similar comment was made by a student studying for a degree in graphic design at a college of higher education who had taken three A-levels at a sixth-form college and passed only one of them. 'I was not informed that I could have gone to my present college of art when I was 17. Having only gained an A-level in Art for two years' work, I feel the time could be said to have been wasted.'

The number of students who subsequently entered employment with A-level qualifications only to find that they were doing jobs which they might just as easily have been offered at 16 also casts doubts on the advisability of studying for A-levels when they are not essential requirements for one's ultimate objectives. 'I regard my sixth-form course at school as a waste of time as it has not helped me at all with respect to my banking career. I obtained one A-level which is not at all useful and I deeply regret not starting in banking at the age of 16.' (Comprehensive.)

This sort of experience not only implies that students should be in a position to consider alternative full-time courses but also that the advantages and disadvantages of entering employment at 16, perhaps with some part-time training involved, should be discussed with them. Given the current employment situation, the assumption that anybody with the ability to stay on should do so should be questioned. The views of students in employment on this and other related issues are discussed in greater detail in Chapter 8.

For the moment we can only endorse the recommendations of the Schools Council's Working Party on sixth-form examinations.[8]

> It is essential that everyone — which means pupils, parents, teachers and employers — is fully aware of all the different courses available to a boy or girl at the end of the fifth year of secondary school. At present, in most areas, information is discovered only by those who make determined inquiries or through an interview with a careers officer. Far too many parents and pupils are quite ignorant of the existence of any alternative to full-time education at school. Some local authorities are producing booklets with details of all school and college courses, but in others no real attempt is made to give pupils either the freedom, or the knowledge to use it, that they should surely have.

> Schools need to work closely with their local college. Teachers in schools and colleges need to appreciate each other's work: merely knowing of the existence of an alternative course is not enough. Teachers who are giving advice about a course must, if possible, have seen it at work and at least know something of what it promises.

ii. *Students on A-level courses in further education*

There were 384 students in the sample who were following full-time A-level courses in colleges of further education (other than tertiary). The most significant difference between the students on A-level courses in further education and those in other types of institution was in their educational background. The types of schools attended by the two groups during their fifth year of secondary education are shown in Table 4.7.

Approximately one third of the FE group had previously attended a secondary modern school, compared with only seven per cent in other institutions. Under a selective system, it is likely that at least some young people with the potential to undertake A-level work will find themselves in secondary modern schools which lack the facilities to offer a full-

Table 4.7: (S1): School backgrounds of FE students (percentages)

Type of school last attended	A-level Students in FE colleges	A-level Students in other Types of Institution	FE and Tertiary Colleges		
			OND Students	City & Guilds Students	Secretarial Students
Secondary modern	31	7	27	42	15
Grammar	19	45	26	10	29
Comprehensive	23	38	30	39	43
Independent	19	5	11	8	12
Other	8	4	7	1	2
Total = 100%	384	2529	322	232	206

range of sixth-form courses. While it may be theoretically possible for them to transfer to the sixth form of a local grammar school, the opportunity to pursue similar goals at a college of further education is probably a more attractive alternative. All of the seven secondary modern schools involved in the fifth-year study (see Chapter 10) reported that local grammar school sixth forms and colleges of FE were available to pupils with the appropriate potential, but in every case less than five per cent of their fifth year entered the sixth form of another secondary school. In contrast, the proportion entering full-time courses in further education ranged from ten to 30 per cent.

Pupils from independent schools were also found in greater numbers among the FE group than in the sample as a whole. There were several possible reasons for this. First, many independent schools find it just as difficult to offer a satisfactory range of A-level subjects as those in the maintained sector, and their pupils may find that an FE college offers them a wider choice. Secondly, young people often grow to resent the rules and regulations that govern their lives at school (this is particularly likely if they attend a boarding school), and may find the college atmosphere more to their liking. Parents will also find relief from the financial burden of fees if their children enter a college at 16. (Although FE colleges have traditionally been the destination of such pupils, in recent years the sixth-form colleges have witnessed an increase in the applications from independent school pupils, and 12 per cent of the sixth-form college sample was made up of students from this background.)

The main reasons given by the two groups of A-level students for entering the particular sixth form or college they now attended are shown in Table 4.8. This shows that the A-level students in institutions other than FE were much more homogeneous in this respect, and were inclined to give somewhat passive reasons for their choice of institution, if in fact the word 'choice' can be used at all in this context. Half were 'happy to stay on at the same school as I attended before' and one quarter said their main reason for entering their current institution was that there was 'no sixth form in my old school'. These findings suggest that the great majority

Table 4.8 (S1): Students in FE – main reasons for entering present institution (percentages)

| | A-level Students in FE colleges | A-level Students in other Types of Institution | FE and Tertiary Colleges | | |
			OND Students	City & Guilds Students	Secretarial Students
Happy to stay on at the same school school as I attended before	–	49	–	–	–
No sixth form in my old school	13	24	14	3	2
Course or subject I wanted not available at my school	18	3	27	25	25
Was not qualified to enter the sixth form at my school	2	–	–	–	1
Wanted a practical course directly preparing for career	4	3	33	50	43
Disliked school, wanted a change	14	2	3	3	7
Failed exams at school, came here to retake them	6	1	–	–	1
Wanted a more adult environment	25	6	9	5	15
Was in employment or abroad, could not go to school	2	–	1	–	–
Total = 100%	384	2529	322	232	206

were happy to comply with whatever arrangements the local authority made for sixth-formers, whether this entailed entering the sixth form of their school or transferring to a sixth-form or tertiary college. The reasons given by A-level students in FE were, in comparison, more varied. One quarter said they had entered the college in search of an adult environment, and a further 14 per cent said they had dislike school and wanted a change. Thus approximately 40 per cent had moved through reasons connected with dissatisfaction with school. A further 18 per cent said they had come to a college in search of subjects which were not available at school, and 13 per cent because their school had no sixth-form provision.

In terms of their educational background students on A-level courses in FE had fewer O-level passes than A-level students in other institutions (an average of 5.8 passes compared with 6.2, p<.001).

The following table (4.9) shows that they were also studying fewer A-level subjects, though it should be borne in mind that a quarter of the FE group was planning to complete an

Table 4.9 (S1)

| | percentages | |
No. of A-level Subjects being taken	FE A-level Students N = 384	Non-FE A-level Students N = 2529
1	6	7
2	35	22
3	54	67
4	3	3
5	1	
mean	2.57	2.67

A-level course in one year and might therefore be expected to be taking fewer subjects. (For a full description of this subgroup and their subsequent performance see *One-Year Courses in Colleges and Sixth-Forms*.[9]) When the actual subjects being taken by the two groups were examined it was found that approximately a quarter of both groups were taking combinations of science and mathematical subjects. However, only 10 per cent of the FE group were taking exclusively arts or languages, compared with 22 per cent of those in other types of institution. The A-level students in FE were much more likely to be taking a social science subject, particularly one or more of the following:

Sociology
British Constitution
Economics
General Principles of English Law
Political Studies
Environmental Studies
Psychology

Thirty nine per cent of the FE group were taking either social science subjects alone or in combination with arts or languages compared with 25 per cent of students in schools and other types of college. There was however no significant difference in the reasons given by students for their choice of subjects. A-level students in general had chosen their subjects either out of interest (40 per cent) or because the subjects were necessary either for their chosen career or for the course they planned to take in higher education (32 per cent). There was some evidence to suggest that the FE group were more career-oriented in their approach to post-compulsory education (see Table 4.10). Whereas 29 per cent said their main reason for staying on in full-time education was in order to obtain the qualifications necessary for their *chosen* career, only 20 per cent of A-level students in other institutions gave this answer, which suggests that they were less likely to have a specific career goal in mind at the outset of their course. The non-FE A-level group more often stated that their desire to go on to higher education was their main reason for staying on (28 per cent gave this reason compared with only 21 per cent of the FE students).

However, there was no significant difference in the ultimate qualifications aimed at by the two groups. Approximately half of all the A-level students hoped to take degree courses, 15 per cent to obtain teaching certificates and 10 per cent

Table 4.10 (S1): Students in FE — main reason for staying on in full-time education after fifth year (percentages)

	A-level Students in FE colleges	A-level Students in other Types of Institution	FE and Tertiary Colleges		
			OND Students	City & Guilds Students	Secretarial Students
Never considered leaving	1	5	2	3	1
Wish to go to higher education	21	28	13	7	7
Interest in subject(s)	3	2	2	13	—
Qualifications necessary for chosen career	29	20	25	33	43
Improving career prospects in general	35	36	45	28	37
Broadening outlook	2	2	3	2	1
Most of my friends stayed on					
Not yet ready to go out to work	2	3	3	2	4
Parental pressure	2	1		1	2
Total = 100%	384	2529	322	232	206

other qualifications. Approximately a quarter either did not intend to take further courses beyond A-level or had not yet decided whether to do so. The FE group was therefore just as likely to be aiming at higher education but was more inclined to see it as a stage in its progress towards career goals rather than an end in itself.

iii. *Students on OND courses*

OND courses are two-year full-time courses designed for young people of above average ability who wish to follow a broadly based course of study within a particular vocational area. The sample of OND students selected to take part in this study was restricted to those taking the examination in either business studies, technology or hotel and catering operations although a number of other options are available. The numbers of students in these groups in the sample were 187, 90 and 45 respectively. All the OND technology students were boys. On the business studies and catering courses boys and girls were found in equal numbers.

Passes in four subjects at O-level are the normal entry requirements for an OND course, and relevant subjects are sometimes specified. For example a pass in English is usually required for business studies and in maths for those intending to study technology. The OND students included in the sample had an average of 4.9 O-levels (SD = 1.9), and over a third had passed six or more subjects. They were therefore the second most highly qualified group after the A-level students.

An OND course entails the study of a number of subjects, some of which are compulsory. In order to qualify for the Diploma students are normally required to obtain a pass in five subjects. On a business studies course, for example, English and economics are compulsory and the rest of the time-table consists of a selection from the following:
Statistics, law, economic geography, elements of computers, accounts, French, German, economic history, mercantile law, function and organization of the office, elements of insurance.

OND students are often given the opportunity to take A-levels in subjects associated with the course, and one third of the sample were taking at least one subject at A-level as part of their course.

While providing a sound background for students intending to embark immediately on a career, an Ordinary National Diploma qualifies a student to enrol for Higher National Diplomas and degree courses in appropriate subjects and also claim exemption from the intermediate examinations of a range of professional bodies. Taking the business studies course as an example again, the following are some of the bodies who will consider exemptions from holders of the Diploma:

> The Association of Certified Accountants
> The Building Societies Institute
> The Chartered Institute of Secretaries and
>   Administrators
> The Chartered Insurance Institute
> The Institute of Bankers
> The Institute of Chartered Accountants
> The Institute of Cost and Management Accountants
> The Institute of Chartered Shipbrokers
> The Institute of Export
> The Institute of Health Service Administrators
> The Institute of Municipal Treasurers and Accountants
> The Chartered Institute of Transport
> The Local Government Training Board
> The Institute of Traffic Administration
> The Savings Bank Institute

In terms of their motivation, OND students were found to be somewhat different from A-level students in further education. They appeared to be less concerned with qualifying for higher education and more interested in improving their immediate career prospects. Their responses to the question 'What was your main reason for staying on in full-time education this year?' were distributed as in Table 4.10 (figures for A-level students in FE and in other types of institution are also given).

Improved career prospects were seen as the most important reason for staying on by nearly half of the OND students.

Only one quarter said the qualifications they hoped to obtain were necessary for their chosen career. It is surprising that the proportion choosing this reason was higher among the A-level students in FE — it might be expected that OND students would be more likely to have decided upon a career, yet only half had done so compared with 63 per cent of the A-level students in further education. Only 13 per cent of the OND students expressed a wish to enter higher education as their main reason for staying on.

In response to an item about further qualifications which they might go on to study for, a quarter of the OND students said they hoped eventually to embark on a degree course, but the qualification most frequently mentioned by this group (29 per cent) was a Higher National Diploma or Certificate. There were very few other students who mentioned this qualification; only three per cent of the A-level students did so.

Table 4.8 shows the reasons given by OND students for entering their present institution compared with those on other types of courses. The reasons most often given by them for entering an FE or tertiary college were either that they 'wanted a practical course directly preparing for career' (33 per cent) or that the 'course or subject I wanted was not available at school' (27 per cent). Considerations concerning the courses available in the different institutions seem therefore to have dominated the deliberations of OND students. They were much less concerned with escaping from the confines of the school atmosphere than the A-level students in FE. Only 12 per cent claimed that they had come to the college in search of an adult environment or because they had disliked school and wanted a change.

No particular type of feeder school was more likely than others to produce candidates for OND courses. Table 4.7 shows that 30 per cent came from comprehensive school backgrounds, and 27 and 26 per cent respectively from secondary modern and grammar schools. When one considers the O-level achievements of this group and their ability compared with other groups in the study, the proportion of ex-secondary modern pupils embarking on OND courses illustrates the standard of GCE work undertaken in many schools of this type.

iv. *Students on City and Guilds courses*

The City and Guilds of London Institute is responsible for developing syllabuses, setting examinations and awarding certificates in a very wide range of technical subjects at various craft and technician levels. Agriculture, construction, forestry, mining and quarrying, food and drink, engineering and water are only a few of the industries for which the City and Guilds offer courses and set examinations.

While many of the courses are available on a day-release basis and this is the pattern of attendance which most apprentices follow at the age of 16, full-time basic craft courses are available in a range of subjects for young people wishing to enter a particular industry. They are 'intended to further the education and development of the student by providing a broad basis of study which will give him or her an introduction of the nature of openings in the industry and the skills necessary in those occupations so that each individual may be guided to an appropriate course of further training and education'.

A total of 232 students on full-time courses leading to City and Guilds examinations were included in the project sample. This number comprised 127 on basic catering craft courses, 57 studying hairdressing, 29 fashion and clothing and 19 computer programming and information processing. 51 of the catering students were on courses of one year's duration but all the other City and Guilds students were on 2-year courses. Girls outnumbered boys on these courses by more than two to one with the exception of computer programming where this ratio was reversed. Entry requirements for City and Guilds courses vary greatly. Students on most of the courses outlined above were required to have a good secondary education and to have achieved a satisfactory standard in relevant subjects, and although GCE and CSE passes were desirable, they were not essential. In the case of computer programming, however, students were required to have obtained either an O-level pass or a CSE Grade 1 in mathematics. In general, this small group were more highly qualified than the other City and Guilds students, and most were being entered for three or even four subjects at A-level — usually maths, accounts, statistics and computing, in addition to their City and Guilds examinations. Overall, the City and Guilds students had an average of 3.2 CSE passes and 1.5 passes at O-level or CSE grade 1. More than 40 per cent of students on this type of course had no O-level passes. Table 4.7 shows that over 80 per cent of the City and Guilds students had attended either secondary modern or comprehensive schools prior to entering the college, and that City and Guilds courses did not attract students from grammar and independent schools in such numbers as did other courses available in FE.

City and Guilds students' main reason for staying on was in order to obtain qualifications necessary for their chosen career. Only among City and Guilds and secretarial students did this reason outweigh 'improving career prospects in general'. Seventy five per cent of the City and Guilds group had already decided upon a career, and this was a higher proportion than among other course groups. However, they also appear to be more subject-minded than other students in FE. Table 4.10 shows that 13 per cent said an interest in the subject had been their main reason for staying on in full-time education, and this was significantly higher than for other groups.

The figures in Table 4.8 support the view of City and Guilds students as very career-oriented. Half said their main reason for entering their present institution was that they wanted a practical course which would prepare them for a career, and a further 25 per cent because the course they wished to follow was not available at their school.

Comparatively few of the City and Guilds students intended to continue their education beyond the qualifications for which they were studying at the time. In answer to a question investigating what further qualifications they hoped to obtain, less than half mentioned one, but 25 per cent of the group said they hoped to go on to take more City and Guilds examinations. Only seven per cent hoped eventually to study for a degree, and four per cent for a teaching certificate.

v. *Students on secretarial courses in FE and tertiary colleges*
    Included in the sample was a number of students on

courses leading to secretarial examinations set by the Pitman Institute, the Royal Society of Arts or the London Chamber of Commerce. In the sample as a whole there were 337 students of this type, all but two of them girls.

Approximately one third of this group was in school sixth forms or sixth-form colleges. Secretarial training had traditionally been one of the very few examples of vocational training offered by the schools, and usually takes the form of a one-year course in the sixth form for girls who do not wish or do not have the necessary aptitude to embark on an A-level course.

Of the 206 girls following secretarial courses in FE and tertiary colleges, 110 were on courses of one year's duration, 56 on two-year courses and 40 were studying for the Medical Secretaries' Diploma, which is also a two-year course.

The girls on secretarial courses in FE and tertiary colleges had an average of 3.5 O-level passes. This was significantly more than the group taking similar courses in schools and sixth-form colleges, who had an average of 2.0 passes to their credit. Many girls in the FE group were in fact very highly qualified, a third of them having five or more O-levels. Those who were on courses designated 'senior secretarial' were frequently taking one or two A-level examinations in relevant subjects, e.g. English, Accounts or British constitution as well as the more usual secretarial examinations.

In terms of their educational background, the largest proportion of the students in this group was from comprehensive schools (43 per cent). However, students from grammar schools accounted for a greater proportion of the secretarial students than for any other course group in FE, 29 per cent of them coming from schools of this type.

Secretarial students in FE and tertiary colleges were more likely than any other group to say that their main reason for staying on in full-time education was to obtain qualifications necessary for their chosen career. Forty three per cent gave this reason, and a further 37 per cent said they hoped to improve their career prospects in general. Comparatively few had any intention of furthering their education beyond their present course. Those that did intend to study for some further qualification most often mentioned GCE A-level

(12 per cent) or more advanced secretarial examinations (nine per cent).

The reasons given by secretarial students in FE and tertiary colleges for entering their current institution are shown in Table 4.8. In common with students on OND and City and Guilds courses, they had entered college in search of a practical course which would directly prepare them for a career. This reason was given by 43 per cent of the secretarial students. A further 25 per cent said the course they wished to follow was 'not available at my school'.

However, secretarial students were more inclined than students on other vocational courses to say they had entered a college because of their desire for an adult environment. 15 per cent chose this as their main reason, and this implies, as is the case with the A-level students, that a proportion of the secretarial students could have stayed on at school to take similar courses but chose to leave through dissatisfaction with the school ethos.

c. Students who opt out of all-through schools

It was possible to identify a substantial number of students in the sample who had left schools with sixth forms in order to enter a college of further education. Of the students in the FE sample, 834 (74 per cent) came from schools which had some form of sixth-form provision, 18 per cent of this group having actually entered the sixth form for a while.

There was very little variation between the various course groups in FE in the proportion transferring from all-through schools. Students from all types of secondary school featured in this category but the proportions from secondary modern and independent school backgrounds were significantly higher than in the sample as a whole. The incidence of ex-secondary modern pupils saying their previous school had a sixth form suggests that while it is common for such schools to offer a limited range of sixth-form studies, they are not able to cater for all their pupils wishing to continue their education, particularly those in search of either vocational qualifications or A-level courses. Table 4.11 shows the main reasons for entry to their current college given by students opting out of 11–18 schools according to the type of school

Table 4.11 (S1): Students in FE opting out of 11–18 schools – main reason for entering FE by type of school attended (percentages)

	Secondary Modern	Grammar	Comprehensive	Independent	Other	Total
Course or subject I wanted not available at my school	36	25	24	22		27
Was not qualified to enter the sixth-form at my school		2	1	1		1
Wanted a practical course directly preparing for career	27	30	31	23		28
Disliked school, wanted a change	6	16	13	11		12
Failed exams at school, came here to retake them	1	3	2	5		3
Wanted more adult environment	13	13	16	24		16
Was in employment or abroad, could not go to school		1	1			1
Total = 100%	201	227	250	124	(32)	834

they had previously attended. Overall, the reasons most frequently given were either that they had wanted a practical course which would prepare them for a career or that the course or subject they wanted was not available at their school. These two reasons predominated for students from all types of feeder school, and were mentioned by approximately half of each group. Other reasons, which indicated a certain disenchantment with school, i.e. 'disliked school, wanted a change' and 'wanted a more adult environment', accounted for most of the remainder. Ex-secondary modern pupils were less likely to express views in this second category than students from other backgrounds. Pupils from independent schools were most likely to say they had entered further education in search of an adult atmosphere. Entry requirements to the sixth form of their school did not seem to have played a significant part in their decision to leave, and very few students said their main reason had been insufficient qualifications for entry to the sixth form.

These findings suggest that the sixth form was available to most of these students in principle but the particular course which they wished to follow was not, and that this, rather than a dislike of the school atmosphere, was the major reason for their rejection of sixth-form education. Table 4.12 shows the reasons for entering their present institution given by this group of students according to the main qualification for which they are now studying. This shows clearly that the group whose reasons for transfer were connected with their dissatisfaction with school was concentrated on A-level courses. The percentage of A-level students in FE saying they had left schools with sixth forms because they 'disliked school' or 'wanted a more adult environment' was 44 per cent. Students on vocational courses were, as might be expected, much more likely to express their wish to follow a practical course as their main reason for entering a college.

The extent to which the school sector can retain students over the school leaving age is inevitably limited by the restricted nature of the technical and vocational courses they are able to run. As long as post-compulsory education in school sixth forms and sixth-form colleges continues to be dominated by A-level there will inevitably be a significant number

Table 4.12 (S1): Students in FE opting out of 11–18 system – main reason for entering FE by type of course (percentages)

	A-level	O-level	OND	City & Guilds	Secretarial	Other	Total
Course or subject I wanted not available at my school	21		34	33	28	23	27
Was not qualified to enter the sixth-form at my school	2		1			3	1
Wanted a practical course directly preparing for career	4		35	50	36	43	28
Disliked school, wanted a change	19		7	5	9	12	12
Failed exams, came here to retake them	6				1	2	3
Wanted a more adult environment	26		8	7	18	10	16
Was in employment or abroad, could not go to school	2						1
Total = 100%	269	(20)	166	122	137	120	834

Table 4.13 (S1): Students in FE opting out of 11–18 schools — enjoyment of fifth year by type pf school attended (percentages)

Enjoyed school in the fifth year	Secondary Modern	other students from same type of school	Grammar	other students from same type of school	Comprehensive	other students from same type of school	Independent	other students from same type of school	Other	other students from same type of school	Total	other students from same type of school
Very much	34	50	21	23	25	26	26	36		29	26	29
Moderately	44	39	44	59	48	57	52	45		51	47	54
Not really	21	11	34	17	25	16	22	17		16	27	16
Total = 100%	201	460	227	1255	250	1523	124	211	(32)	165	834	3614

Type of school attended in the 5th year

of young people whose needs can only be catered for in FE establishments.

On the other issue, that of resentment of the school atmosphere, while it is true that the development of sixth-form colleges and an increasing tendency on the part of all-through schools to allow their sixth-formers greater freedom may in future depress the number of students moving to FE through dissatisfaction with school, this cause for transfer to FE should not be underestimated. Although the majority of students stated they had left for curricular reasons, a certain dissatisfaction with the school ethos may also underlie their actions.

The questionnaire included an item which asked students to indicate the extent to which they had enjoyed their last year at school. The responses to this item are given in Table 4.13 for students leaving schools with sixth forms and other students from the same background. Overall 27 per cent of the students leaving schools with sixth forms said they had not really enjoyed school in the fifth form, compared with 16 per cent overall. For every type of secondary school, the proportion leaving for FE saying they had not enjoyed school was higher than for other students who had attended the same type of school. Although the proportion giving this answer was higher for all types of school, it is the grammar schools, above all, which contribute to this expression of discontent. One third of leavers from grammar schools said they had not really enjoyed their last year at school, and grammar schools seem in general to have been less popular than other types of schools. Not surprisingly, students who had left all-through schools were more enthusiastic in their general support of a college system for 16- to 19-year-olds. When asked whether they thought a school sixth form or a college was the more appropriate form of education for students of this age, 56 per cent of all students said they preferred colleges, but for those in FE who had left schools with sixth forms, the proportion in favour of colleges was 76 per cent.

One interesting point to emerge very clearly from the administration of the first student questionnaire was the strength of feeling expressed by students in this group on this particular issue. The opportunity to express freely their

views on any topic covered by the questionnaire was often
used by students in FE to compare their present situation
favourably with that of a school sixth form and to stress how
much happier they now were. Students in this position will
obviously have an advantage over their contemporaries in
school sixth forms in that, having experienced both school
and college, they are able to compare the two. Nevertheless,
it was noticeable how many comments of the following
nature were made, and indeed how many of those from
school sixth-formers (particularly those in grammar schools)
expressed equal discontent.

> I hold a very high opinion of colleges of further edu-
> cation as opposed to a sixth-form education. I left my
> old school at the end of the lower sixth for three main
> reasons:
>
> 1. I made the wrong choice of subjects.
> 2. They did not provide facilities for the subjects I
>   wanted to do.
> 3. I found the sixth-form atmosphere intolerable — also
>   the fact that I had no idea what to do because there
>   had been very little career guidance. Having attended
>   for one year the college of further education I am
>   still at, I feel a much greater need for continuing
>   my education:
>
> 1. Because I am on a course which interests me.
> 2. It is a course which broadens my outlook on life —
>   this is due to varied subjects which constitute the
>   course.
> 3. There is much to be said for the adult atmosphere
>   in a college of further education — the teachers
>   treat you as adults.
>
> The opportunities are certainly available — it is up to
> the individual whether or not he wants to make use of
> them. (Ex-grammar school pupil.)

I went to a public school in Lincolnshire. In the fifth

form I only passed three O-levels, there was some discussion as to whether or not I would be accepted for an
A-level course. During this time I decided to attend
————FE College and when the school said I could
go back I decided not to. At the end of my first year at
college I had a grade 1 O-level in a subject I wouldn't
have taken at school, and an A-level which I wouldn't
have taken till the following year. I hope this goes to
show that a college of this form *can* be most beneficial.
I know, before I came here I looked down on technical
colleges, and their type of education, and I'm sure many
others do. A college of this sort is what you make it
but the amenities are here for a good, social, educational
and recreational year, and should not be sneered at.
(Ex-independent school pupil.)

Sixth-forms in schools cannot work because you are not
treated in a responsible adult way but expected to conform and behave the same as the younger members of
the school. You are not prepared for life by staying on
in school as life there is too sheltered.

In colleges there are no need for petty rules because
students are treated with a reasonable attitude, and that
they are people with ideas of their own. (Ex-grammar
school pupil.)

d. Organizational influences upon staying on

i. *Introduction*
One of the most important implications of different forms
of post-compulsory provision is their effect on the attitudes
and aspirations of fifth-year pupils. A number of arguments
both for and against 16+ colleges have been raised which
focus on the bearing this system has on the decisions of fifth-
formers, particularly the decision they make at 16 to leave or
to continue their education.

An often-voiced fear about enforcing a break at 16 is that
certain pupils may be put off continuing their education if
they are obliged to transfer to a new institution. It has been

suggested that this may be particularly true of pupils from working-class backgrounds where no tradition of post-compulsory education exists. Such pupils might be more likely to enter a sixth form where they would be taught by teachers whom they have known for a number of years and with whom they have built up a relationship. If that relationship were to be severed they would, it is claimed, prefer to take a job than to continue their education elsewhere.

> If you asked fifth-year youngsters in my school how many would want to go on or want to stay, I would guess that an awful lot would want to stay. They've made their roots, they know us, they trust us — even if they distrust us, they trust us in their distrust — they know where they are. I think for quite a number it's a disruptive break. It would be interesting to know how many people don't go on, who would have gone on had they been able to stay in the same place. (11—16 comprehensive school headmaster.)

On the other hand, there may exist in the schools a significant number of pupils who feel they have outgrown school, who have possibly soured their relationship with teachers and would therefore welcome an opportunity to make a fresh start. This group would perhaps not be willing to stay on in the sixth form of an all-through school. Pupils who have done well at school may also look forward to entering a college. The range of subjects and courses on offer, the chance to mix with contemporaries from a variety of backgrounds and to study in an atmosphere more in keeping with their near-adult status are all features likely to attract the able student.

> It is difficult to assess how well a pupil might have done in a different situation. Certain individuals will thrive on the independent attitude to study which is practised by the colleges. I think that the college really benefits the more able child because he finds there a flexibility, a breadth and combination of courses and so on and probably high-calibre staff, which he wouldn't even find in the old grammar school. (11—16 comprehensive school head.)

It has also been suggested that the presence of the sixth form in a school acts as an inducement for younger pupils to stay on. They see that the sixth form has prestige; that, in exchange for carrying out duties, sixth-formers are granted certain privileges and may even play a significant role in the daily running of the school. All this is visibly taking place and therefore encourages a fifth-former to look forward to the time when he may enjoy the same status. If the school does not have a sixth form, then staying on becomes a step into the unknown. The following comments from teachers illustrate opposing views on this point.

> Children who are not automatically going on to further education, but who *might* consider it, don't have the experience of seeing it going on as they would in an 11—18 school with a sixth form.

> I don't think it is a carrot. Children will stay on because of their own particular designs to advance their own career. I think it might be a severe distraction for the 11—18 school, where you have to cope with a certain, specific area (i.e. the sixth-form) which does not comply with the normal rules and regulations of the school. It's easier to give them up.

> I've recently moved from a grammar school which changed to comprehensive. When it was a grammar and most people stayed on, the sixth form seemed a natural progression through from the lower school, but when we had a comprehensive intake feeding the sixth form, the sixth form seemed more of a separate appendage and this is why I sense that the 11—16 system is sensible.

Relatively little research has been carried out which investigates the numbers of pupils entering post-compulsory education within different systems of secondary organization. Benn and Simon[14], in a study conducted in 1968, found that 11/12—16 schools had significantly lower staying-on rates than other types of comprehensive school. However, at the time of their survey there were very few sixth-form colleges and no tertiary colleges in existence. These schools normally co-existed with all-through 11–18 schools and were often ex-secondary modern schools. The lower than average ability of the pupils concerned was therefore thought to contribute to the poor staying-on rates in these schools as was the social composition of the neighbourhood served by the school. Eggleston[15], in a study of non-selective schools in eight local authorities found that pupils were more likely to stay on in schools with superior material environments and in catchment areas of superior socio-economic status.

More recently King[16] undertook a study of 16 'short-course' comprehensives in a single local authority whose post-16 provision was concentrated in sixth-form colleges. The CSE and GCE results of these schools compared favourably with results from comprehensive schools in general, and more pupils continued their education than did so nationally. In *School and College* King[3] examines further the complex relationship between the social composition of a school, local authority provision and pupil attainment. Using data from the same study he reports a negative relationship between material provision and pupil attainment but points out there may be a number of benefits other than pupil performance from positive discrimination towards schools in working-class areas. He concludes that 'most of the fears about the academic viability of such schools, in terms of provision of courses and examination success are not substantiated in at least one local education authority'.

To repeat a survey such as that carried out by Benn and Simon would be a useful exercise now that most LEAs have reorganized their secondary education, and sixth-form and tertiary colleges have been in existence for a number of years in some areas. However, these studies show it would be hazardous to estimate how much of the variation between staying on rates in different areas and between different schools is directly attributable to the types of post-compulsory provision available to pupils. To date no research has been undertaken of students' perceptions of the options available to them at 16+ and the part considerations concerning these options play in their decision whether or not to remain in full-time education.

ii. *Attitudes of fifth-form pupils*

In order to investigate the relationship between pupils' plans to terminate or continue their education and the types of post-compulsory education available to them, a subsidiary study was undertaken which concentrated on fifth-year pupils and their teachers. The main purposes of this study were as follows:

1. To ascertain the effect of different systems of post-compulsory education on the decisions of fifth-year pupils, and to survey the views of senior staff in 11–16 schools on this issue.
2. To determine the effects of the presence or lack of a sixth form within a school on the attitudes and experiences of pupils in the fifth form.
3. To investigate in general the views of senior staff in 11–16 schools on the advantages and disadvantages of this form of secondary provision.

This section of the report will deal with the first of these items. Findings on items two and three are discussed in Chapter 10, '11–16 Schools'.

It should be noted here that an original intention of this study was to investigate pupils' image of the options available at 16+, i.e. the sixth form, the FE college and, where appropriate, the sixth-form or tertiary college. However, a number of problems were encountered during the trials of questionnaires which led to the conclusion that pupils had a very confused picture of these and were not always able to differentiate between the alternatives. For example, pupils were not able to state with any degree of certainty whether statements concerning such items as the amenities, courses, rules and regulations etc. might be applicable to the sixth form or the colleges which were open to them. There were a number of possible reasons for this confusion. First, the questionnaires were in most instances piloted during the autumn and spring terms which may have been prior to pupils' being informed in any detail by their school of the opportunities available. It also became apparent that there existed a good deal of confusion on the part of pupils (and teachers sometimes) in the definition and nomenclature of different colleges. The term 'sixth-form college' had been used at times to describe what were in reality sixth-form centres, sixth-form blocks in all-through schools and tertiary colleges. It was therefore decided to abandon this aspect of the study and to concentrate on the objectives itemized above.

Method

A questionnaire was administered to a sample of fifth-formers in a cross-section of secondary schools during the summer term of 1977. The following types of schools were included:

1. comprehensive schools with their own sixth form
2. grammar schools
3. 11—16 comprehensive schools feeding sixth-form colleges
4. 11—16 comprehensive schools feeding tertiary colleges
5. secondary modern schools.

In the first two categories, i.e. all-through comprehensive and grammar schools, questionnaires were administered to a random sample of fifth-formers in the schools whose sixth-formers had participated in the main study. In the second two categories, a number of comprehensive schools was selected which feed the sixth-form and tertiary colleges taking part in the main study, and the same questionnaire administered to a random sample of their fifth year. It was decided to include in the study only those pupils in secondary modern schools who were engaged in sufficient O-level and CSE work to suggest they might have the potential to continue their education at 16-plus. Local authorities where secondary modern schools still existed were asked to nominate schools in their area which were likely to contain a number of such pupils. A number of these schools were then approached and the questionnaire administered to a sample of their fifth-formers meeting this criterion.

The fifth-year questionnaire contained items on

a) the options available at 16+
b) pupils' plans on completion of their fifth-form course

c) number of O-level and CSE examinations being taken
d) experiences of life in the fifth form — responsibilities, privileges, etc.
e) the extent to which factors which might dissuade pupils from staying on applied to them personally.

Respondents were also invited to give any further comments they thought relevant to topics covered by the questionnaire.

At the same time, the head teachers of the 11—16 comprehensive schools were asked to complete questionnaires covering the following items:

a) whether the school had had a sixth form prior to reorganization
b) the destinations of last year's fifth-form leavers
c) methods used for informing fifth years about opportunities in 16-plus education
d) effect of absence of sixth form on staff recruitment.

Both heads and senior members of staff were asked to give their views on the proportion of pupils lost or gained to full-time education because of a break at 16 and the advantages and disadvantages of separate educational provision at 16+.

Results

Table 4.14 shows the intended destinations of the 417 pupils completing the questionnaire according to the type of school they attended. Overall, 44 per cent intended to leave and take a job, 25 per cent to enter the sixth form of their present school, 23 per cent to enter a college of further education and the remainder to continue their education elsewhere. As might be expected, the grammar schools contained the lowest proportion of pupils intending to leave, and secondary modern schools the highest (18 per cent and 58 per cent respectively). Sixty eight per cent of the grammar school pupils intended to enter the sixth form at their present school, compared with 45 per cent of all-through comprehensive school fifth-formers. Of the seven secondary modern schools in the sample, two had their own sixth form and seven per cent of the pupils in this type of school were intending to enter the sixth form. Secondary modern school pupils were the only ones planning to transfer to another school (usually the sixth-form of the local grammar school), 10 per cent of them falling into this category.

Pupils intending to enter colleges of further education were found in all types of secondary school. The largest proportion in this group was in comprehensive schools feeding tertiary colleges where, by definition, no alternative in the form of a school sixth form is available. Fifty five per cent of the fifth-formers in this type of school were aiming to enter further education. For pupils in secondary modern schools, approximately one quarter were planning to enter colleges of further education and this was the most likely destination for pupils in such schools wishing to continue full-time study. For pupils in areas served by sixth-form colleges, a choice exists between this type of college and a college of further education. In most areas, this means that pupils are split into two groups — those wishing to follow a general, academic course who enter the sixth-form college, and those opting for training in a particular vocational field and who therefore enter further education. However, it is possible that in some areas both the sixth-form college and the college of further education may offer the same course — this is particularly likely in the case of A-level — and a student must then base his choice on considerations other than the courses offered. Of the students in the sample in schools in areas served by sixth-form colleges, 36 per cent were planning to enter this type of college and 16 per cent a college of further education.

With the figures available here it is possible to compare the percentage of pupils planning to continue their education in comprehensive schools with and without sixth-forms. Of the pupils in all-through comprehensives, 63 per cent were planning to do so (45 per cent in their own school and 18 per cent elsewhere). For comprehensive schools without sixth forms, the corresponding figures were 54 per cent for those feeding sixth-form colleges and 55 per cent for those feeding tertiary colleges. However, these differences were not statistically significant and therefore do not point to the presence of a sixth form in a school being an important factor in determining pupils' plans.

Table 4.14 (P5): Expected destinations of pupils completing fifth-year questionnaire (percentages)

	All-through Comprehensive School	Grammar School	11–16 Comprehensive School Feeding Sixth-form College	11–16 Comprehensive School Feeding Tertiary College	Secondary Modern School	All Schools
Leave school and take a job which will involve some kind of training	30	18	31	33	49	35
Leave school and take a job which will not involve any further training	6		16	13	9	9
Enter the sixth form at present school	45	68			7	25
Enter the sixth form in another school in the area					10	3
Enter a sixth-form college			36			5
Enter a full-time course in a college of further education	15	11	16	55	24	23
Enter some other form of school or college	3	3	2		1	2
Total = 100%	152	38	58	55	114	417
No. of schools	13	6	9	5	7*	40

* Of these seven schools, two had their own sixth form.

Pupils were asked to give the number of O-level examinations which they would be taking at the end of the fifth-year. Table 4.15 shows the average number for each destination group. Pupils leaving school to enter employment were taking significantly fewer O-levels than those who were continuing their education, 1.5 compared with 4.8 ($p < .01$). Those intending to enter a sixth-form college or the sixth form in their own school were the most academic groups, taking 6.1 and 5.8 subjects respectively. This finding is very much in line with those of a recent DES report which stated[17]:

> The association between academic orientation of fifth-formers and their intentions at the end of compulsory education was so strong that the rest of the results are best viewed as an indication of factors other than intrinsic ability which may influence this academic orientation, or which exercise a relatively small independent effect on pupils' intentions.

Table 4.15 also gives the percentage distributions of boys and girls according to their expected destinations. Over half the boys and one third of the girls were planning to take a job, and boys were more likely than girls to take one involving further training. This tendency for girls to be more positive than boys in their attitude to continued full-time education may be a reflection of the paucity of opportunities for day-release in jobs normally associated with girls. Whereas there is a considerable range of crafts and trades offering day-release for boys, girls wishing to train, for example, as secretaries may find a full-time course in further education the best and most available means of doing so.

When we examine the reasons pupils give for not continuing their education, we find that considerations of institutional arrangements and academic ability are not recognized by them as important factors in their decision. Pupils who were not continuing their education were presented with a list of possible reasons for this, and asked to indicate to what extent each had influenced them. Table 4.16 gives the responses to these items. The factors which they said had been most likely to influence their decision to leave were as

Table 4.15 (P5): Intended destination of fifth-formers by number of O-levels being taken and by sex

	Average no. of O-levels being taken	N	Boys %	Girls %
Leave school and take a job which will involve some kind of training, e.g. an apprentice scheme; a job involving day release	1.7	144	47	21
Leave school and take a job which will not involve any further training	0.6	35	6	12
Total leavers	1.5	179	53	33
Enter the sixth form at your present school	5.8	103	21	30
Enter the sixth form in another school in the area	4.6	11	3	3
Enter a sixth-form college	6.1	21	2	8
Enter a full-time course in a Technical or Further Education College	3.3	93	20	25
Enter some other form of school of college	5.3	7	2	2
Total stayers	4.8	235	48	68
Total = 100%			215	196

follows: 'I am very keen to start a particular job or career'; 'It is better to take a job if you get the chance'; 'I would not be earning any money'.

Over half the students said they had been very much or moderately affected by these considerations. Clearly, eagerness to begin work is uppermost in pupils' minds and most of them are keen to start work and earn money at the earliest possible opportunity.

It is also probable that the present employment situation, particularly in some areas of the country, may persuade young people to grasp the opportunity of a job should a suitable position become available, rather than risk facing unemployment in the future.

> The job situation as it is now is unstable so I would think it a good thing to get out and get some work, e.g. join the forces than stay on and lose a year, although it might be beneficial. There again you might not pass any O-levels or CSEs or A-levels. (11—18 comprehensive school fifth-former.)

'I would lose the chance to become an apprentice', although not highly rated overall, was a very important factor for a number of pupils, particularly boys. The fact that most apprenticeships are only offered to 16-year-olds has caused many schools to consider very carefully whether they are always right in persuading pupils to stay on, as these comments from teachers in 11—16 schools illustrate.

> Over the past few years it's become increasingly apparent to me that more and more able boys who would in the past have gone on to A-levels without any difficulty are not in fact doing so because they have the opportunity of continuing their education through an apprenticeship scheme.

> It's a frightening decision to have to make. Whether to advise a child to go on to college; traditionally we've done this with the brighter ones and thought nothing of it. But now I hesitate in many ways because I feel in my bones that the right answer is sometimes for the brighter child to get into industry, particularly with a good firm.

It should not be assumed that the intention to take a job necessarily implies a rejection of school. Many pupils express satisfaction with school life yet do not plan to enter the sixth form.

Table 4.16 (P5): Extent to which various factors influenced pupils against continuing their education (percentages) N = 182

		1 Very much	2 Moder- ately	3 Slightly	4 Not at all/ Does not apply
a.	It is better to take a job if you get the chance	57	24	15	3
b.	My parents are against the idea of my staying on	9	5	10	75
c.	I would be separated from most of my friends	7	13	30	50
d.	I would have to go to a different school or college	9	5	15	72
e.	I would have to stay on at this school	12	9	5	75
f.	The subjects I want to study are not taught at any of the schools or colleges in this area	10	5	10	75
g.	I would not be earning any money	38	20	20	22
h.	I would lose the chance to become an apprentice	29	19	18	34
i.	So far I have not benefited very much from my education	9	18	24	49
j.	I might not get on well with some of the teachers who would be teaching me	10	7	32	51
k.	It would mean being treated like a child for at least another year	20	14	23	43
l.	It would involve much hard work	24	22	27	27
m.	It involves carrying out too many special duties and responsibilities apart from work	8	15	30	47

Table 4.16 (cont.)

n.	I would not get as much free time as I would like	19	21	28	32
o.	I am very keen to start a particular job or career	77	15	5	2
p.	It is difficult to know what the life in the sixth form or at the college would be like until I got there	21	22	30	27
q.	It would involve getting used to new surroundings	15	16	23	46
r.	The standard of teaching is not very high	8	13	14	66
s.	There are no courses or examinations that I would be able to do	7	5	15	73
t.	I would have to be taught by new teachers	19	9	18	54
u.	I am not good enough at school work to qualify for any of the sixth-form or college courses	14	18	25	44
v.	It would involve a long or inconvenient journey every day	10	13	22	55

I am only leaving school because I want to get started on a job and I would like to have a nice career ahead. I think school is a nice place to go but if I stay on I will not be able to earn money or get settled down in a particular job. (Secondary modern school pupil.)

I have thoroughly enjoyed my fifth year at school, and we have the right amount of privileges. My plans for next year are to work in a bank and do extra education in the evenings or on day release. (11–16 comprehensive school pupil.)

Pupils were less inclined to attribute their decision to leave to reasons connected with their academic ability. One third said they had been very much or moderately affected by the fact that 'I am not good enough at school or college work to qualify for any of the sixth-form or college courses'. On the other hand, three quarters of the students said that either 'there are no courses or examinations that I would be able to do' did not apply to them or that this factor had not affected their decision to leave.

There was no difference between the two items which were specifically included to test the effect of a break at 16, i.e. 'I would have to go to a different school or college' and 'I would have to stay on at this school'. Three quarters of the pupils in the study said these factors had not influenced them at all. However, there was a slight tendency for pupils to display a fear of the unknown in that nearly half said they had been very much or moderately affected by the consideration that 'It is difficult to know what life in the sixth form or at the college would be like until I got there'.

It is perhaps indicative of the low importance attached to different forms of sixth-form education by fifth-formers that so few of them made any comments on this aspect of the questionnaire. Whereas approximately 10 per cent of the respondents used the back page of the questionnaire to express their views on life in the fifth form — the privileges they receive etc. — very few made any comment on the options available at 16+, and those that did voiced somewhat conflicting opinions, as these two pupils from the same school demonstrate:

> I feel that as I will be able to choose the subjects I want at college, I'll work harder and more enthusiastically at them. I'll also be glad to be freer as a full-time student and decide more about my education instead of the teacher choosing for me.

> I think schools should have a sixth-form education. When we finish in our fifth year and we want to carry on with our education, we should be able to carry on in the same school. It would save a lot of bother, what with all new forms to fill in and trips to the college and making sure what course we are doing.

During preliminary discussions with fifth-year pupils it became clear that many who eventually decided to continue their education were conscious of having weighed up the advantages or the disadvantages of staying on and had reached this decision having recognized and evaluated the drawbacks. A good deal is already known about the reasons pupils give for entering post-compulsory education — the desire to improve career prospects, to enter higher education or to qualify for a particular occupation or profession, but it is not known to what extent factors which persuade pupils to leave also feature in the decisions of those who decide to stay on. Therefore, the pupils in the sample remaining in full-time education were asked to indicate to what extent the same factors listed in Table 4.16 applied to them. The deterrent factors which pupils appeared to be most aware of were that the course they were about to embark on would involve a lot of hard work and, to a much lesser extent, that they would not be earning any money and they might not get as much free time as they would like.

To summarize these findings, it appears that the major difference between leavers and stayers at 16 is in their academic potential, although those planning to leave do not consider that 16+ education has nothing to offer them or that they have failed to benefit from their education to date. Their intention to leave is dominated by a desire to start work and earn money. Whether the school they attend has a sixth form or not seems to have very little effect on their decision. The disadvantages of staying on as seen by pupils who plan to do so are, overwhelmingly, the prospect of hard work, lack of money, and free time. It is interesting to note that these remain the major disadvantages as seen by students in their first year of post-compulsory education.

iii. *Views of teachers in 11—16 schools*

In order to ascertain the effect, from the teachers' viewpoint, of the absence of a sixth form on staying-on rates, the heads and senior staff of the 11—16 comprehensive schools taking part in the study were asked to estimate:

a. the proportion of the previous year's leavers who might

have continued their education if they had the opportunity to do so in a sixth form in the school

b. the proportion of the previous year's pupils entering a college who might not have continued their education if they had no choice but to enter a sixth form in the school.

Before looking at the responses to these questions, it is worth considering first some background information on the schools concerned. Of the 14 schools involved (nine feeding sixth-form colleges and five feeding tertiary colleges) 10 had been secondary modern schools prior to comprehensive reorganization, two had been grammar schools, one had been a technical school and the other had been formed by the amalgamation of a secondary modern and a grammar school.

The three grammar schools and the technical school had lost sixth forms ranging in size (during the year prior to reorganization) from 70 to 240 pupils. Three of the ex-secondary modern schools had also had a small sixth form at that time.

Techniques which were used by all the schools to inform their pupils about opportunities in 16-plus education were:

1. talks by visiting staff from the sixth-form or tertiary college
2. circulation or display of literature and prospectuses from sixth-form and tertiary colleges
3. talks on 16 plus opportunities by people other than college staff.

All but two of the schools made arrangements for their fifth-formers to visit the local sixth-form or tertiary college. This comment from a student approaching the end of his second year in a sixth-form college illustrates the importance of close co-operation between feeder colleges and the college.

In the hope that this will be read I would just like to say that I have really enjoyed my time at college but it would be foolish of me to encourage someone else to enter college on the strength of my own experiences as everyone has different views, ambitions and abilities.

Therefore I think it is essential that a college, such as my own, should have an effective liaison system with its 'feeder' schools to enable pupils in the fifth form to have an opportunity of visiting the college and discussing their ambitions and hopes with the staff and the college administrators. This I feel is essential, otherwise pupils who come to the college from the fifth form with few if any definite ideas as to their future career could well 'waste' their first year by constantly changing their course and by being generally unsettled due to the lack of a goal or ambition which they can aim at.

My own case was somewhat similar and as a result I have chosen to stay on an extra year to make up for time and work which was lost during an initial period in my first term when I was unsettled academically. I hope this will be of some help to you in your research.

As well as head teachers, the questionnaire was also sent to senior staff with a special responsibility for fifth-year pupils. A total of 51 heads and teachers completed the questionnaire, and their responses to item a. and item b. above were distributed as follows:

Table 4.17 (T5:) Teachers' estimates of percentage of pupils who left last year for employment and who might have continued their education if there were a sixth form in the school

% Estimated	No. of Teachers
None	24
10% or less	20
20% or more	2
Don't know	5

Teachers' estimates of percentage of pupils who entered a college last year who might not have continued their education if they had no choice but to enter a school sixth form

% Estimated	No. of Teachers
None	17
10% or less	21
20% or more	8
Don't know	5

Table 4.17 (cont.)

No. of teachers saying more pupils gained than lost	18
No. of teachers saying no difference	18
No. of teachers saying more pupils lost than gained	10
Don't know	5

The figures show that overall, teachers felt there were more pupils who stayed in full-time education because they had to enter a college than dropped out for the same reason. At least one third thought there was no difference in either direction. Amongst those who felt that the system had some effect on pupils' decisions, the majority considered the percentage involved was very small (10 per cent or less).

Chapter 5

Characteristics of Students on Entry to Post 16 Education

The last chapter discussed some of the factors affecting the decision which pupils face at the age of 16 as to whether to continue their full-time education or not, and paid particular attention to those choosing to enter colleges of further education. This chapter will consider some of the chief characteristics of the entire student sample on their entry to post-compulsory education. Much of the information discussed has already appeared in the project's report on *One Year Courses in Colleges and Sixth Forms*[9] but while the focus there was on differences between students on one- and two-year courses, in what follows the emphasis will be on the similarities and differences between students in different types of institution.

a. Reasons for entry to post-compulsory education

When asked to select their main reason for staying on in full-time education, the students' responses were distributed as shown in Table 5.1. The three reasons selected by students above all were 'improving their general career prospects' (35 per cent), 'obtaining qualifications necessary for their chosen career' (26 per cent) or 'for higher education' (21 per cent). There was little difference in the proportions of students staying on to improve their general career pros-

Table 5.1 (S1): Main reason for staying on in full-time education this year (percentages)

	Comprehensive School	Grammar School	Sixth-form College	Tertiary College	FE College	Total
Never considered leaving	4	3	4	5	1	3
Wish to go on to higher education	25	26	24	18	14	21
Interest in subject(s)	2	3	2	3	4	3
Qualifications necessary for chosen career	25	20	23	26	35	26
Improving career prospects in general	34	36	37	33	34	35
Broadening outlook	1	2	3	2	2	2
Most of my friends stayed on		1				
Not yet ready to go out to work.	3	4	3	4	2	3
Parental pressure	1	2	1	1	1	1
Total = 100%	981	866	946	530	1125	4448

pects among the different types of institution. In all types of institution, other than FE, more students chose this as their main reason for staying on than any other. Students in FE were most likely to see their current course as a means of entering the career they had already decided upon, reflecting the presence in this group of a significant number of students following vocational courses. A wish to go on to higher education was therefore of less importance to FE students than those in school sixth forms and sixth-form colleges.

Very few students were staying on for reasons associated with the intrinsic value of education. This is shown by the very small proportions (less than five per cent in each case) saying they had stayed on primarily to 'broaden their outlook', because of an 'interest in the subjects' they would be studying or because they were subject to either parental or peer group pressure. These responses demonstrate the very practical, instrumental approach students have towards their continued education. The majority were concerned not with the immediate benefits of continuing their education but with the effects that doing so would have on their long-term career plans. The fact that over half the students in the sample were hoping to enter higher education yet only 21 per cent gave this as their main reason for staying on suggests that a significant proportion also see higher education primarily as a means of improving their career prospects. However, these findings should not be taken as proof that students are completely indifferent to the more idealistic reasons. The design of the question did not allow for considerations of secondary importance to be identified, but the following paragraph which discusses course choice suggests that, for some students at least, 'interest in subjects' would have been one of them.

b. Course choice

Responses to an item investigating course choice showed that more idealistic reasons than those described above do feature in many students' decisions, at least at the stage of choosing a particular course.

Students were asked to select from the list given in Table

Table 5.2 (S1): Main reason for choosing particular course or combination of subjects by type of course (percentages)

	A-level	O-level	OND	City & Guilds	Secretarial	Other	Total
Subjects form an acceptable combination	7	8	9	1	4	2	7
Subjects I am most interested in	40	17	10	48	11	19	33
Subjects were best compromise considering choice offered	5	6	5		4	3	4
My earlier qualifications allowed few alternatives	4	10	3	2	6	2	4
Subjects I have been best at	9	5	2	3	1	4	7
Course/subjects necessary for chosen career or higher education	32	46	66	34	72	67	40
Total = 100%	2913	439	322	232	337	205	4448

5.2, their main reason for choosing the course or combination of subjects they were studying. While 'course or subjects necessary for chosen career or higher education' (40 per cent) was the most important single reason given, nearly as many students (33 per cent) said they had chosen their course out of interest. On this question, differences between institutions could be attributed to the presence of students on a particular type of course. The table therefore presents the more meaningful breakdown, that of the reason for course choice selected by students following a particular type of course.

The figures show that choice based on interest was particularly prevalent among those studying for A-levels and City and Guilds examinations and that a greater proportion of students on these courses chose this reason than any other (40 per cent and 48 per cent respectively). All other courses had been chosen by students primarily for their relevance to future career or higher education plans.

Further investigation of the characteristics of the two main groups within A-level and City and Guilds courses, i.e. those choosing their course out of interest, and those choosing it for its relevance to their career plans, showed that their original reasons for staying on had been different. The interest groups were less likely to have decided upon a career, and were therefore more likely to stay on in order to improve their career prospects in general. They were also more inclined to be staying on through 'interest in subjects' or to 'broaden their outlook' than those choosing their course through necessity. There was a clear tendency for students in the latter group not only to have already chosen a career but also to be more ambitious in terms of its socio-economic status.

The differences underlying choice of courses thus proved symptomatic of wide-ranging differences. The group who chose out of interest could be characterized as clearly less definite in their attitude to their educational and occupational future, and probably less ambitious where they had made plans. Those who chose out of necessity were much more likely to have formed specific future career or educational plans which appear to have been the conscious basis for entry to post-compulsory education. Their career aspirations were also generally higher than those of students in the 'interest' group who had formed career plans. These differences are indicative of the presence of somewhat contrasting groups within A-level and City and Guilds courses which deserve to be taken into account by those providing and planning them.

Why the students following O-level, OND or secretarial courses should be so much less inclined to choose their courses out of interest is not entirely clear, particularly as there was some overlap between the subjects studied. For example, students following catering courses appear in both the City and Guilds and the OND groups although they account for different proportions of these groups. As the data were not adequate for fuller analysis of the nature of differences in specific subjects and courses, this finding suggests a fruitful line for future research.

c. Disadvantages of staying on

The students in the sample were also asked to say what, if any, were the disadvantages of staying on in full-time education beyond the age of 16 (see Table 5.3). Overall one third felt there were no disadvantages, although there were differences between students in different types of institution in this respect. There was a slight tendency for students in grammar schools and in FE and tertiary colleges to be more aware of disadvantages than those in comprehensive schools and sixth-form colleges. Students in all types of institution were most aware of 'shortage of money' as being the main drawback to continued full-time education, and this was particularly true of students in tertiary and FE colleges. No doubt the fact that students attending colleges of this type are mixing with day-release and part-time students who are earning money has the effect of making them more aware of sacrifices they are making.

There was evidence that some students were subject to considerable conflict between the pressures of education and employment.

> During the summer holidays I worked in an engineering works and I enjoyed it, even though it was dirty. I en-

joyed it because it was different. I was earning money
and I knew I would only be there for a short time.

Now that I have come to this college, I am not earning
money, which I dislike, and it is just like being back at
secondary school, which I disliked, although the atmosphere is much better here. I dislike the course because
it is uninteresting for me, and when we go in the work-
shop we are back at the filing stage. If somebody
offered me a reasonable job with some prospects I
would start next Monday! I would take it because there
is less work involved. College is 9—4.30 and homework
and you are unpaid. I would work because next March
I am 17 and I want a motorbike, and what use is an
OND anyway, if you aren't going to get a BSc or HNC?
It means you are virtually tied down to engineering,
which I don't like — either being tied down or engineering. I don't intend to get a BSc because a) have I the
ability? b) can I be without any real cash or private
transport for the next five years or so? NO! (Tertiary.)

(Readers may be interested to learn that, in this instance,
education triumphed. This student passed OND technology and is now studying for a BSc in vehicle engineering at a polytechnic.)

But for some students the temptations proved too strong.
The following remarks were made by a boy in a grammar
school sixth-form who subsequently left school before taking
his A-level examinations.

It gets me very annoyed and even depressed when I
see people with a lot of money. The other people who
stay on at school have either cushy jobs or rich mothers
and fathers who give them loads of money. I only get
£1 a week which is not enough for a night out. I believe
the State should give pupils between £10 and £15 a
week (tax free) with increases in parallel with inflation.
There is a boy at school called N who gets lots of money
and just bought a leather mack which is really neat. I

Table 5.3 (S1): **Main disadvantage of staying on (percentages)**

	Comprehensive School	Grammar School	Sixth-form College	Tertiary College	FE College	Total
None	34	29	34	30	31	32
Lack of practical experience/sheltered life	4	9	4	2	2	4
Shortage of free time	2	5	2	2	2	3
Shortage of money	25	21	28	33	34	28
No chance to learn a trade	1	1	1	1	1	1
Dependence on parents	9	11	12	9	13	11
Continuing exam pressure	8	7	6	4	3	6
Time wasted if I fail exams	13	11	10	12	8	11
Lost contact with friends who are now at work	1	1	1	1	1	1
Total = 100%	981	866	946	530	1125	4448

have to wear a crummy cromby when it's cold. K works in a shipping office and has lots of money and can afford to go in pubs every day and he's got Sally and I'm very, very jealous. I've got a big inferiority complex about neat dollies and staying on at school doesn't help.

This student's request for a grant for everyone in post-compulsory education was one which was universally endorsed. There were innumerable comments from students in all types of institution of which the following are typical:

A grant is needed by sixth-form pupils. This would enable them to have some independence and a small social life. Contact is lost between pupils and their working friends through lack of funds. (Comprehensive.)

I think that students attending sixth-form colleges should get a grant. It is said that they cannot have one because they are continuing school education so why should students at technical colleges get grants when sixth-form college students can't? Do they realise parents cannot keep us for ever, making us dependent upon our parents when we are old enough to earn a living but instead chose to go to college so that we could get better job opportunities. (Sixth-form college.)

All students should have a grant of some sort, because many students lose interest in study if earning is more important. Why should the Government waste money on unnecessary issues when the future brains of the country have to pay to give their services? (Tertiary.)

Considerations of secondary importance to students were 'continuing exam pressure', 'time wasted if I fail', and dependence on parents' although the latter implies financial dependence and is therefore difficult to separate from 'shortage of money'.

Fewer grammar school sixth-formers than other groups thought shortage of money was the main disadvantage of staying on but they were slightly more inclined to be concerned about the 'lack of practical experience/sheltered life' and 'shortage of free time' than students in other types of institution although the proportions involved were very small (less than 10 per cent in each case).

d. Reasons for entering present institution

We have already considered in Chapter 4 some of the motives of students in FE in entering that particular type of institution and compared these with students taking similar courses elsewhere. Table 5.4 shows the responses of the entire sample to the item which asked them to select their main reason for entering their current institution.

The great majority of school sixth-formers had not, in fact, made a choice at 16. They were happy to stay on in the same school they attended up to the age of 16. Over 70 per cent of comprehensive and grammar school sixth-formers gave this response. A small proportion of the grammar school sample was made up of students (mainly from secondary modern schools) who had previously attended schools with no sixth-form provision.

The largest single group of students in sixth-form and tertiary colleges is also one which revealed a lack of conscious choice of institution by stating that their main reason for entering the colleges was that their previous school had no sixth form.

(The 11 per cent of students in sixth-form colleges who said they were 'happy to stay on at the same school' were in new colleges which were developing from all-through schools and would not therefore need to transfer to a different institution at 16.)

One quarter of the tertiary college sample was, however, made up of students for whom the FE sector has traditionally catered, i.e. those in search of a practical course which would directly prepare them for a career. Students who had entered their current institution because they had disliked school and wanted a change and because they wanted a more adult environment were found in all three types of college, particularly in colleges of FE, but in relatively small proportions. In general, therefore, the majority of students were happy to comply with the educational provision made by the

Table 5.4: (S1): Main reason for entering present institution (percentages)

	Comprehensive School	Grammar School	Sixth-form College	Tertiary College	FE College	Total
Happy to stay on at same school	77	72	11			33
No sixth form in my old school	3	9	43	42	8	18
Course or subject I wanted not available at my school	1	1	5	12	24	9
Was not qualified to enter sixth form at school			1	1	1	
Wanted a practical course directly preparing for career	4	2	7	22	28	12
Disliked school, wanted a change		1	5	2	10	4
Failed exams at school, came here to retake them	2	1	5	2	3	3
Wanted a more adult environment	1	1	12	7	15	7
Total = 100%	981	866	946	530	1125	4448

local authority, whether this was in all-through schools or in tertiary or sixth-form colleges. Students in FE were most likely to have left the secondary system in search of a vocational course. Students who were discontented with the school ethos were fewer in number, and were also to be found in other types of college.

e. Expectations of life in the sixth form or at college

Students were asked to select, from the list given in Table 5.5, in what respect they would most like their life in the sixth form or at college to differ from that in the fifth year. Of the alternatives offered, the one which students were most likely to choose was 'to be treated more like adults generally'. This applied to all groups of students, the proportions giving this response ranging from 34 per cent in colleges of further education to 40 per cent in sixth-form colleges. However, it is worth noting that at least two of the other alternatives listed, i.e. 'more responsibility given to students in the running of the school or college' and 'fewer rules concerning behaviour, attendance, dress etc.', can be counted as part of a general desire for adult treatment. The small number of students choosing them should not therefore be taken to indicate that they were of low priority, but that students were more inclined to seek a general change in their status, rather than particular manifestations of it. There was a slight tendency for grammar school sixth-formers to opt for 'fewer rules' more often than students in other types of institution, but with this exception there was little variation in students' responses to the question.

We shall see in the next chapter to what extent students felt, after two years in the sixth form or at college, that their experiences matched these expectations. But although students had only been in post-compulsory education for two months or less when they completed the first questionnaire, there were already signs of strongly-held views on this issue and differences in their views on this important aspect of their educational experience.

I would like to make it clear that contrary to what many people believe and what we were told before-

Table 5.5 (S1): **Most important respect in which students would like the sixth form or college to differ from the fifth form (percentages)**

	Comprehensive School	Grammar School	Sixth-form College	Tertiary College	FE College	Total
Higher standards in subjects in which I am interested	10	9	10	8	12	10
More optional subjects to choose from	5	4	7	5	6	5
Better amenities	13	11	11	10	10	11
Better relationships with staff	9	7	7	7	8	8
More responsibility given to students in the running of the school/college	6	4	5	4	4	5
More free time/private study periods	7	8	6	10	10	8
To be treated more like adults generally	36	37	40	39	34	37
Fewer rules concerning behaviour, attendance, dress etc	9	14	9	8	10	10
Total = 100%	981	866	946	530	1125	4448

hand, sixth formers, in our school at least, have very little say in school matters and are not generally treated differently from the lower school.

Not enough freedom is given to sixth-formers to mould their own desired type of sixth-form community. (Grammar.)

I prefer college to school but we have too many rules and regulations, at times it is more like school than the fifth-year at my last school. I disagree with the treatment of a student who has been absent or missing from a lesson and I disagree with compulsory integrated studies. A college should be a college not a 'scholege'. We have chosen to continue our education and should be treated as such. If lessons are not attended it is the student's loss. I do not think they should be singled out, and asked to account for their absence. (Tertiary.)

For all the claims this 'college' tries to make, it is still a school. Many of the traditions and customs of a school are continued i.e. registration, insistence on attendance, restrictions on leaving the college during the day etc. etc. In fact the whole college was grossly misrepresented by my former school. (Sixth-form college.)

Sixth-formers should be given more adult treatment i.e. no uniform, permission to leave school at lunchbreak, permission to smoke in common room, etc. Personal appearance (e.g. hair length) should not be decided by an old-fashioned board of governors or headmaster. (Grammar.)

Although I have said I didn't enjoy the fifth-form at school, life in the sixth-form is much better and I like being made responsible and treated as an adult. (Comprehensive.)

I believe the sixth-form to be a good thing. We are given responsibility and a chance to lend a helping hand in the running of the school. It also gives younger members of the school a good example to look up to and follow. (Comprehensive.)

The sixth-form college is excellent in that relationships with teachers, facilities, rules and regulations and choice of subjects are agreeable. The idea of a sixth-form college is good because it allows boys and girls of varying educational and social backgrounds to mix and exchange opinions so giving people a wider outlook on life. (Sixth-form college.)

f. Difficulties encountered on present course

One of the items in the first questionnaire was designed to elicit information on any difficulties students were encountering on their course. Sixty two per cent of students said they were having no difficulty in coping with their new course. Those that were having difficulty with some aspects of it most often mentioned 'the amount of homework or private study' (11 per cent), 'working on my own' (7 per cent) and 'the high standard of work required' (six per cent). Problems connected with academic study therefore predominated, and other difficulties were only mentioned by a negligible proportion of students.

Institutional differences on this item were found not to be as great as those between students on different types of courses. A-level students were the most likely to admit to problems. The figures shown in Table 5.6 which suggest that grammar school sixth-formers were most likely to be encountering difficulties merely reflect the preponderance of A-level students in this group. Fifty eight per cent of students on A-level courses said they were having no difficulties compared with 64 per cent of secretarial students, 67 per cent of those on City and Guilds courses and over 70 per cent of OND and O-level students.

'The amount of homework or private study' was the A-level student's biggest problem (mentioned by 14 per cent) followed by 'working on my own' (nine per cent). While these were also the major difficulties for other groups of students, they were mentioned with less frequency.

Table 5.6 (S1): Main difficulty encountered on present course (percentages)

	Comprehensive School	Grammar School	Sixth-form College	Tertiary College	FE College	Total
None	59	52	64	65	68	62
High standard of work required	7	6	6	6	6	6
Amount of homework/private study	14	17	11	7	5	11
Teachers who do not know me	1	2	1	1		1
Working on my own /organizing my own work	6	10	9	4	4	7
The amount of free time	3	2	1	2	5	3
Making new friends		1	1	2	1	1
Absence of younger pupils						
Lack of community spirit/ impersonal atmosphere	3	2	3	5	4	3
Total = 100%	981	866	946	530	1125	4448

Some comments from students showed that they were at a loss to know how to make the best use of the free time which they now had at their disposal, and wanted more guidance from teachers in this respect: 'Too much relied on students' private study. How do we know what to study?' (comprehensive); 'Reading around is suggested — too vague — what do we read? A whole book or most of it may be wasted by being irrelevant' (comprehensive).

At the same time there was some indication that very strict supervision of private study would not be welcomed.

> In the sixth-form we should be allowed to use our private study time as we think best. If continuous check-ups are made to see if everyone is either reading or writing during private study time, it will not result in any extra study being done as students will do their homework anyway and being made to work all the time will lead to resentment. (Grammar.)

At the time the first questionnaire was completed students had been in the sixth form for a comparatively short time, and their attitudes and ideas were only just beginning to take shape.

By the time students had spent two years in post-compulsory education they had formulated well-defined ideas about most aspects of their course. Study problems proved to be one of these, and Chapter 9 of this report is entirely devoted to a discussion of the expressions of problems connected with academic study elicited from students at that stage.

g. Summary

On many of the important characteristics of students discussed in this chapter there were areas of broad agreement between those in different types of institution. For example, underlying the majority of students' decisions to stay on was a belief that in doing so, they would significantly enhance their career prospects. Students intending to go on to higher education did not generally see this as an end in itself but as a vital stage in their progress towards worthwhile and rewarding employment.

The decision to stay on is the most immediate one students are faced with, and practical issues dominate their deliberations. It is at the next stage — that of course choice — that more idealistic factors such as an interest in particular subjects come into play, particularly for students on some courses whose future plans are still uncertain.

The issue of course choice is in many instances compounded by that of choice of institution. Some students will decide first on the course they wish to follow or perhaps the area in which they would like to receive vocational training, and then select the institution which offers the relevant course. This is the most likely pattern for the majority of students in further education. For those in school sixth-forms 'choice of institution' is a misnomer, as the intention to stay on in the sixth is probably uppermost in their minds and only afterwards do they choose their course and their subjects from what the school has to offer. It is also possible to identify a third group — those who first decide on a particular course but then choose their institution on the basis of its 'adult atmosphere' rather than on the courses available.

In sixth-form and tertiary colleges students of all three types were found in varying proportions. There was greater variation between students in their reasons for attending a particular type of institution than in any other. In terms of their reasons for continuing their education, their perceptions of the disadvantages of staying on and their expectations of sixth-form or college life, the different students groups were in broad agreement.

Chapter 6

Students' Evaluation after Two Years

a. Method
A major aim of the study was to investigate students' evaluation of the course they had followed as it neared completion and to examine the different experiences and opinions of students in different institutions. This chapter will examine responses to the questionnaire (S2) completed by students in the research sample during summer term 1976 as they approached the end of their second year in post-compulsory education.

i. *The S2 sample*
Of the 4,448 students in the original sample, 3,646 stated they were on courses of two years' duration. These, together with the 201 students who had originally embarked on one-year courses but subsequently stayed on in the same school or college, formed the target sample for this exercise. Three schools (one comprehensive and two grammar) were not able to take part in this and subsequent stages of the project, and their students were therefore lost. A total of 3,687 questionnaires were finally administered. Institutions were given a choice in the means of administration of the questionnaire. Either:

1. a member of the research team would visit the school or college and all the students concerned assemble to com-

plete the questionnaire in their presence, or
2. the school/college could arrange a date for a member of their staff to administer the questionnaires and return them *en bloc*, or
3. the questionnaires could be distributed to the individual students and completed and returned by them at their own convenience.

The final response rates for the different types of institution were as follows:

No. of Questionnaires	Administered	No. Returned	Response Rate (percentage)
Comprehensive	719	439	61
Grammar	725	549	76
Sixth-form college	845	563	67
Tertiary	492	296	60
FE	906	464	51
Total	3687	2311	63

Because of the difficulty of arranging a date on which it was possible to bring together students from a number of different departments, most colleges of FE chose to distribute the questionnaires and leave the students to return them, i.e. option three. This may be the reason for the somewhat lower response rate from FE students compared with the other types of institution.

Because of this and also because the students on one-year courses who had left full-time education had been eliminated from this study, the composition of the sample, in terms of the courses followed, was somewhat different from the sample completing S1. The respondents to the second questionnaire were distributed as in Table 6.1.

This shows that overall, A-level students account for more than three quarters of the sample and those following vocational courses(i.e. OND, City and Guilds, and Secretarial courses) form only 17 per cent of the students completing the questionnaire. However, when we consider the composition of the sample within different types of institution,

Table 6.1 (S2): Type of institution attended and type of course followed by respondents to second student questionnaire

Main qualification	Comprehensive School		Grammar School		Sixth-form College		Tertiary College		FE College		Total	
	No.	%	No.	%	No.	%	No.	%	No.	%	No.	%
A-level	407	93	542	99	541	96	182	61	154	33	1826	79
O-level	24	5	3	1	14	2	11	4	7	2	59	3
OND							60	20	120	26	180	8
City & Guilds							21	7	64	14	85	4
Secretarial	5	1	4	1	8	1	17	6	70	15	104	5
Other	3	1					5	2	49	11	57	2
Total	439	100	549	100	563	100	296	100	464	100	2311	100

we see that students on A-level courses account for over 90 per cent of those in comprehensive and grammar schools and in sixth-form colleges. For FE and tertiary colleges this proportion was significantly lower (61 and 33 per cent repectively). Two thirds of the respondents in FE and one third in tertiary colleges were therefore on courses other than A-level.

Since much of the discussion which follows in this chapter will be devoted to comparing responses from different types of institution, the variation in these proportions should be borne in mind. However, where a student's course appears to have a greater bearing on his or her attitudes than the type of institution attended, course differences are discussed.

ii. *The questionnaire*
The questionnaire investigated the following areas:

1. Views on the differences between being in the fifth form and being in the sixth form or at college
2. The advantages and disadvantages of staying on after the fifth year
3. Preference for a school or college environment at 16+
4. The benefits of higher education
5. Evaluation of the advice given on higher education and employment
6. Evaluation of the help received with study techniques and problems.

All the issues listed above were investigated by means of attitude statements to which students indicated the extent of their agreement by circling a number on a precoded scale. Although the use of this technique enables a large amount of data to be collected and processed quickly, it allows the respondents no opportunity to express themselves freely on any topic. Nor does it give any indication whether the topics being investigated are those with which the respondents feel most concerned. It was decided therefore that some open-ended items be included in the questionnaire which would both give respondents an opportunity to air their views and also act as a check that the topics dealt with in the questionnaire were indeed those that students consider important.

To provide some structure for the answers it was decided to use sentence-completion items. Students were asked to 'complete the following statements so that they express your own feelings as honestly as possible, using as few or as many words as you wish'.

1. The most valuable thing I have gained from being at school or college this year is . . . .
2. The least satisfactory part of my course has been . . . .
3. If I were starting my college or sixth-form course over again I would . . . .
4. The greatest difficulty I encountered on my course was . . . .

As on the first questionnaire, if they had any further comments to make which they felt were relevant to the project, students were invited to write them on the back page. Where appropriate, responses to these items and other comments made have been used to illustrate particular points. Some items were deliberately worded to coincide with those asked in the questionnaire completed by students at the very beginning of their course, so that direct comparisons could be made between pupils' expectations of their course and their subsequent experiences. Where such comparisons are possible, they have been made.

b. Expectations and experiences

Students in the sample had been asked at the beginning of the project in which respect they would most like life in the sixth form or at college to differ from that in the fifth form. The responses described in Chapter 5 showed that most students were looking forward to being 'treated more like adults generally' and that the proportion giving this answer varied relatively little between different types of institution. Aspects of sixth-form life of secondary importance were 'better amenities', 'fewer rules concerning behaviour, dress, attendance' (the latter of more importance to grammar school sixth-formers) and 'higher standards in subjects in which I am interested'. Items which evoked least response were 'more optional subjects from which to choose' and 'more responsibility in the running of the school/college'.

At the end of two years, students were asked to indicate to what extent their experience of the sixth form or college *had* differed from the fifth form. In order to investigate more closely the degree of opinion on each item, the question was expanded so that students were asked to rate each item on a precoded scale from 'Not at all' (1) to 'Very much' (5). The mean responses on this scale to each of the items investigated are presented in Table 6.2.*

It should be noted that, with one exception, all the items covered in question 1 achieved mean ratings of at least 2.5 for students in each type of institution, i.e. the midpoint on the scale. This shows that all of the features of the sixth form or college mentioned had been experienced, at least to some extent, by the great majority of the students in the sample. Where differences in responses between those in different types of institution are discussed, we are only comparing opinions within a fairly narrow range, even though these differences were in themselves statistically significant.

i. *Specialist subjects*

'It provided a higher standard in subjects I was interested in' was the aspect of sixth-form or college life which students felt had been most satisfied. On the 1–5 scale it obtained a mean rating for all students of 4.0. Apart from those in FE, there was very little difference between types of institutions in this response. This is one of several items where it may be less meaningful to explore variations between institutional types than between course types, as variations in attitude will probably be more associated with the latter. For example, the slightly lower score on this item for students in FE

---

* It is recognized that there are limitations to questions of the type used in S1, which allow respondents to select only one answer from a list of alternatives. Because it was essential to collect a considerable amount of factual information from the students on the first questionnaire about their course, previous educational experience and attainment, it was necessary to use items of this type in order to keep the questionnaire to a manageable length. The second questionnaire completed by the students at the end of their course was considerably shorter and it was possible at this stage to investigate comparable issues in greater depth, and it is for this reason that different formats have been used.

Table 6.2 (S2): Extent to which sixth-form or college course differed from the fifth form

Mean ratings by students in different types of institutions (1 = Not at all, 5 = Very much)

	Comprehensive School	Grammar School	Sixth-form College	Tertiary College	FE College	Total
It provided a higher standard in subjects I was interested in	4.1	4.0	4.1	4.0	3.8	4.0
It provided plenty of optional, non-examination subjects to choose from	1.9	1.9	2.7	2.4	2.0	2.2
It provided satisfactory amenities such as a common room and rooms for private study	3.6	2.8	3.9	3.3	2.9	3.3
It gave more responsibility to students in the running of the school or college	2.9	2.6	3.5	3.1	2.7	3.0
It provided plenty of free time and study periods	3.8	3.4	3.7	3.6	2.8	3.5
It made it possible for students to be treated like adults	3.2	2.7	3.7	3.9	3.8	3.4
It had fewer rules concerning behaviours, attendance, dress	3.0	2.2	4.1	4.3	4.0	3.4
Total	439	549	563	296	464	2311

reflects the presence in this sub-sample of students on OND, City and Guilds and Secretarial courses, where the concept of 'subjects' may have less meaning than for those following A-level courses. This was borne out when the mean scores for these three groups on this item were found to be 3.7, 3.9 and 3.8 respectively compared with 4.1 for all A-level students.

There were a number of responses to the open-ended items which showed that many students are highly subject-oriented and that the opportunity to pursue their chosen specialist subjects was an important feature of their sixth-form experience. There were several answers of the following nature:

> The most valuable thing I have gained from being at school or college this year is that the greater one's favourite topic is studied in depth, the more enjoyable it becomes, with greater satisfaction and understanding. It also brings out the 'power' or beauty of the subject being studied such that the student is able to appreciate the subject more. Teachers at college also show much more interest than at school in the subjects they specialise in. (FE.)

> My interest has deepened in the subjects I have been studying and I have learned to appreciate them in a different and more fulfilling way than before. I find this has been reflected in my attitudes towards other topics with which I have come into contact. (Tertiary.)

ii. *General studies*

Most institutions recognize the need to counteract the effects of over-specialization and to provide some form of general studies for their students. As well as fulfilling a compensatory role, courses of this nature can also provide opportunities for students to develop new interests and leisure-time activities.

Students were asked in this item to indicate the extent to which their sixth-form or college course had provided a range of non-examination subjects for them to choose from. Students in every type of institution rated this item lower than any other. Overall, it achieved a mean rating of only 2.2, and for school sixth formers the rating was as low as 1.9. This would suggest that all students, but particularly those in schools, were presented with a very limited choice of non-examination subjects. Sixth-form colleges and tertiary colleges appear to have the means at their disposal to offer a somewhat wider range of courses. Only 19 and 27 per cent respectively of students in these types of institution said that their course did not differ at all in this respect from the fifth form, compared with 40 per cent or more in others. It may be, however, that these figures more accurately reflect a widespread negative attitude towards general studies than the degree of choice presented to students.

Information was sought in the institutional background questionnaire about the nature of the general studies provision made by the schools and colleges in the sample. As the position of FE and tertiary colleges regarding general studies appears to be somewhat different from the schools and sixth-form colleges, these two groups are discussed separately. There was considerable diversity in the nomenclature of non-examined studies. Core studies, integrated studies, electives, minorities, options, liberal studies, recreational studies were all phrases used to describe this aspect of the curriculum. Although each suggests slightly different approaches and philosophies, the phrase 'general studies' has been used throughout to avoid confusion.

Schools and sixth-form colleges

Despite minor variations, it is clear from the data provided in the institutional background questionnaire that the schools and sixth-form colleges in the sample can be divided into three broad categories in terms of their general studies provision.

a) The first group comprises institutions which enter their students for a general studies examination. In most instances this is an A-level paper, but students in some institutions were taking the O/A general paper. In institutions adopting this procedure, the students have no choice. Attendance at the general studies classes, usually two to three periods per week, is compulsory, and they follow a syllabus determined by the requirements of the examination. Approximately a quarter of the schools, but none of the sixth-form colleges, fell into this category.

b) A small number of institutions require their students to attend a general studies course which does not lead to an external examination but whose content is largely determined by the staff in charge, although students' preferences may sometimes be taken into account. This was the least common approach. Only three schools and one sixth-form college operated general studies schemes of this nature. While not insisting that their students entered for a general studies examination, two of the schools said pupils could do so if they wished.

c) The approach most commonly adopted is for students to be required to allocate a certain proportion of their timetable to general studies but allowed to choose the subjects which make up their course from a range of options. In most cases the aim is not to prepare students for an examination, although where appropriate, for example in language classes, students might be encouraged to enter for O-level or some similar qualification. In several institutions, students are required to change their options each term so that, over a two-year course, they would attend classes in six different subjects. Others prefer students to commit themselves to a subject for a whole year, on the assumption that one term is not long enough to reap any benefit from it.

Some institutions simplify the operation by concentrating all general studies courses in one half-day per week so that there are no timetabling constraints on students regarding the general studies options available to them. Where this system does not operate, students' choice will be limited to the general studies options that coincide with his or her free periods. It is worth noting here that the institutions in this category usually included a range of sporting activities among their general studies options. Students may therefore choose not to take part in any physical education or games. However, in institutions in the other two categories games and PE are regarded as separate from the general studies programme, and are in most cases a compulsory component of the timetable.

No systematic data were collected concerning the number of subjects from which students were able to choose. An examination of the school and college prospectuses, many of which contained this information, indicated that the sixth-form colleges, in general, are able to offer more general-studies options than the schools. Whether a wide range of options is intrinsically beneficial is, however, open to question. There is no evidence to suggest that choice alone engenders a more positive attitude towards general studies on the part of students.

The picture of general studies is further complicated by the fact that some institutions differentiate between general studies and leisure or recreational activities. There were at least three schools and one sixth-form college where students' non-examination work was divided into two distinct groups. They were required to attend both a 'general studies course' and in addition choose from a range of 'recreational activities' for a further two to three periods per week.

Only one school, a boys' comprehensive, did not offer any form of general studies. The sixth-formers in this school had three periods of games per week but the rest of their time-table was devoted to examination classes or private study. Of over 40 respondents to the questionnaire from this school, only two displayed any dissatisfaction with this arrangement, one of them complaining of the 'sheer waste of time, due to the fact that we had *too many* free periods with no provision of optional subjects to choose from'. In view of the attitudes towards general studies which are discussed later in this section, this is not surprising. No doubt many other students in the sample would envy the boys in this school their single-minded pursuit of examination goals.

FE and tertiary colleges
The nature of general studies courses provided in a college of further education will be determined to a great extent by its departmental structure. Where general studies is organized centrally, across departments, students are offered a range of options to choose from, in the same way as schools and colleges in category c) above. If colleges operate in this way, one half-day per week is normally devoted to general studies,

and all full-time students participate. A general studies class will therefore contain a cross-section of students from different courses who would otherwise have little contact with each other.

Many colleges do not appoint general studies lecturers as such but expect their staff to contribute to the general studies programme as part of their normal teaching requirement.

If, on the other hand, departments are responsible for the general studies teaching of their particular students, sometimes through the appointment of staff with a special responsibility in this area, students may have comparatively little choice, and their courses be more in line with those described in category b) on p. 152. A detailed and informative account of the functioning of general studies within different colleges is contained in Watson's *Liberal Studies in Further Education.*[18]

The majority of the FE colleges in the sample fell into the first of these categories. They offered a range of activities, some of them of considerable variety, from which all full-time students were required to choose. One college, where each Wednesday afternoon was devoted to these activities, publishes a brochure which contains information on some 50 courses on offer. These cover sports — sailing, horse riding, squash, rifle shooting, yoga — creative arts, film studies, theatre and music and a number of other activities such as community service, foreign languages, electronics, typing etc.

Of the three tertiary colleges, two operated general studies schemes sufficiently unusual to be worth describing in some detail. The first, in the belief that if general studies is treated as separate from the examined curriculum, it will enjoy only low esteem among staff and students alike, does not differentiate between the two. All students on A-level courses are required to take a 'key subject'. This key subject has twice the normal time allocation for an A-level subject, and the tutor is required to make use of this extra time to incorporate a general studies course within the subject. He may call upon other members of staff to assist in this. In this way an A-level syllabus acts as a springboard from which general studies develop. Students are therefore encouraged to view general studies as an integral feature of the curriculum and not as a superfluous extra whose purpose is to fill the gaps in their timetable. In addition the college offers a range of 'activities'. These include athletic, aesthetic and other options, and all full-time students take part in the programme. The other tertiary college enters its A-level students for general studies A-level but offers a number of alternative courses which students can choose to take if they wish. These include fluency courses in Spanish, Italian, French and German, a pre-education course for intending teachers, and college diploma courses in communications and physical education. In common with the other colleges, a number of recreational options are available from which all full-time students are free to choose.

Students' attitudes to general studies

Given the great diversity of practice in general studies, students' views on the matter were surprisingly uniform. It was an issue which aroused strong reactions. The great majority of the comments made regarding this topic were critical and students in general seem to have a very unfavourable attitude towards this aspect of their course. Over three hundred students (approximately 13 per cent of the sample) mentioned general studies in their responses to the item describing 'the least satisfactory part of my course'. 'A waste of time' and 'boring' were the phrases which occurred most frequently in this context. Most of the students adopted the attitude that examination work was all-important and anything which, in their view, did not contribute directly to their final examination performance was resented.

> I think too much importance is placed on giving us a general education i.e. core studies. If we want to learn about these sorts of things we can do without being forced to listen to a teacher lecturing on what he wants to. We come to school, really, to study for exams. (Grammar.)

> The least satisfactory part of my course has been the times when we've done absolutely nothing in lessons, e.g. music, drama, social studies, in other words, general

studies. It makes one feel it's a waste of time and we
could be doing private study or having longer periods of
other more appropriate subjects. (FE.)

The least satisfactory part of my course has been having
to do things like general studies when this time could be
put to greater use i.e. for study, especially during the
second year in the spring and summer terms. (Sixth-
form college.)

Some students complained that sometimes their teachers
appeared equally unenthusiastic about general studies.

The least satisfactory part of my course has been the
general studies programme. Non-examination subjects
seemed to collapse almost at the start of the sixth-form
course due to the non-existence of interest on behalf of
teacher and pupils. I speak only with knowledge of my
situation where I had supposedly two periods a week.
One teacher never turned up and the other never knew
what to do. (Comprehensive.)

One or two of the sessions were interesting because of
the teacher's enthusiasm over what he was talking
about. In others I got the impression that the teacher
was just as fed up with having to give up his free periods
as we were. (Grammar.)

In view of their reluctance to value anything which does
not lead to some form of external examination, it might be
concluded that students would be more inclined to take
general studies seriously if it were an examined subject. There
was evidence that in one or two schools students wished this
were so and had asked to be allowed to take A-level general
studies. However, those that were entering for the examination
showed no more favourable an attitude, mainly, it appears,
because they did not feel the lessons directly prepared them
for it.

I doubt if I shall pass the general studies A-level, and do

not need it. The lessons teach very little which help with the exams. I could spend the time on something much more valuable such as work for my Spanish O-level, which I am doing in addition to my A-levels. (Comprehensive.)

The four periods per week set aside for general studies lessons have been an extremely tedious aspect of school life for the past two years. Most of the time there is less than half the number of pupils at each lesson — showing that there is something amiss with the courses they have to offer which in any case are usually a teacher trying to make reluctant pupils enter an irrelevant, boring discussion about what the teacher happens to be interested in. No advice has yet been given as to the manner of answering the general studies A-level paper, although there are copies for us to take home and thumb through. (Comprehensive.)

Another frequently voiced complaint was the lack of choice or consultation students were allowed in the general studies courses.

The least satisfactory part of my course has been that one has no say whatever in the optional choices in the syllabus and that one was unable to do what the majority of the class wanted but was forced to do by a teacher because of her own personal preference. We were never consulted as to our preferences. (Comprehensive.)

I should like to say that general studies periods should be arranged at the beginning of each term by discussing the proposed topics which are of particular and general interest to the pupils. Otherwise many pupils find the general studies periods very boring — this may be a crucial factor in determining the 'taste' for school of a person. (Grammar.)

The least satisfactory part of my course has been useless minority subjects in which I have no interest. For instance, I am forced to do mathematical statistics, which is ridiculous as I failed maths O-level. I can do one sum a period and I ALWAYS get that wrong — rather disheartening to say the least. (Comprehensive.)

Even the fortunate ones who were presented with a considerable range of general studies options showed little gratitude for the opportunities available. The following comment is from a student in a college of FE where there were 30 subjects on offer.

The least satisfactory part of my course has been the electives system. For two hours a week we had to partake in a chosen elective. The choices were fairly limited and although most students managed to find one which was interesting, a new subject had to be chosen each term. The second choice was invariably something that was not really interesting to them at all. This then led to students skipping this lesson which led to bad feeling all round.

Where this attitude was widespread, it obviously spoilt the classes for the few students who were willing to participate actively in them: 'The least satisfactory part of my course has been general studies periods where other students have been apathetic and unwilling to join in as they foolishly chose courses in which they had little or no interest.' (Sixth-form college).

Total antipathy to the whole concept of general studies was shown by some students in spite of their freedom of choice, as this rather extreme example illustrates:

The least satisfactory part of my course has been some irrelevant additional courses such as 'options' which meant wasting several hours a week doing totally unnecessary subjects which had no relevance to my course (compulsory options on a Wednesday afternoon, i.e. cooking, badminton, tennis, making handbags etc.).

> If I were starting my college or sixth-form course over again I would not attend at all on Wednesday afternoons because we don't do any relevant *work*.

> The greatest difficulty I encountered on my course was attending options on a Wednesday afternoon 'cos a) they are boring, b) I'd rather drink coffee, c) we knicked off so many times that if I went now they'd tell me off.

> The main wrong thing about college is the emphasis on options which are a complete waste of time. They don't seem to serve any useful purpose. They consist of several *compulsory* alternatives ranging from golf to chess to making handbags (!) to silversmithing to life saving etc. and they waste the entire Wednesday afternoon. The only thing to do about options is not go. But this is against the college rule! (so instead we go for coffee as far from college as possible). (FE.)

There were very few suggestions on how the nature or content could be changed for the better. The overall impression created by students' comments is that they would prefer to avoid general studies altogether. Where suggestions were made, they were normally demands for advice on practical, everyday matters.

> I think that we should have a much wider course of minority subjects. These should be things which will be relevant to us when we leave school. Possibly things like bank accounts, how to fill in tax forms, politics, etc. (Comprehensive.)

> The least satisfactory part of my course has been an utter omission of extra-curricular activities which I consider to be of extreme importance, i.e. a basic grounding in politics, current affairs and a fundamental knowledge of economics. (Sixth-form college.)

> I feel that these lessons have proved a vain attempt to

broaden one's outlook and instead have merely caused boredom and frustration. It would have been preferable to develop practical skills rather than talking on philosophical and hypothetical levels which are in my opinion fruitless and dull. (Grammar.)

We will see in Chapter 8, which discusses the views of students when they have spent several months in employment or higher education, that they are then aware of certain gaps in their knowledge or experience which in their view might have usefully been filled by general studies courses, and that pleas for practical advice of this nature are common.

iii. *Amenities*

It is common practice for schools to set aside a room for the exclusive use of the sixth form. This is something more than the usual 'form room' in that lessons will not normally be held there and sixth-formers can therefore make use of it at any time of the day when they have no timetabled lessons (although some schools limit the amount of time that may be spent in the common room in any one week). Sometimes the common room is used exclusively for relaxation – record players, refreshment facilities, magazines etc. are frequently provided – but in some schools, where accommodation is at a premium, students wishing to do private study may find the common room the only place available.

A number of schools have, as a result of comprehensive reorganization, had to cope with a significant increase in the size of their sixth form. In some instances this has necessitated the building of extra accommodation for the sixth form, sometimes the addition of a new sixth-form block. The young people attending these may have a whole suite of rooms at their disposal – common rooms, study booths, discussion and tutorial areas, sixth-form libraries etc.

The facilities in grammar schools are unlikely to be so extensive. Normally these schools are housed in older buildings and, with a sixth form of a fairly constant size, have, for the most part, to make do with existing accommodation.

Where sixth-form colleges have been introduced there is a difference in this respect between those which have been purpose-built and those which are housed in existing school buildings. Whereas the former will have been designed with the specific nature and requirements of sixth-form study very much in mind, the latter will, as far as possible, have to adapt buildings which are designed for younger pupils to meet their new function.

Colleges of FE are in most parts of the country having to cope with considerably more full-time students than they were designed to accommodate. Most colleges give the impression of bursting at the seams. Several of the FE colleges in the sample had more than 1,000 full-time students, and it is difficult to see how common room and private-study facilities could be adequately provided for such numbers. As a result some colleges allow their students to study at home. They therefore have no registration regulations and insist only that their students attend timetabled lessons. This was also true of the three tertiary colleges in the sample. While most schools require their sixth-formers to be on the premises throughout the school day, there was some variation between institutions in their policy regarding attendance, and a number, perhaps those conscious of the lack of quiet space, allowed students to go home to study when they had no lessons.

For these reasons, it was concluded that differences between institutional types in students' rating of the item on amenities was less meaningful than differences between individual institutions. The views of students in comprehensive schools in particular, were found to vary considerably. The two schools where this item, 'it provided satisfactory amenities such as a common room and rooms for private study', was rather highest (4.4 and 4.3) both had recently completed purpose-built sixth-form blocks, and two other schools where this item achieved a mean grade of more than 4.0 housed their students in a suite of rooms set apart from the main school. All but three of the comprehensives required their sixth-formers to be on the premises throughout the school day, and several students expressed resentment of this restriction.

When a study period happens to be in the morning

session, it is compulsory for us to arrive at the normal registration time of pupils aged 11. This is very annoying. (Comprehensive.)

The least satisfactory part of my course has been the fact that one is not supposed to leave the school and work at home despite the fact that one may have a free afternoon or morning. (Comprehensive.)

The least satisfactory part of my course has been over-rigid discipline. I feel sixth-formers should be allowed to spend free time as they wish and not be forced to remain in school. This would be more like college/ university and would also fit better with the idea that sixth-formers are adults, not children being constantly watched. (Comprehensive.)

The greatest difficulty I encountered on my course was organizing private work. Private study facilities in our school are pathetic. We have a ROSLA block but due to general overcrowding, our block has been infiltrated by children. Consequence — a lot of noise. Also, we don't have a common room. (Comprehensive.)

The grammar school students, in general, did not rate this item as highly as those in comprehensives. The highest rating achieved by any grammar school was 3.5. This was a school purpose-built 15 years prior to the survey. The lowest rating for all institutions was a grammar school on the verge of going comprehensive, where the buildings ranged in age from early Tudor to modern terrapin.

There was less variation among the three types of college than among the schools. Students in sixth-form colleges were most satisfied with the amenities provided and the highest degree of satisfaction (4.6) was, surprisingly, associated with one of the colleges housed in ex-grammar school buildings.

College of FE students were similar to grammar school students in their comparatively low rating of this item and a number were critical of the amenities provided, both for recreation and private study.

The greatest difficulty I encountered on my course was meeting other people from different courses. The social amenities at my college were disgusting, consisting of one common room, measuring originally approx. 15' by 25' and later partitioned into two separate rooms — one for pinball machines and one of about 12' by 14' for armchairs etc. As the furniture was awful, I very infrequently went in the common room and so if I hadn't known people already before I went to college, I would have spoken to no-one other than the people on my own course. (FE.)

iv. *Student autonomy*

A chance to take an active part in the running of the school has always, it is claimed, been a hallmark of the sixth form. However, this phrase is open to interpretation, and it is probable that in different institutions this responsibility has taken a variety of different forms. For some, it may involve an active participation in decision-making via a school or college council which has real power to change the rules and regulations which govern students' lives. For others, this type of body may exist only in an advisory capacity, in which case the head or principal has the final word. In other schools, sixth-formers' responsibilities may be limited to the running of school societies and mundane duties connected with the supervision of younger pupils.

The size of the institution may also be an important determinant of the extent to which students feel they play a significant role in its functioning. In small institutions, it may be possible for all students to have the opportunity to share in a democratic process. In some of the larger colleges, where only a small minority can be actively engaged in Student Union affairs, the decision-making machinery may seem remote to the majority of students.

The institutional background questionnaire provided information on the existence of prefect systems, school and college councils and student unions. Prefect systems were in operation in all but four of the schools in the sample. Schools councils were a less common phenomenon. Sixteen of the 27 schools had some form of council in operation on which students were represented. Sometimes membership of the council was restricted to representatives of the sixth form or senior pupils, but in most cases, all pupils voted for the representatives of their year group. The existence of such a council was found to have a significant effect on the views of school sixth-formers on whether they had been granted sufficient responsibility in the running of their school. Students in schools with councils rated this item significantly higher than those in schools without. The mean rating for these two groups on this item, i.e. 'it gave more responsibility to students in the running of the school or college', were 3.0 and 2.5 respectively ($p = <.01$). Several students complained of the lack of opportunity to exercise responsibility within the school. 'A sixth-form student of 16 years of age has made up his or her own mind to remain at school or go on to college. I feel they should therefore be treated as responsible individuals. It would be nice if we could have more of a say in the running of the sixth form as it involves two important years in our lives.' (Comprehensive.)

Although there was also some evidence that students were not totally satisfied with the way in which the council functioned.

> Our 6th form was run very much from above by the head of the upper school. As well as causing some resentment on such trivial issues as whether ties should be worn, it meant that an opportunity to develop students' responsibility and social awareness was wasted. We did in fact have a 6th form committee but, having served on this for one year and been thwarted in any attempt ever to bring up contentious issues, I am sure that this body has no power. The students on it are treated like children and there is no voting. The only way anything can be achieved by it is by persuading the head that it is right, which is virtually impossible. (Comprehensive.)

There were, on the other hand, a number of comments from sixth-formers which suggest that they find the opportunity the all-through school structure provides for supervising younger pupils a valuable experience.

> The most valuable thing I have gained from being at school or college this year is an appreciation of responsibilities to myself, the staff, and of the running of the school and instilling discipline in the lower school. (Grammar.)

> A sixth-form college would give people freedom from younger pupils but valuable experience can be gained from supervising junior pupils if a person wants to go on to teacher training. Also, a sixth-form college, with only ages 16—18, could restrict association with other people of different ages and narrow one's outlook. (Grammar.)

> 6th formers could be involved further in the running of the school as opposed to just being 'disciplinary' prefects. I feel that the traditional method of a 6th form at school to be the best method, as it gives the chance for 6th formers to run societies and activities for younger children. (Grammar.)

However, students in sixth-form colleges rated this item higher than any other group. All of the institutions of this type in the study had a student council in operation, and in the majority of cases a representative of each tutor group was elected to the council. The opportunity this system provides for a high proportion of students to participate in a decision-making process may be a contributory factor in the high rating achieved on this item by students in sixth-form colleges. The following is a typical statement of the aims of the council in a sixth-form college:

The objectives of the Student Council may therefore be seen as:-

> (i) To promote the general welfare of students and encourage co-operation for social, educational, cultural and athletic activities.

> (ii) To provide a channel of communication and con-

sultation with the principal and staff.
(iii) To support and encourage community service work.
(iv) To establish and administer a fund.
 (v) To establish a social committee and to assist in the organization of refreshment facilities in the common room.
(vi) To support and encourage all recognized clubs and societies of the college.

All of the FE and tertiary colleges in the sample had a students' union, and all but two of these were affiliated to the National Union of Students. A question investigating the major activities in the colleges in which the student unions were involved revealed that all were responsible for organization of community and voluntary work. All but two of the colleges said that the students' union was represented on the academic board and on committees dealing with college regulations. Five colleges stated that the union was fully represented on the board of governors. Although students in tertiary colleges rated it higher than those in other colleges of FE, it was difficult to discern any corresponding differences in the policies in operation. For those individuals who had been deeply involved in student union activities, this experience was very highly valued.

> The most valuable thing I have gained from being at college this year is my role played in the students' union as NUS secretary and president. Although the work was very demanding, I have gained a great deal of experience both with the students' union and my communication with other people. I also think that after being in an adult atmosphere for two years that I am more prepared for polytechnic than school students. (Tertiary.)

v. *Free time*
This is another issue where students' views were found to be less dependent on the type of institution they attended than on the type of course they were following. It has traditionally been accepted that students studying for A-levels will spend a significant proportion of their time in private

study. Although the way this time is spent is usually left to the individual student, they are expected to spend it constructively, e.g. by making notes, in relevant background reading, going over the ground recently covered – in general, to develop the habits of academic study normally required in higher education.

On the other hand, students studying for vocational qualifications such as City and Guilds may find that their timetable contains comparatively few free periods, and that teacher-contact time accounts for a very high proportion of their week.

There were significant differences between course groups in their responses to the item 'it provided plenty of free time and study periods'. The mean ratings for each course group were as follows:

Type of Course	Mean Rating
A-level	3.7
O-level	3.8
OND	2.5
City and Guilds	2.7
Secretarial	2.4
Other	2.3

These figures show that there was a sharp distinction between academic courses (i.e. A- and O-level) and vocational courses in the amount of free time and study periods students had at their disposal, the academic group rating this item significantly higher than those on vocational courses.

In fact a number of students on vocational courses did complain that the demands of their course left them relatively little time for private study or for relaxation.

> The greatest difficulty I encountered on my course was the fact that five subjects have to be studied to a standard which was equivalent to that of A-level. This allowed little time for social activities and consequently they had to be sacrificed. Because five subjects have to be covered, little time could be spared to indulge in the subject one enjoyed the most. (OND business studies student).

The least satisfactory part of my course has been little
time for private study so all homework had to be done
at home leaving little free time for recreation. (Medical
secretary.)

The least satisfactory part of my course has been that
we did not get any free periods to do our project in and
it has to be done in our own time which was very difficult after 7 to 8 hours continuous study. (Pre-Health
Service student.)

Although there were a considerable number of comments
from A-level students on the exacting nature of these courses,
comparatively few actually complained about the number of
free periods they had been allocated.

vi. *Adult treatment*

Responses to the two items 'it made it possible for students
to be treated like adults' and 'it had fewer rules concerning
behaviour, attendance, dress' will be discussed together
because they are closely interrelated and because the pattern
of responses to them was very similar. On both items there
was a clear difference between the responses from school
sixth-formers and college students, the latter rating both
items significantly higher than pupils in either comprehensive
or grammar schools.

'It had fewer rules concerning behaviour, attendance,
dress' was for students in FE and tertiary colleges, the aspect
in which their present situation *most* differed from the fifth
form. Sixth-form college students rated it equally high with
'it provided a higher standard in subjects I was interested in'.
The grammar school group, however, rated this item very low.
With a mean score of 2.2, only the item concerning non-
examination subjects was rated lower by grammar school
sixth-formers. In fact, 38 per cent of grammar school sixth-
formers said this statement did not apply at all to them
compared with only 15 per cent of comprehensive school
sixth-formers and two and four per cent respectively in sixth-
form colleges and FE. In tertiary colleges there were *no*
students saying this did not apply at all in their experience.

A similar pattern of responses emerged for the item 'it made it possible for students to be treated like adults', where colleges, particularly the tertiary colleges, achieved a significantly higher rating than either of the school types. When we recall that all groups of students had hoped at the beginning of their course above all 'to be treated like adults' it is clear that the school sixth-formers and particularly those in grammar schools had been disappointed in their expectations.

The importance young people attach to this aspect of their sixth-form or college experience should not be underestimated. At all stages of the study there were innumerable comments from students about the extent to which they had been granted the treatment, privileges and responsibilities they felt their adult status warranted. It would be misleading to say that all the comments from college students on this issue were favourable and those from school sixth formers, unfavourable. However, it is undoubtedly true that the majority of comments were in this direction. There were many complaints from school sixth-formers that they had not been treated in quite the way they had been led to expect. The following remarks are typical:

> The rules at this school are far too strict for 6th formers. A reasonable relaxation of these rules would make for a better atmosphere and more ability and willingness to work. (Grammar.)

> I think that if pupils are to be encouraged to return in the 6th form then staff should be made to recognise them as *adult* students who are continuing their studies voluntarily, and not as merely an extension of the 5th form who can be pushed around and treated with no respect whatsoever. If this was done, then I think a lot more people would be prepared to stay on for higher education and the school would be far more harmonious in its operation. (Grammar.)

> Although it may just seem like sour grapes, I feel rather disillusioned with my sixth-form course. One is led to believe that relations with staff will improve, one will

instantly be treated as an adult and one will have ample time for private study when in actual fact I found none of this was so. One is still restricted unnecessarily and expected to abide with petty rules. (Grammar.)

> The greatest difficulty I encountered on my course was the frustration and boredom of having to submit to a great number of petty rules and regulations, and the irritation of being treated almost exactly the same as the 12 year olds. (Grammar.)

Similar criticisms from comprehensive schools were far less frequent, although where they occurred, they tended to be of the same nature.

> This school tends not to change its attitude to 6th formers completely from its attitude to 5th formers. In the sixth form we are generally treated more like adults but certain petty regulations still hold. For example boys must still wear ties and although the uniform standards have changed, it became usual to see the 5th formers allowed more concessions in uniform than the sixth. And those 5th formers of lesser intelligence who plainly abused the concession demonstrated that they were not worthy of it. (Comprehensive.)

In contrast, college students frequently mentioned the benefits to be gained from being subject to fewer restrictions, many of them pointing out that this had encouraged them to acquire self-discipline and was therefore a more appropriate preparation for higher education than an authoritarian structure.

> The most valuable thing I have gained from being at college this year is . . .

> . . . that I feel I have been able to develop my personality more than had been possible in a strict school atmosphere. Also I now feel that I can take on greater responsibilities and organize and handle situations with greater efficiency and confidence. (Sixth-form college.)

... being able to work on my own but to ask for help and advice when it has been needed. And also to work in, and be part of, an adult, friendly, atmosphere. (Sixth-form college.)

... learning how to adjust to the adult world during this transitional stage and also learning how to mix with other people. (Tertiary college.)

... a broadened outlook due to the way in which a technical college is run. This includes qualities of self discipline which have to be exercised in a situation where there is little formal discipline. (Tertiary college).

c. Advantages and disadvantages of post-compulsory education

An important objective of the second student questionnaire was to investigate students' perceptions of the advantages of staying on beyond the age of 16. Two groups of advantages were investigated — the immediate, short-term advantages already experienced, and the anticipated, long-term advantages. The mean ratings on both groups by students in different types of institution are given in Table 6.3. Although the short-term advantages received moderate recognition, the higher ratings for the second group of items show that students are more aware of the long-term advantages of their course.

The short-term advantage most highly rated was 'it has allowed me to study subjects which interested me'. This achieved an overall mean rating of 4.0 with comparatively little variation between institutional types. When differences between course groups were examined it was found that the highest ratings on this item were those of students on City and Guilds and secretarial courses. This is a somewhat surprising result when one considers that A-level students, within certain limits, choose the subjects which make up their course, but students on City and Guilds and secretarial courses have less control over the content of their courses. A number of students mentioned this in responses to open-ended items.

The most valuable thing I have gained from being at school or college this year is it has provided me with an opportunity to study the subjects I am interested in alongside my friends. (Grammar.)

The most valuable thing I have gained from being at school or college this year is finishing my A-level English course — this is my best and favourite subject, which has helped me to develop and mature my opinions and attitudes generally — not only in the literary field. (Comprehensive.)

The most valuable thing I have gained from being at school or college this year is the opportunity to study subjects I enjoy in an adult atmosphere. (FE.)

Students also felt that their experience of post-compulsory education had generally 'broadened their outlook' and this was the second most important short-term advantage of staying on. This was particularly true of those in colleges, where this attitude seemed to be associated with the opportunities colleges provided for mixing with a greater cross-section of young people.

The most valuable thing I have gained from being at school or college this year is . . .

. . . I have lost a lot of my previous shyness, met more people and made new friends and have generally broadened my outlook. (FE.)

. . . A broadened outlook on life and perhaps in June a sense of fulfilment at having worked hard and achieved something. In many ways a broadened social outlook through meeting with a lot more people of my own age than I would otherwise have done. (Sixth-form college.)

. . . A broader outlook on life. I have been taught to question and not to accept too readily. I've been made to try to look at all matters of importance with an objective view. (FE.)

Table 6.3 (S2): Advantages of staying on in full-time education after the fifth form

Mean ratings by students in different types of institution (1 = Not at all, 5 = Very much)

	Comprehensive School	Grammar School	Sixth-form College	Tertiary College	FE College	Total
It has allowed me to study subjects which interested me	3.9	3.9	4.1	4.0	4.0	4.0
It has broadened my outlook	3.2	3.2	3.6	3.6	3.9	3.5
It has allowed me to be with my friends	3.1	3.3	3.3	3.0	2.8	3.1
It has given me a chance to get ready to go out to work	2.3	2.2	2.7	2.9	3.4	2.7
Long-term advantages of staying on in full-time education after the fifth form						
Earning qualifications enabling one to enter higher education	4.4	4.4	4.4	4.1	4.0	4.3
Earning qualifications necessary for one's chosen career	4.2	4.3	4.2	4.4	4.4	4.3
Improving career prospects generally	4.2	4.2	4.2	4.3	4.2	4.2
Getting a good all-round education	3.2	3.4	3.6	3.5	3.5	3.4
Total	439	549	563	296	464	2311

'It has allowed me to be with my friends' was seen as a somewhat less important advantage of having stayed on, although a rapport with fellow-students was sometimes mentioned in responses to the open-ended items: 'The most valuable thing I have gained is the friendliness of my fellow students as we all face the rigours of work together.' (Grammar.) This item was of least importance for students in FE where a large number of students would have been separated from most of their fifth-form contemporaries on entry to college: 'I have also discovered that one should not expect school friends who go into employment to remain close friends and therefore I have learnt to make new friends.' (FE.)

'It has given me a chance to get ready to go out to work' was an item which drew a sharp distinction between A-level and vocational courses. The mean responses to this statement for each of the main course groups were as follows:

A-level	2.4
O-level	3.2
OND	3.2
City and Guilds	3.8
Secretarial	4.2

The A-level students clearly felt that studying for this type of qualification had not prepared them for employment in the same way that the City and Guilds and secretarial students did. The traditional view of A-level as an entry requirement to various fields of higher education and not a direct entry into a particular occupational field is obviously accepted by students. Although most A-level students thought studying for these qualifications enhanced their general career prospects, they were comparatively unconvinced as to their preparedness for employment as the next step. We will see in a later chapter of this report how the A-level students who did not go on to a course of higher education fared in their search for appropriate employment.

Students on vocational courses, however, often expressed their confidence regarding the relevance of their present course to the job they intended to do.

> The most valuable thing I have gained from being at school or college this year is . . .
>
> . . . a wider realisation that the course is applicable to working life. An increasing awareness that what I am doing in theory work is applicable to working life. (Secretarial student.)
>
> . . . a wide and varied appreciation of different aspects of the business world. (OND business studies student.)
>
> . . . the chance to improve and develop my talents towards my chosen career. Also the extra knowledge I have gained to prepare me for my City and Guilds exam. I would like to say that the hairdressing facilities are excellent and the staff are very helpful. I would not hesitate to recommend my two-year course to anyone wishing to take up hairdressing as a career.

An overall scrutiny of the evaluation of these short-term advantages suggests that school sixth-formers did not, in general, rate them as highly as those in colleges. Is this because those in schools did not find the experience as immediately enjoyable as the college students, but are willing to complete their course because of the promise of the opportunities this will lead to?

The long-term advantages of staying on were very much more highly rated than the short-term advantages. There was however a clear distinction between students in schools and sixth-form colleges who thought 'earning qualifications enabling one to enter higher education' was the most important long-term advantage, and those in FE and tertiary colleges were 'earning qualifications necessary for one's chosen career' was rated highest. Once again these differences reflect differences in the qualifications aimed at by these groups. The mean scores on these items for the various course groups were as follows:

Table 6.4 (S2)

	Earning Qualifications Enabling One to Enter Higher Education	Earning Qualifications Necessary for One's Chosen Career
A-level	4.4	4.2
O-level	4.2	4.3
OND	4.1	4.3
City and Guilds	3.5	4.4
Secretarial	3.5	4.7

These show that for students on City and Guilds and secretarial courses, 'earning qualifications necessary for one's chosen career' was a much more important advantage than 'earning qualifications enabling one to enter higher education'. Students studying for OND rated the latter item slightly higher but still considered that obtaining the qualifications which were necessary for entry to their chosen career was the most important gain from post-compulsory education. The very high rating by A-level students on the first of these items shows how oriented this group are towards higher education.

'Improving career prospects generally' was rated almost as highly as the two previous items, and there was no significant difference between either institution or course groups in their rating of this item: 'The most valuable thing I have gained from being at school or college this year is the chance to leave school with some decent qualifications under my belt, so as to better my long-term career prospects.' (Comprehensive.)

'Getting a good all-round education' was not seen by students as an important advantage of staying on. In fact, there was some evidence to suggest that students did not see this as the purpose of post-compulsory education at all.

> Staying on after the fifth form generally involves either a retake of previous subjects, a secretarial course, or as most people choose, studying for A-level subjects. Therefore, studying for two or three subjects (usually on the basis that these subjects have been studied to a lesser degree before) would by no means give any of

> us 'a good all-round education', but this phrase would have already been in our interests during our first five years at school. (Comprehensive.)

> The least satisfactory part of my course has been the time we have spent on lectures that have no real relevance to the course but have to be taken to broaden one's education. (FE.)

Most students seem content to study either a subject or a limited range of subjects which they had chosen to coincide with their own interests and abilities. Despite some misgivings about their choice of subjects and some criticism of the limitations placed on the range of subjects or combinations available in certain institutions, there was no quarrel with the concept of specialization *per se*. The negative attitudes to general studies described earlier in this chapter only serve to endorse this view of students as subject- or specialist-minded.

Table 6.5 shows students' evaluation of the disadvantages of staying on in full-time education. This shows that overall, shortage of money was the greatest single disadvantage of staying on, and that students in FE and tertiary colleges rated this item significantly higher than those in other types of institution. These two groups' contact with part-time and day release students who are in employment may help to exacerbate their feelings on this matter. FE students may also incur expenses in the purchase of textbooks or stationery.

> I have found that one of the major difficulties I have encountered by carrying on with further education after the fifth form is that of financial support. This has created problems connected with both the course at college and my own social life. I have had to buy all of my own textbooks, files etc. and spend a small fortune on paper. From the point of view of my own social life, this problem seems apparent when I go out with friends of mine who are now out at work. The only way I have found to overcome this problem is to work as many hours as possible in the summer vacation and hope to save enough to carry me through the autumn and spring term to the next vacation. (FE.)

Table 6.5 (S2): Disadvantages of staying on in full-time education

Mean ratings by students in different types of institution (1 = Not at all, 5 = Very much)

	Comprehensive School	Grammar School	Sixth-form College	Tertiary College	FE College	Total
Shortage of free time	2.6	2.9	2.8	2.5	2.7	2.7
Lack of practical experience/ sheltered life	2.8	3.2	2.7	2.6	2.5	2.8
Shortage of money	3.8	3.8	3.8	4.1	4.1	3.9
Loss of chance to learn a trade	2.1	2.1	2.3	2.0	2.0	2.1
Dependence on parents	3.6	3.5	3.7	3.7	3.8	3.7
Continuation of exam pressure	3.7	3.8	3.8	3.7	3.7	3.7
Time wasted if I fail	3.2	3.2	3.3	3.4	3.2	3.2
Loss of contact with friends who are now at work	2.2	2.1	2.2	2.3	2.4	2.2
Total	439	549	563	296	464	2311

Although there were frequent pleas for small grants and concessions to be made available to sixth-formers and FE students, these were fewer in number than they had been on the first questionnaire. Perhaps after two years in post-compulsory education students had got accustomed to their impecunious situation or perhaps they now had less contact with contemporaries in employment and thus felt the comparison less.

> It is very unfortunate that pupils who opt to stay on in the sixth form are to be short of money for two years. For instance our contemporaries in jobs are earning while we have to rely totally on our parents and perhaps a Saturday job (which the teachers frown on) for a few pounds to spend. Surely it would be fair to introduce cheap bus fares for school students and perhaps even cheap entry to cinemas etc. (Comprehensive.)

'Dependence on parents', and 'continuation of exam pressure' were also seen as major disadvantages of staying on. The first of these is clearly closely allied to 'shortage of money' in that dependence on parents implies financial dependence. However, in this case there were no significant differences between students from different types of institution in their responses.

Many students were conscious of being subject to extreme pressure as their final examinations approached. In fact, there were a number of heartfelt pleas for the A-level examining system to be revised in order to incorporate some form of continuous assessment.

> Exam pressure can lead to nervous instability which I have noticed more in people who are intelligent and very likely to pass the exam with a good grade. Another fault with condensing two years study into 2–3 hours is that 'parrot fashion' learning is encouraged. A continual assessment system would therefore be desirable which would stimulate constant revision and remove the fact that everything depends on the performance during a final short period.

> There are many people I feel who could justifiably be awarded an 'A' or 'B' on their record over the past two years without the need for them to sit a final exam. (Grammar.)

Although students, particularly those in sixth-form and tertiary colleges, were less inclined to think that their time would have been wasted if they failed their examinations, there were a number who considered exam passes were the only benefit to be gained from staying on: 'The most valuable thing I have gained from being at school or college this year is the chance to gain higher qualifications which will enable me to follow my chosen career. If I do not pass my exams, I have gained absolutely nothing from staying on at this school, and will consider my time spent here to be completely wasted.' (Grammar.)

'Lack of practical experience/sheltered life' was not seen as a major disadvantage of staying on except by grammar school sixth-formers who rated it significantly higher than other groups. We have already seen that college students were more inclined to feel that their horizons had broadened, that they had mixed with a greater cross-section of the community and that they were more in touch with the realities of working life. The grammar school sixth-formers on the other hand seem particularly conscious of the artificiality of their surroundings. One aspect of 16—19 education which has not yet been discussed, but which may have a bearing on this attitude, is the question of whether an institution is mixed or single-sex. Whereas the majority of grammar schools in the sample were single-sex, all the colleges and all but three of the comprehensives were mixed. Many students who had transferred to colleges from single-sex schools stressed the effects of this transition.

> It is a distinct advantage that the college is mixed — you don't mention this in the questionnaire. People fail to realise, when they themselves are past 25, what a sudden shock, wrench or disturbance this produces in the unsuspecting, unfortunate children who had to go to non-mixed schools. It is BAD that people who are segregated

from the opposite sex for five years should have to cope with this as well as new study patterns, independence and a new, anonymous institution like the college. (Tertiary.)

As the college is co-educational it provides interesting diversions from the normal school curriculum and opportunities arise for a person to get to know someone of the opposite sex better and to meet them more easily than would have been possible before when the school was all-male. It seemed a strange thing at first to have girls in the same class and doing the same subjects but one soon got used to it. (Sixth-form college.)

There was a tendency at all stages of the study for some boys in single-sex schools to display flippant attitudes in their responses to the questionnaire which were quite lacking in mixed schools and in colleges. These were often manifested in comments which included obscenities or catch phrases from favourite television comedy series (such as Monty Python). Although small in number, these were sufficiently associated with particular schools for the project team to speculate on whether this kind of immaturity is a reflection on the absence of adult treatment which pupils in grammar schools so frequently complained of, and whether it is particularly likely to flourish in an all-male atmosphere.

The following is one of the more amusing (and printable) examples. It is typical in that it starts out to make a serious point but gradually the opportunity to pour out his feelings on paper leads the author to an uncontrolled outburst.

I stayed on at this school only because I was here and settled in (etc.). But I just can't stick the academic, cold, snobbish atmosphere that I am in now. I would much rather have gone to a *mixed* college but I would leave friends etc. and have to pay for books and be more on my own as far as getting work done goes. Also change of teachers might be a bit difficult, but I would really prefer going to a college. I disagree with this school as the last-surviving grammar school in ————.

This school is going for a public school image for the
benefit of its own name and so the pupils have to suffer.
The main decisions are made by out-of-touch governors
who haven't got a clue and waste vast amounts of
money on unnecessary amenities (statues, swimming
pools, classics libraries etc.). What we need is equal
status for pupils — no, not equal status — the pupils
should rule! PUPIL POWER and BLOODY REVOLU-
TION is what we need!!! Soon the lads will be on the
march, first ————— School, then Parliament, then
the United Nations! Yes, we'll take over the world, the
time is coming, just you wait. Your surveys won't do
any good then . . . Sorry, I got carried away.

d. Students' preference for a school or college

The preference of students for either a school or college
system for the 16—19 age group was investigated in all
three questionnaires administered to the students in the
sample. The responses to this item in the second questionnaire (S2) are shown in Table 6.6. Overall, two thirds of
students felt it was better for young people to be educated
in colleges, 21 per cent opted for schools and 13 per cent
did not know. However there were significant differences
between institutional groups in their attitudes to this issue.
In sixth-form or tertiary colleges and colleges of FE, over
80 per cent felt that colleges were preferable. There were
numerous testimonials from students in colleges saying
how satisfied they were, and the following extracts are
presented to illustrate the type of comments made.

I feel very strongly that sixth-form colleges should
become part of the normal educational set up. They
prepare a student to cope with the independence of
university life, but also give good help and guidance.
Also the amount of freedom given to the individual
student will lure school leavers into remaining to gain
higher examination qualifications. Students that are
able, yet dislike school-like discipline will be encouraged
to remain in an educational establishment. The sixth-
form college is unique in allowing students to develop

Table 6.6 (S2): Students' preferences for a school or college for the 16–19 age group (percentages)

	Comprehensive School	Grammar School	Sixth-form College	Tertiary College	FE College	Total
Colleges	34	44	88	81	85	66
Schools	45	36	6	10	6	21
Don't know	21	19	6	8	8	13
Importance of reasons for preferring a college						
Mean rating by students in different institutions (1 = Not at all, 5 = Very much)						
N =	151	244	493	239	392	1519
Wide choice of courses	4.0	4.0	4.1	4.2	4.3	4.1
Adult atmosphere	4.5	4.5	4.2	4.2	4.2	4.3
No younger pupils	3.4	3.3	3.6	3.4	3.4	3.4
Few rules and regulations	3.6	3.9	3.7	3.7	3.5	3.7
Importance of reasons for preferring a school						
N =	197	199	35	29	26	486
Small teaching groups	3.9	3.8	3.8	3.6	3.6	3.8
Familiar environment, known to teachers and friends	4.0	3.9	4.2	3.8	3.5	3.9
Contact with/responsibility for younger pupils	3.6	3.6	3.9	4.1	3.5	3.7
Example of sixth form important for lower forms	3.3	3.3	3.4	4.0	3.8	3.4

their personalities in friendly surroundings. The discipline is just enough to check wayward students, but not enough to cause annoyance to the majority. Having experienced a sixth-form college I can honestly state that these institutions are highly effective in obtaining the right balance between academic and personal development. (Sixth- form college.)

I have enjoyed being at my college very much. The course overall is very interesting and my lecturers are very understanding, helpful and considerate. The whole atmosphere at college was more 'adult' and students/ teacher relationships are much nicer and on more friendly terms. (FE.)

In attending the college I have found it useful from a social point of view and educationally beneficial. I can only say that I have enjoyed almost every minute of college life and have found it much more conducive to work than school. The atmosphere is relaxed, yet enough discipline exists for the college to run smoothly. (Tertiary.)

On the whole I think that a college is much better than carrying on in a school. You are treated as an adult, not as a child. You learn and are expected to use your own initiative. A much greater understanding is gained of people and of the world. Much more general knowledge is gained not just about your career but about life as a whole. You learn to mix with people more than you would at school. You meet different people of varying backgrounds and altogether it is much more interesting. (Tertiary.)

Sixth-form colleges are much better than a sixth form tacked on to a secondary school, because by implication several schools will contribute students to the college. The area from which students are drawn is large and the sixth form itself is larger. Being larger there is a better mixture of students of widely varying views, talents etc.

all which help the atmosphere and character of social life. Also economically sixth-form colleges have more money for equipment and text books, without some being reallocated by the head to 5th forms. (Sixth-form college.)

I find the small groups and close relationships with tutors helpful, as well as the fact that each group is under the care of a tutor who keeps a check on progress, even though students are encouraged to work independently without being told to work all the time. So although 'pastoral care' is given, and tutorial guidance is a strong feature of the college, students are treated as adults and are expected to organize their work of their own accord. (Tertiary.)

School sixth-formers on the other hand were considerably less enthusiastic about their present situation. Of the students in comprehensive-school sixth formers, 45 per cent felt schools were preferable, 34 per cent opted for colleges, and 21 per cent did not know. Only in grammar schools were there fewer pupils in favour of their present system than opposed to it. Of the grammar school sixth-formers, 44 per cent said they thought the age group should be educated in colleges and only 36 per cent that a school sixth form was preferable. As might be expected, there were more pupils in the school sixth forms who felt unable to give an opinion than those in colleges. The latter had previously been at school and even though most had no direct experience of the sixth form, were more likely to feel able to compare the two. The results for grammar schools seem even more noteworthy, in that pupils who considered a college system, of which they have no direct experience, would be preferable to the one in which they now find themselves formed the largest single group.

When we examine the reasons given by students for their preferences in this matter we find that colleges were most popular because of their 'adult atmosphere'. School sixth-formers who stated a preference for a college system were particularly inclined to give this as the main reason for their choice.

A high percentage of sixth-formers at my school feel that although the education has been good over their A-level subjects, though virtually non-existent on a broader basis, that they would have been far happier in a less-restricted, more adult atmosphere. One of the big advantages of our system is the sense of stability and continuation gained from remaining in the sixth form. (Grammar.)

I think that a special sixth-form college has advantages over a school as the staff, because of the absence of younger children, would treat you more like an adult and less like an irresponsible twelve year old. The sixth form do not get any privileges and still have to wear the same uniform and have the same rules. (Grammar.)

It seems to me that students studying A-level courses are expected to work in a way which is half-way between school work and university/college work. It is therefore as unrealistic to make them conform to a school curriculum, the rules etc. as it is to put them straight into a university. Sixth-form colleges, although I have had no personal experience of them, would seem to be the answer. School is very repressive for 17 and 18 year olds. (Grammar.)

The wide choice of courses available in a college was another important reason for students' preferences for this type of system. This was particularly true for students in FE and tertiary colleges where a number of the respondents were following vocational courses which are not available in institutions run under schools regulations. Even so, some school sixth-formers felt they might have had a wider choice of A-level subjects had they attended a sixth-form college: 'I would have preferred to attend a sixth-form college because it would mean a wider range of subject choices. I would have liked to have done A-level law or international politics which I did not get the chance to do here.' (Comprehensive.)

The absence of rules and regulations in a college was not seen as quite such an important reason for preferring this system, although it is significant that it was the grammar schools sixth-formers for whom this was a more important factor than other groups.

It was decided not to investigate more deeply the particular *type* of college students would most prefer, i.e. a sixth-form college as opposed to a tertiary college, as there appears to be considerable confusion over their definition. Indeed, a number of students in tertiary colleges referred to them as sixth-form colleges. There was only one comment from a student which revealed any awareness of the different regulations which govern institutions.

> The fact that the college is still secondary education means that the student is still very limited and prevented from taking advantage of all benefits that could be offered by the college system of sixth forms. There is still too much 'secondary' red tape and this also means that not only students but staff as well are made to comply with some regulations relating to secondary schools that are totally inapplicable to such a college. (Sixth-form college.)

Overall, the ratings achieved by the reasons given for preferring a school system were not quite as high as those for colleges, which suggests that the feelings of students opting for a school system were somewhat lukewarm in comparison. Students thought the chief virtue of the school sixth form was that it provided continuity in a familiar environment.

> The most valuable thing I have gained from being at school or college this year is a feeling of belonging to a group of people — both friends and teachers. Being able to make contact with younger pupils by being form counsellor, taking folk group etc. Feeling of security before having to face the rest of the world. (Comprehensive.)

Even some students who would opt for a college if given a choice, recognized that the small, close-knit community of a school had its advantages.

Although I would go to college if I had the chance, I am not dissatisfied with my school. The reason I did not attend college instead was my feeling of security in school. I knew my environment. Some girls who did the first questionnaire did leave the sixth form after the first year and went to college. Although I was secure in the sixth form I was given a number of responsibilities which in themselves were a change in my life. I am not sure if going to college would have made me mature more quickly or not. I hope this information is helpful. (Grammar.)

It is difficult to answer the question of whether education in sixth-form colleges or at schools is better because having only attended a college I have no knowledge of what life in a school sixth form is like from personal experience. My friend found life in a school more advantageous after leaving the college. In a good, well-organised, small school, where the sixth form can get to know all of the lower school this system would probably work better as long as they had their freedom of dress and of private work. (Tertiary.)

The smaller teaching groups in schools, and contact with and responsibility for younger pupils were the second most important reasons for choosing this system. The necessity of the presence of a sixth form in order to set an example for lower forms was not rated so highly. There were no significant differences between the comprehensive and grammar school sixth-formers in their reasons for school preference. The students in colleges who opted for a school system seemed more inclined to stress the relationship between the sixth form and the younger pupils, but the numbers involved were rather too small to draw any general conclusions from this.

An investigation of the differences between students' preferences for a school or college system at the beginning and at the end of their course revealed some interesting changes (see Table 6.7). Of the students who had opted for schools in the first questionnaire (only 18 per cent of the

Table 6.7 (S2 and S1): Changes in students' preferences for a school or college for the 16–19 age group

		On entry to 16+ education		
		Colleges	Schools	Don't know	Total
After two years in 16+ education	Colleges	85	34	47	66
	Schools	8	51	28	21
	Don't know	6	15	24	13
	Total	56	18	26	100
	N = 100%	1289	415	607	2311

total), one third had decided, in two years' time, that colleges were preferable. Nearly half of those who said at the outset of their course that they had no opinion on this matter had decided in favour of colleges, and 28 per cent in favour of schools. In comparison, very few of the majority of students who had been in favour of colleges from the beginning changed their minds during the course of their 16+ education.

e. Careers guidance and perceptions of higher education

Students were asked to indicate whether they had received careers guidance during their course or advice on applications to university, polytechnic etc. either as an individual or as a member of a group, and also to rate the helpfulness of this advice. Responses to these two items are presented in Tables 6.8 and 6.9. These show that over 80 per cent of students had been given advice on opportunities in higher education, but only two thirds had been given corresponding advice on careers and employment. Sixth-form colleges appeared to have been most effective in this area. Ninety four per cent of their students said they had received advice on higher educa-tion and 84 per cent on careers and employment oppor-tunities. Both the comprehensives and the grammar schools were significantly more likely to have given their sixth-formers advice on higher education than on careers; only just over half the school sixth-formers said they had been given advice on the latter. The proportion of students in tertiary colleges saying they had received help in these two respects were approximately equal. Only in colleges of further educa-tion were students more likely to have been given advice on careers than on higher education.

This reflects the high proportion of students in FE in the sample on vocational courses who were unlikely to be con-sidering higher education and for whom such advice would be redundant. For this reason it was felt more meaningful to investigate to what extent institutions had offered advice on matters appropriate to the immediate aspirations of their students (although it could be argued that if students are intending to follow a course in higher education this should not preclude the need to focus their attention on the types of employment which will be available to them afterwards). The

Table 6.8 (S2): Whether students given advice on opportunities in higher education (e.g. courses at universities, colleges and polytechnics) (percentages)

	Comprehensive School	Grammar School	Sixth-form College	Tertiary College	FE College	Total
Yes	87	84	94	79	65	83
No	13	16	6	20	34	17
Whether advice given individually or as part of a group						
Group	20	24	17	21	31	22
Individually	19	24	23	29	20	22
Both	61	52	60	50	50	55
Helpfulness of advice						
Very helpful	18	12	22	15	16	17
Fairly helpful	41	41	50	52	42	45
Of limited help	26	33	21	24	28	27
Not really helpful	15	14	7	9	13	12

Table 6.9 (S2): Whether students given advice on careers and employment opportunities (percentages)

	Comprehensive School	Grammar School	Sixth-form College	Tertiary College	FE College	Total
Yes	59	56	84	73	75	69
No	41	44	15	26	25	30
Whether advice given individually or as part of a group						
Group	17	19	24	26	40	26
Individually	40	41	31	32	21	32
Both	42	39	45	42	39	42
Helpfulness of advice						
Very helpful	12	12	16	17	13	14
Fairly helpful	35	31	44	45	46	41
Of limited help	35	33	26	25	25	29
Not really helpful	18	24	13	13	17	17

Table 6.10 (S2): Advice given relevant to students' plans

	No. of Students Planning to Enter Higher Education	Percentage Receiving Advice on Higher Education	Percentage Finding this Advice either Very Helpful or Fairly Helpful
Comprehensive school	316	91	61
Grammar school	414	84	54
Sixth-form college	408	97	75
Tertiary college	174	90	74
FE college	223	80	64
Total	1535	89	65

	No. of Students not Planning to Continue their Education Beyond their Present Course	Percentage Receiving Advice on Employment	Percentage Finding this Advice either Very Helpful or Fairly Helpful
Comprehensive school	46	70	56
Grammar school	48	69	42
Sixth-form college	66	89	68
Tertiary college	46	83	71
FE college	127	81	63
Total	333	80	62

proportion of students within each type of institution who had been given advice appropriate to their intended destination, and the extent to which they found this advice helpful, are presented in Table 6.10. Over 80 per cent of students intending to enter courses in higher education had received relevant advice. In sixth-form colleges virtually everybody who was aiming at university, polytechnic or colleges of education had been given information and advice on courses in these types of institution. Students in sixth-form colleges were also, together with those in tertiary colleges, the most likely to have found this advice either 'very helpful' or 'fairly helpful' (75 and 74 per cent respectively).

In all types of institution other than colleges of further education, students who intended to enter employment at the end of their course were less likely to have been given advice on jobs than were the higher education group on university and college courses. In comprehensive and grammar schools, only 70 per cent said they had done so, and the school sixth formers were also less likely to have found the advice helpful than the corresponding groups of students in the colleges.

While recognizing that these data are based on subjective judgments and that what one respondent may classify as 'advice', another student may not, these figures give a general indication of the emphasis in both schools and colleges on the dissemination of information on courses in higher education rather than on jobs. Only colleges of further education appeared equally likely to provide their students with information on jobs as on university and college courses. Grammar schools, particularly, came in for criticism from students for their narrow approach to this topic.

> Careers advice was very patchy. You only got advice applicable to your problems if you arranged interviews yourself with external careers adviser who visited the school. Encouraged to go on to university but polytechnics regarded as second choice. Any unusual ideas for careers i.e. acting, woman mechanics, motorbike riding or very competitive courses — commercial art, degree in drama — are discouraged greatly. Only other careers advice is for teaching (in spite of serious situation of surplus of teachers without work) or typing. It makes one wonder if there is anything else for a female to do apart from teaching or typing. (Grammar.)

> Many of my friends in the sixth form and myself found that we were pressurised into applying for a university place. There was little interest in those wishing for advice concerning sponsors for polytechnic courses etc. and many of those who did not intend to go on to further education were brushed aside. It was a case of sorting it out for oneself. This is the only serious criticism I had of the sixth form. Apart from this it was a fairly enjoyable two years. (Grammar.)

There was also some evidence to suggest that students

felt career decisions could not be temporarily postponed just because they were proposing to continue their full-time education.

> More help should be given to students before they leave the sixth form. They should be encouraged to work for qualifications for a career in which they feel worthwhile — and not just be told to go to university because that's the easiest thing one can say, as advice, or so it would seem. We need much more advice on careers. (Comprehensive.)

A number of items were included in the questionnaire with the aim of investigating the views of students who were planning to embark on courses in higher education on the necessity of having some ultimate career in mind. They were asked to indicate whether they were in agreement with the following statements:

a. 'People who go to university should think carefully about the kind of career it will lead to.'
b. 'Most people who wish to continue their education at university need not think too seriously about a career while they are still at school or college.'
c. 'Any degree, or other course in higher education, should prepare the students for a career later on.'
d. 'Education after A-level should be followed for its own sake, not just because it might be useful to an employer afterwards.'

The responses to these items according to the type of institution attended by students aiming at higher education are given in Tables 6.11 and 6.12. Approximately two thirds of students agreed with statements a and c. The proportions agreeing and disagreeing with the statement 'education after A-level should be followed for its own sake, not just because it might be useful to an employer afterwards' were approximately equal. Only one quarter agreed that 'most people who wish to continue their education at university need not think too seriously about a career while they are still at school or

Table 6.11 (S2): **Percentage of students intending to enter full-time higher education agreeing with statement**

| | *People who go to university should think carefully about the kind of career it will lead to* | | | | | |
	Compre- hensive School	Grammar School	Sixth- Form College	Tertiary College	FE College	Total
Agree	63	67	59	70	71	65
Disagree	19	16	22	12	14	17
Unsure	18	17	19	18	15	18
	Most people who wish to continue their education at university need not think too seriously about a career while they are still at school or college					
Agree	23	21	27	17	22	23
Disagree	62	64	58	68	65	63
Unsure	14	15	15	15	13	14

college'. In general, the responses to these items show that students look beyond the immediate future and are aware of the implications their choice of higher education may have for their subsequent employment. The idea that the opportunity to study at university should never be passed up, regardless of its relevance to one's ultimate career, gained little support among the students. They appeared to have a much more hard-headed approach and to evaluate courses in higher education more in terms of their practical application than their intrinsic value. It is interesting to note that the students in tertiary and FE colleges were particularly inclined towards this view. They were most likely to agree that 'people who go to university should think carefully about the kind of career it will lead to' and that 'any degree or other course in higher education should prepare students for a career later on'. They were also most likely to disagree that 'education after A-level should be followed for its own sake'. Sixth-form college students were the most likely to subscribe to the 'education for education's sake' view. It is possible that the atmosphere of FE where many of the staff have had

Table 6.12 (S2): Percentage of students intending to enter full-time higher education agreeing with statement

| | *Any degree or other course in higher education should prepare students for a career later on* | | | | | |
	Compre-hensive School	Grammar School	Sixth-Form College	Tertiary College	FE College	Total
Agree	60	61	57	68	70	62
Disagree	27	23	24	18	15	23
Unsure	14	16	19	15	15	16
	Education after A-level should be followed for its own sake, not just because it might be useful to an employer afterwards					
Agree	39	42	40	32	33	39
Disagree	36	37	32	42	40	36
Unsure	25	21	29	26	27	25

industrial experience and where students have more contact with part-time students in employment is more likely to engender this instrumental attitude towards education than the relatively academic surroundings of the sixth-form college.

In order to investigate this issue further, students were presented with a number of long-term benefits of higher education and asked to evaluate them, and also a number of aspects of university or college life which they might consider desirable. Table 6.13 shows that the long-term advantages were rated very highly. In line with the other findings on this topic, students considered that obtaining qualifications which prepared them for a chosen career or improving their general career prospects were more valuable benefits than the general intellectual training or the social experience. Only on the last of these items was there a significant difference between the responses from students in different types of institution. Those in FE and tertiary colleges were less likely to consider 'social contact, confidence and experience' as a very valuable benefit than school sixth-formers or students in sixth-form colleges. Perhaps the former group feel that their

Table 6.13 (S2): Long-term benefits of a university, college or polytechnic course

Mean ratings by students intending to enter full-time higher education (1 = Not at all valuable, 5 = Very valuable)

	Comprehensive School	Grammar School	Sixth-form College	Tertiary College	FE College	Total
A qualification preparing me for my chosen career	4.5	4.4	4.3	4.4	4.3	4.4
A qualification which will improve my career prospects generally	4.3	4.2	4.2	4.3	4.3	4.3
A general intellectual training	3.8	3.9	4.0	3.8	3.9	3.9
Social contact, confidence and experience	4.2	4.2	4.2	3.8	3.9	4.1
Desirability of different aspects of life at college, university or a polytechnic *(1 = Not at all desirable, 5 = Very desirable)*						
Opportunity for interesting and advanced study	4.3	4.3	4.3	4.1	4.3	4.3
Opportunity to live away from home	3.4	3.4	3.6	3.3	3.1	3.4
Social and recreational activities, dances, societies and clubs	3.9	3.9	3.9	3.7	3.6	3.8
Living in a community with so many people of one's own age and outlook	3.8	3.8	3.9	3.6	3.6	3.8

present situation is more akin to higher education and that the latter expect and probably hope that there will be a marked contrast between the sixth form and university.

The more immediate short-term gains of entering higher education were not rated quite so highly overall. 'The opportunity for interesting and advanced study' was the item most highly valued in this group, achieving a mean rating of 4.3. The social life and the opportunity of living in a community of young people were equally sought after, particularly by the school sixth-formers and those in sixth-form colleges. These students were also more likely to be looking forward to moving away from home than those in FE and tertiary colleges. It is significant that students in FE and tertiary colleges are in general less enthusiastic about the social implications of going on to higher education. Perhaps they feel they are already enjoying many of the opportunities and responsibilities that their sixth-form contemporaries are so looking forward to. If, as has been suggested, the colleges act as a half-way house between school and HE, then it is likely the greater contrast will be experienced at 16 rather than 18 by their students.

Chapter 7

Examination Results

In much of its work the research project placed considerable emphasis upon criteria which cannot be directly measured, such as the students' own perceptions and evaluations of their courses. Nevertheless the more tangible criterion of examination success cannot be ignored. Accordingly, this chapter examines the performance of students in the public examinations they entered in 1976. The emphasis of the discussion is upon GCE A-level examinations as these provide the most direct common criterion by which schools and colleges can be compared and are generally regarded as having considerable instrumental value in respect of higher education and career prospects. Examination results were sought for 2,875 students who were expected to take A-level examinations in summer 1976. These results were provided by 40 of the original 45 institutions.

a. Entries for A-level examinations

Just over half the students entered three or more subjects in the summer examinations; 22 per cent entered two subjects only, and four per cent entered only one subject. A further 23 per cent did not sit any A-level examinations. The proportion entering more than three subjects was in fact very small — just under three per cent — and all but two of these students offered four subjects. The two exceptions were a comprehensive school student and a student in one of the FE colleges, who each entered five subjects.

There were variations in this overall pattern, although the three-subject entry group was predominant in all types of institution. The second largest group in the grammar schools, tertiary colleges and FE colleges comprised those entering two subjects, whereas in the comprehensive schools and the sixth-form colleges such students were exceeded in number by those who did not take any A-level exam. The main differences between types of institution can be seen by examining the numbers of students entering no subjects and those entering two or more (Table 7.1). For example, 82 per cent of the grammar school students entered at least two subjects whereas this applied to only 66 per cent of the comprehensive school students. The discrepancy of 16 per cent is almost wholly reflected in the larger proportion of comprehensive school students who did not enter any subjects. Very few — as in the A-level group as a whole — entered only one subject. This pattern is generally repeated across all the institutional types, although slightly more sixth-form college and FE college students entered just one subject. Slightly larger proportions of students in the tertiary and FE colleges entered exactly two subjects.

The no-subject entry group is of some interest in view of its relative size — almost a quarter of all the A-level students. No direct information was obtained to account for students' individual reasons for withdrawing from the course, but in most cases the institutions reported that the student had left the school or college altogether. The strength of performance at O-level appears to have some bearing on the matter, although the group as a whole contained a very wide range of academic ability in terms of O-level passes held at the start of the course. Nine tenths of the group were fairly evenly distributed over the range of O-level passes from none through to seven; only those with eight, nine or more passes to their credit were comparatively few in number.

However, the fairly even distribution of O-level attainment within this group masks the fact that relatively more less-qualified students withdrew than those with higher O-level attainments. For example, 18 per cent of the entire A-level group had possessed three or fewer O-levels at the start of

Table 7.1: Numbers of A-level examination subjects entered by students on main A-level courses

Number of subjects entered	Comprehensive Schools	Grammar Schools	Sixth-form Colleges	Tertiary Colleges	FE Colleges	All Students
	%	%	%	%	%	%
0	30.8	15.4	24.0	19.4	26.2	23.3
1	3.2	2.3	7.2	2.9	4.5	4.3
2	17.5	19.4	21.9	26.0	31.0	21.6
3	46.7	58.8	44.4	48.4	36.7	48.1
4	1.7	4.0	2.5	3.3	1.3	2.6
Totals	100%*	100%	100%	100%	100%*	100%

* One student in each of these types of institution entered five subjects at A-level

their course, but such students accounted for 49 per cent of the 'premature' leavers. Furthermore, of all the three or fewer O-level pass students in the entire A-level group, 62 per cent were discovered to have withdrawn, compared with 15 per cent of those with higher O-level attainments.

The larger proportions of A-level students who withdrew from the comprehensive schools and the sixth-form colleges can be related to this tendency for less-qualified students to leave before completing the course. These two types of institution, in particular, had had many more students with three or fewer O-level passes enrolled on A-level courses in September 1974. Approximately 25 per cent of their A-level students had been so qualified, compared with between eight and 13 per cent of those in the other three types of institutions. Proportionally more of these students left the comprehensives and the sixth-form colleges. Whereas the grammar schools and the tertiary colleges 'lost' 49 and 50 per cent, respectively, the corresponding figures for the comprehensives and the sixth-form colleges were 72 and 59 per cent respectively.

The FE colleges, while beginning with almost the same proportion of A-level students with three or fewer O-level passes as did the tertiary colleges, 'lost' comparatively more — 63 per cent.

The figures suggest that the tendency for A-level students

to withdraw before completing a two-year course is fairly closely related to the number of O-level passes achieved by the start of the course, although there is no evidence to suggest that relatively low O-level attainment is the sole, or even the main, reason why the majority of these students withdrew. Interestingly, of the two hundred students with three or fewer O-levels who did not withdraw, 138 went on to take two or more subjects in the A-level examinations. The success of all the A-level students is discussed in the next section.

As the sixth-form colleges and the comprehensive schools in the sample had relatively more students with three or fewer O-level passes enrolled on A-level courses, it is perhaps not surprising, therefore, that they also had more students withdrawing. Just why they, and the FE colleges, also 'lost' relatively more of their less-qualified students is not clear. It may be that such students in these institutions became more dispirited, or received more acceptable advice about alternative career paths, or both. The selective policies over admission to the sixth form in some of the grammar schools may be seen as serving partly to mitigate the number of false starts and possible 'wastage' — if such they be — during the sixth-form course in these schools.

b. A-level results

Tables 7.2 and 7.3 present details of the A-level results, and, in particular, the percentage pass rate in each type of institution. It can be seen that both the mean number of passes obtained and the percentage pass rate are highest in grammar schools although the results for tertiary colleges are almost as high. In contrast the performance of students in FE colleges is markedly lower than that in other types of institution.

Of course such results should not be interpreted as demonstrating the superiority of A-level teaching in grammar schools. In particular it is important to check how far the ranking of institutions in these two tables is a function of initial differences in the ability of the students involved. It has already been observed that the grammar schools were much more selective in their admissions policy for the sixth

204   *The Sixth Form and its Alternatives*

Table 7.2: Numbers of A-level subjects passed by students in each type of institution

No. of Subjects Passed	Comprehensive Schools	Grammar Schools	Sixth-form Colleges	Tertiary Colleges	FE Colleges	Total
0	76	62	80	20	36	275
1	107	98	155	37	72	469
2	121	134	160	66	63	544
3	184	297	228	95	55	859
4	7	23	19	2	5	56
5	1	0	0	0	0	1
Mean no. passed	1.88	2.20	1.92	2.10	1.66	1.99

Table 7.3: Overall pass rates in each type of Institution

	Comprehensive Schools	Grammar Schools	Sixth-form Colleges	Tertiary Colleges	FE Colleges	Total
Total No. of A-levels attempted	1333	1696	1640	582	574	5825
Total no. of A-levels passed	934	1349	1235	462	383	4363
Percentage pass rate	70	80	75	79	67	75

form than were the other types of institution.

The present research study did not seek to measure directly the general ability of students in the sixth form, and so in order to assess the relative performance at A-level it is necessary to look to an indirect measure. In the circumstances the most appropriate controlling variable appeared to be the number of GCE O-levels passed in the fifth year. An analysis of these data revealed a correlation of 0.76 between the mean number of A-levels passed in each individual school or college and the mean number of GCE O-levels gained by the students concerned during their fifth year. In other words the institutions with the better A-level results tended to be those whose students had more O-level passes — a not unexpected result — and thus it is essential to take this relationship into account when assessing the relative success rate of the different types of institution.

Figure 7.1 plots the mean number of A-level passes against the mean number of O-level passes previously earned by A-level candidates for each of the institutions in our sample. The regression line in the figure gives the predicted number of A-level passes for different numbers of O-level passes based on the sample as a whole. It is clear that there is a considerable spread of points in this figure, with examples of most types of institution coming both above and below the regression line. Tables 7.4 and 7.5 present the results of an analysis of variance applied to deviations from the linear regression (in effect, an analysis of covariance). This shows that once the influence of prior attainment (at GCE O-level) is removed, then the differences in A-level success rates between types of institution are not statistically significant.

The preceding analyses were repeated using 'average A-level grade' in place of 'mean number of A-level passes', but the pattern of results was similar and it is not repeated here. Once again when prior O-level performance was taken into account no one type of institution proved significantly more or less successful in securing high GCE A-level grades.

The use of a linear regression model in the paragraphs above assumes a particularly simple relationship between O-level and A-level performance. There are a number of alternative hypotheses, and one at least appears to deserve specific consideration. It might be argued that the less selective institutions at 16-plus would have developed teaching procedures and skills which were particularly appropriate for those students with fewer O-level passes in helping them to cope with A-level work. For this reason we made a special study of the A-level performance of all those students embarking on an A-level course with six or fewer O-level passes. The results, presented graphically in Figure 7.2, suggest that overall the tertiary colleges were more successful in dealing with this type of student. There is little to choose between

Figure 7.1: Mean no. of O- and A-level passes for students in each institution

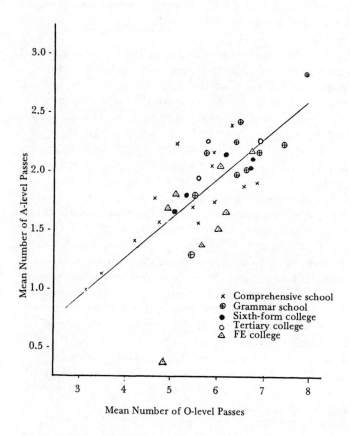

Table 7.4: Examination results by type of sixth form

Type of Sixth Form	Mean Number O-level Passes	Mean Number A-level Passes	No. of Institutions in sample	No. of Students in Sample
Comprehensive	6.3	1.88	14	497
Grammar	6.9	2.20	10	614
Sixth-form college	6.4	1.92	5	406
Tertiary college	6.3	2.10	3	220
FE college	5.9	1.66	8	231
Total	6.4	1.99	40	2068

Table 7.5: Analysis of variance: examination results by type of sixth form (deviations from linear regression)

	Sum of Squares	Degrees of Freedom	Mean Square	F
Between types	.3968	4	.0992	1.35 (n.s.)
Within types	2.5634	35	.0732	
Total	2.9602	39		

the other types of institution, although it should be noted that the comprehensive schools appeared to be achieving rather poorer results than the rest. The sample of tertiary college students was comparatively small, and so the figures presented for tertiary colleges in Figure 7.2 cannot be generalized with a high degree of confidence. Nevertheless the finding that tertiary colleges achieve better results than do the other types of institution appears both statistically and educationally significant, and would seem to deserve further study.

Additional information was gathered concerning the performance of A-level students in a number of additional or subsidiary examinations. These results are displayed in Table 7.6, and show that over 30 per cent of the A-level student sample passed at least one O-level subject during the sixth-form course, and that about 10 per cent of them passed an

Figure 7.2: A-level success for students with six or fewer O-level passes

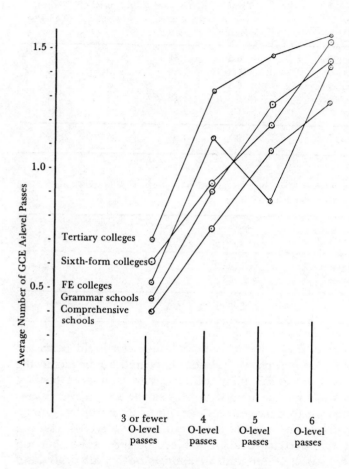

Qualifications of Students at Entry to Sixth Form

Table 7.6: Percentage of A-level students passing other examinations

Type of Examination	Compre-hensive Schools	Grammar Schools	Sixth-form Colleges	Tertiary Colleges	FE Colleges	Total
One or more O-levels	37.4	39.7	34.3	20.5	22.5	30.9
One or more CSEs	4.2	0.0	10.4	1.4	6.1	4.8
Use of English	0.8	17.4	4.1	0.0	1.3	6.4
A-level General Studies	11.5	13.2	5.1	18.2	1.3	9.7
Secretarial	2.2	0.0	2.8	0.0	0.0	1.3
N	497	614	642	220	231	2204

A-level General Studies examination. A small number also passed one or more subjects at CSE, or an examination in the Use of English or in secretarial studies. The results do not provide any particularly notable contrasts, although it does appear that the tertiary and FE college students were less likely to earn additional O-level passes, and that overall the grammar school students were somewhat more likely to have acquired additional qualifications by the end of their course than those studying elsewhere.

c. Non-A-level students

Of the total sample of students followed up in 1976, 812 were not following main A-level courses. These students were entirely confined to the FE and tertiary colleges, which makes it difficult to make any direct comparison of the five different types of institution. Nevertheless, there are some interesting indirect comparisons which can be made with the pattern of A-level results. For example, roughly a quarter of those who had commenced OND or City and Guilds courses did not actually enter the examination, a proportion similar

Table 7.7: Percentages of non-A-level students passing additional examinations

Main Course	One or More O-level Passes	One or More A-level Passes	Secretarial Qualifications	N
OND	34.8	23.5	14.2	247
City and Guilds	0.0	8.1	0.0	148
NNEB	0.0	0.0	0.0	32
Pre-nursing	47.6	0.0	0.0	21
Art Foundation	7.5	37.5	0.0	40
Other courses	50.0	18.4	10.5	38
Secretarial	21.8	10.9	55.8	147

to that for the main A-level students. The pass rates in the non-A-level examinations were somewhat higher, at 84 per cent for OND and 88 per cent for City and Guilds.

The pattern of additional examination results for this group is also worth consideration, if only in passing. In Table 7.7, the GCE and secretarial qualifications gained by students in the various non-A-level courses are presented. The actual numbers involved are, for the most part rather small, but the evidence shows that those on OND and secretarial courses tended to complete their courses with a relatively more diverse set of qualifications than other types of student.

d. Summary

The evidence presented in this chapter has shown that there is some relationship between type of 16—19 provision and examination performances: the grammar schools generally perform better in this respect, and the FE colleges do least well. The analysis also shows that this hierarchy may have little to do with differences in the quality of teaching that is provided, but much to do with differences in the ability of the students who enter different types of institution. It thus follows that generalizations about the superiority of one form of provision over another must be made with caution. The adoption of any particular pattern, whether it is selective, comprehensive or involves separate 16—19 provision, does not guarantee that a particular standard of public examination performance will follow. What does appear from these results is that no one method of 16-plus organization would have the disastrous consequences that its critics might claim; students working for A-level in very different environments, given that they have similar abilities, appear to obtain similar examination results. Thus, for example, the possible distractions of working for A-level alongside less academic students in a comprehensive school, or part-time and vocational students in a tertiary college, do not seem to have adverse effects. Nor indeed do the more strictly academic and homogeneous surroundings of the grammar school sixth forms appear to be a *sine qua non* for effective A-level work.

In closing this chapter, it would be as well to draw attention to the generality with which the examination results have been treated. Distinctions between different examining boards have not been made, and nor has account been taken of differences in the types of subjects entered. The results of the present study thus have relevance in general terms, but had a more detailed and intensive study been possible some interesting exceptions and qualifications to the overall pattern might have been identified.

Chapter 8

Students in Higher Education and Employment

---

a. **Destinations, summer 1976**

On completion of their second year in post-compulsory education, the students' destinations and examination results were recorded. The number of students involved at this stage was 3,687 as 601 students had left as planned in summer 1975 and a further 160 students were 'lost' to the project due to their schools' (two grammar and one comprehensive) being unable to participate further.

The destinations (Table 8.1) reveal that approximately 38 per cent of the 3,687 students were transferring to courses in higher education, with a further nine per cent remaining in full-time education at a non-advanced level, either in schools, sixth-form colleges or further education institutions. Approximately a quarter of the students were taking up full-time employment, while another 11 per cent were either still seeking employment or their final destinations were not known to their institutions. The remaining 18 per cent (679 students) were discovered to have left their various institutions during the two years between 1974—1976 despite their original intention to remain for two years. More girls than boys had left — 21 per cent of all girls compared with 16 per cent of all boys — and proportionally more students had left from pre-nursing, secretarial, art foundation and 'other' courses than from the remaining types (Tables 8.2 and 8.3).

Table 8.1: Destinations of students by type of institution, summer 1976

Destination	Comprehensive School		Grammar School		Sixth-form College		Tertiary College		FE College		Total	
	N	%	N	%	N	%	N	%	N	%	N	%
Higher education:												
university	168	23	202	28	184	22	61	12	46	6	661	18
Polytechnic	40	6	66	9	58	7	49	10	66	7	279	8
College of HE or advanced course at college of Further Education	21	3	21	3	40	5	10	2	28	3	120	3
College of Education	49	7	41	6	71	9	31	6	16	2	208	6
Other higher education	20	3	13	2	17	2	10	2	4	0	64	2
Deferred entry (unconditional place)	8	1	24	3	11	1	4	1	8	1	55	2
Total higher education	306	43	367	51	381	45	165	34	168	19	1387	38
Employment	130	18	121	17	159	19	165	34	324	36	899	24
Full-time 'non-advanced' course	67	9	69	10	79	9	38	8	67	7	320	9
Unemployed or destination unknown	37	5	68	9	126	15	29	6	142	16	402	11
Left school or college before summer 1976	178	25	101	14	100	12	95	19	205	23	679	18
Total	718	100	726	100	845	100	492	100	906	100	3687	100

Table 8.2: Destinations of students by sex, summer 1976

Destination	Boys		Girls		Total	
	N	%	N	%	N	%
Higher education:						
University	419	23	242	13	661	18
Polytechnic	185	10	94	5	279	8
College of HE of advanced courses at college of FE	60	3	60	3	120	3
College of Education	51	3	157	9	208	6
Other full-time higher education	23	1	41	2	64	2
Deferred entry (unconditionsl place)	25	1	30	2	55	1
Total higher education	763	42	624	34	1387	38
Employment	358	20	541	29	899	24
Full time 'non-advanced' course	221	12	99	5	320	9
Unemployed or destination unknown	206	11	196	11	402	11
Left school or college before summer 1976	289	16	390	21	679	18
Total	1837	100	1850	100	3687	100

Table 8.3: Destinations of students by type of course, summer 1976

Destination	A-level	OND	City & Guilds	Secre- tarial	NNEB	Pre- Nursing	Art Founda- tion	Other Courses	All Students
Higher education:									
University	637	22	1	1	0	0	0	0	661
Polytechnic	207	54	4	0	0	0	14	0	279
College of HE or advanced course at college of FE	95	20	1	0	1	0	1	2	120
College of Education	206	1	0	0	1	0	0	0	208
Other higher education	59	0	0	0	0	0	5	0	64
Deferred entry (unconditional place)	54	0	0	0	0	0	0	1	55
Total higher education	1258	97	6	1	2	0	20	3	1387
Employment	516	117	132	92	18	3	4	17	899
Full-time 'non-advanced' course	285	19	3	3	2	3	2	3	320
Unemployed or destination unknown	334	27	10	4	13	5	0	9	402
Left school or college before summer 1976	482	61	47	47	3	10	14	15	679
Total	2875	321	198	147	38	21	40	47	3687

There were significant differences between the destinations of the boys and girls in the sample. A greater proportion of boys went on to higher education or remained in full-time non-advanced education, while proportionally more girls entered employment or had already left, as previously mentioned. Almost nine-tenths of the 3,687 students had been on A-level or OND courses, and these general differences reflect differences between the destinations of boys and girls from these two courses. There were no significant differences between the destinations of boys and girls from any of the other courses.

Forty-four per cent of A-level students went on to higher education compared with 50 per cent of art foundation course students, 30 per cent of OND students and very small numbers of students from other courses (Table 8.3). Between 60 and 70 per cent of City and Guilds and secretarial course students entered employment on completion of their course, the majority of the remainder of these students having already left their course by the summer 1976. The proportion of A-level students entering employment was 18 per cent, and that for NNEB, OND and 'other' course students was between a third and a half.

Half of the students leaving grammar schools went on to higher education, slightly more than those from sixth-form colleges and comprehensive schools. All three of these types of institution had about a further tenth of their students remaining in full-time non-advanced education and between 17 and 19 per cent of their students entering employment. More students (25 per cent) had left comprehensive schools during the two years than from any of the four other types of institution, although the proportion from the FE colleges was only slightly lower at 23 per cent. Not surprisingly, more students entered employment from tertiary and FE colleges — just over a third in each case — than from the other types of institution, and fewer remained in full-time education, whether at a higher or a non-advanced level. The number of tertiary college students known to be entering employment was exactly the same as the number entering higher education. The respective numbers for the schools and the sixth-form colleges showed that considerably more of their students went on to higher education than took up employment, while for the FE colleges the reverse was true (Table 8.1).

i. *Students in higher education*

The 1,387 students who left to enter higher education included 25 boys and 30 girls who were deferring entry until the following academic year. The majority of those taking up places immediately entered three main types of higher education institutions: universities (50 per cent), polytechnics (21 per cent) and colleges of education (16 per cent). The remainder entered other institutions including colleges of higher education and colleges of further education which offered advanced courses. Almost 60 per cent of the grammar school pupils who entered higher education went to universities while a further 19 per cent went to polytechnics. These figures compared with 56 per cent and 13 per cent for the comprehensives and with 50 per cent and 16 per cent for the sixth-form colleges. The proportions for the tertiary and FE colleges were lower for universities but higher for polytechnics — 38 and 30 per cent and 29 and 41 per cent respectively. Almost a fifth of the students entering higher education from sixth-form colleges and tertiary colleges went to colleges of education, compared with 12 per cent and 10 per cent respectively of grammar school and FE college students (Table 8.1).

The majority of all the students going on to higher education (91 per cent) had been on A-level courses at their previous institution. (This compares with a proportion of 78 per cent of A-level students in the whole sample of 3,687). Seven per cent and one per cent respectively had been on OND and art foundation courses. Half the A-level students entered universities for their higher education and a further third were evenly divided between polytechnics and colleges of education. A much lower proportion (23 per cent) of the OND students entered universities but many more — over half — entered polytechnics.

There were significant differences ($p<.01$) between the destinations within higher education of the A-level boys and girls, but this did not apply to the OND boys and girls. More A-level boys went to university and polytechnic while

Table 8.4: Destinations of boys by type of course, summer 1976

Destination	A-level	OND	City & Guilds	Art Foundation	Other Courses	All boys
Higher education:						
University	401	18	0	0	0	419
Polytechnic	132	46	3	4	0	185
College of HE or advanced course at college of FE	41	16	1	1	1	60
College of Education	50	1	0	0	0	51
Other higher education	20	0	0	3	0	23
Deferred entry (unconditional place)	25	0	0	0	0	25
Total higher education	669	81	4	8	1	763
Employment	249	62	45	1	1	358
Full-time 'non-advanced' course	207	11	2	1	0	221
Unemployed or destination unknown	181	20	2	0	3	206
Left school or college before summer 1976	240	28	17	3	1	289
Total	1546	202	70	13	6	1837

Table 8.5: Destinations of girls by type of course, summer 1976

Destination	A-level	OND	City & Guilds	Secretarial	NNEB	Pre-Nursing	Art Foundation	Other Courses	All Girls
Higher education:									
University	236	4	1	1	0	0	0	0	242
Polytechnic	75	8	1	0	0	0	10	0	94
College of HE or advanced course at college of FE	54	4	0	0	1	0	0	1	60
College of Education	156	0	0	0	1	0	0	0	157
Other higher education	39	0	0	0	0	0	2	0	41
Deferred entry (unconditional place)	29	0	0	0	0	0	0	1	30
Total higher education	589	16	2	1	2	0	12	2	624
Employment	267	55	87	92	18	3	3	16	541
Full-time 'non-advanced' course	78	8	1	3	2	3	1	3	99
Unemployed or destination unknown	153	7	8	4	13	5	0	6	196
Left school or college before summer 1976	242	33	30	47	3	10	11	14	390
Total	1329	119	128	147	38	21	27	41	1850

more girls entered colleges of education. The proportion of A-level girls entering colleges of education was more than three times greater than the proportion of boys (Tables 8.4 and 8.5). The mean number of A-level passes obtained by all the students entering higher education was 2.36. That for the boys at 2.48 was significantly higher (p<.001) than that for the girls at 2.22, and reflects the fact that more girls than boys entered with one, two or no A-level passes. The tendency for more girls than boys to enter colleges of education was again apparent when the students were grouped according to the numbers of A-level subjects passed, the destinations of the boys differing significantly (p<.01) from those of the girls. Despite the larger numbers of girls at all levels of A-level qualification entering the colleges of education, there was no significant difference between the group of boys and the group of girls who entered these colleges in terms of A-level qualification, although there was greater variety among the girls' qualifications. Almost nine-tenths of the boys entering these colleges had either one or two A-level passes, compared with seven-tenths of the girls.

ii. *Students in employment*

The total of 899 students who left their 16+ institutions to enter employment in the summer of 1976 consisted of 358 boys and 541 girls, representing approximately 20 per cent of all boys and 29 per cent of all girls (Table 8.2). Fifty-seven per cent of these students had been on A-level courses, and between 10 and 15 per cent each had been on OND, City and Guilds and secretarial courses. The mean number of passes for the A-level students was 1.33. That for the boys was 1.35 and that for the girls 1.30 (Table 8.6) which unlike the corresponding figures for the HE group were not significantly different. Identical proportions of the A-level boys and girls entering employment had two or more A-level passes — 43 per cent in each case. Of the remainder, there were slightly more boys with a single A-level pass, 31 per cent compared with 27 per cent of the A-level girls.

Excluding those students (almost all girls) for whom a pass or fail classification was not applicable, 81 per cent of all the non A-level students had successfully completed their

Table 8.6: Mean A-level passes of A-level students by sex and destination, summer 1976

Destination	Boys			Girls			Total		
	N	Mean Number of A-level passes	S.D.	N	Mean Number of A-level passes	S.D.	N	Mean Number of A-level passes	S.D.
Higher education:									
University	401	2.86	0.52	236	2.87	0.54	637	2.86	0.53
Polytechnic	132	2.15	0.83	75	2.32	0.76	207	2.21	0.81
College of HE or advanced course at college of further education	41	1.41	0.97	54	1.33	1.06	95	1.37	1.02
College of Education	50	1.60	0.70	156	1.62	0.92	206	1.61	0.87
Other higher education	20	1.55	0.89	39	1.54	0.97	59	1.54	0.93
Deferred entry (unconditional place)	25	2.52	1.00	29	2.52	0.95	54	2.52	0.97
Total higher education	669	2.48	0.85	589	2.22	1.00	1258	2.36	0.93
Employment	249	1.35	1.07	267	1.30	1.06	516	1.33	1.07
Full-time 'non-advanced' course	207	1.26	1.28	78	0.96	1.12	285	1.18	1.24
Unemployed or destination unknown	181	1.09	1.20	153	1.11	1.13	334	1.10	1.16
Left school or college before summer 1976	240			242			482		
Total	1546			1329			2875		

two-year 16+ course. The proportions for boys and girls separately were 71 per cent and 85 per cent respectively.

Seventy-one per cent of the OND students who entered employment had successfully completed their course, and a further seven per cent had been 'referred'. The remainder of the OND students had either failed or had not taken the examination at the end of the course. The pass rate for the City and Guilds students, who formed the largest single group of students entering employment, was 86 per cent. The differences between the non A-level boys and girls in terms of their examination results were statistically significant (p<.01) reflecting, in addition to the difference in pass rates, the larger proportion of boys (18 per cent) who failed outright (compared with 10 per cent of the girls) and the relatively larger group of boys who did not enter for their examination — six per cent compared with one per cent of the girls.

iii. *Achievement of original objectives*

Information was sought from students on their entry to post-compulsory education on whether they hoped to continue their education beyond their present course and, if so, what further qualifications they hoped to obtain and in what type of institution they hope to study for them. It was therefore possible when data on examination results and destinations were collected to investigate the extent to which students in different types of institution had fulfilled their original intentions.

Approximately half of the 3,687 students for whom both sets of data were available planned at the outset of their course to continue their education further, although this proportion varied between the different course groups, e.g. from 57 per cent of A-level students to 10 per cent of secretarial students. Among the A-level students there was little difference between the proportion planning to go on to higher education from different types of 16+ institution.

Table 8.7 shows the ultimate destinations of the students who hoped at the outset of their course to enter either a university, college of education or polytechnic. A breakdown by type of institution attended is given for university

Table 8.7: Destinations of students planning to enter universities, colleges of education and polytechnics at the outset of their course (percentages)

Destination	Universities				FE College	All Students Planning to Enter University	All Students Planning to Enter Colleges of Education	All Students Planning to Enter Polytechnics
	Comprehensive	Grammar	Sixth-form College	Tertiary College				
University	46	44	44	31	16	39	6	8
Polytechnic	7	9	8	13	12	9	3	17
College of HE or FE (adv.)	2	2	2	1	6	3	5	3
College of education	2	2	3	4	1	2	28	2
Other higher education	2	1	2	3		2	2	1
Deferred entry (unconditional place)	1	5	2	2	3	3	1	1
Total higher education	60	63	61	54	38	58	45	32
Employment	11	8	11	13	17	11	21	28
Full-time non-advanced course	12	16	11	12	9	12	4	7
Unemployed/not known	6	7	11	6	23	10	10	10
Left before summer 76	10	7	6	14	15	9	19	23
Total = 100%	310	377	329	155	199	1370	488	348

aspirants but not for the other two groups where the numbers involved are smaller. Thirty nine per cent of the students who hoped to enter a university eventually did so, and a further 16 per cent entered some other form of full-time education. The proportion of students who originally planned to enter either colleges of education or polytechnics and who achieved these aims were 28 and 17 per cent respectively. The university aspirants were less likely to drop out of their course and less likely than the other groups to enter employment.

A higher proportion of the students aspiring to polytechnics took jobs on completion of their course than other groups, and there was also a higher drop-out rate (23 per cent) amongst students in this category. Overall only nine per cent of the university aspirants failed to complete the course, compared with 19 per cent of those aiming at teacher training and 23 per cent at polytechnics. Amongst the students aiming at university there was a significant difference between the proportions achieving this aim in school sixth forms and sixth-form colleges and those in FE and tertiary establishments. Over 40 per cent from institutions in the former categories entered a university but only 31 per cent from tertiary colleges and 16 per cent from colleges of FE did so. However, students from tertiary colleges were more likely to enter polytechnics than other groups, and the total percentage entering full-time higher education from this type of institution was not very much lower than for the secondary institutions.

It is possible but unlikely that the proportions entering higher education from colleges of further education are depressed through the number of students whose destinations were unknown as colleges would have been asked for references concerning applications to higher education. It appears therefore that the A-level students in FE who aspired to university courses were more likely to fail to reach this objective than those in other types of institution. However, the data presented in Chapter 4 showed that students taking A-levels in further education were less well qualified in terms of their O-level attainment and that the colleges are providing A-level opportunities for young people who might otherwise be denied them.

b. Students' evaluation of their course

i. *Introduction*

The remainder of this chapter will be devoted to an account of the results of the questionnaire administered to students in spring 1977, during their first year of employment or higher education.

The students followed-up in this third phase of the study were deliberately chosen to include a greater proportion of those in higher education than in employment. Every student who had completed the second questionnaire and whose destination was reported to be some form of full-time higher education was sent a copy of the third student questionnaire (S3). Only half of the students who completed the second questionnaire and who subsequently entered employment were asked to complete S3. Questionnaires were either forwarded by schools and colleges to the students' home address or, in the case of students in higher education, via the registry of their university or college.

A total of 1,707 questionnaires were sent and 1,070 completed, a response rate of 63 per cent. The students who returned completed questionnaires were distributed as follows:

Table 8.8: Respondents to third student questionnaire (S3)

	N	%
In full-time higher education or on the education part of a sandwich course	700	65
In full-time employment	317	30
Still studying full-time for A-level qualifications	37	3
On the employment part of a sandwich course	5	—
Unemployed	7	1
Situation unknown	4	—
	1070	100

The section which follows immediately deals with the
views of all the students on various aspects of their course.
Sections c) and d) are specifically concerned with the views
of the two major sub-groups on the effectiveness of their
course in preparing them for higher education or employment.

ii. *School/college preference*

The students taking part in the third phase of the study
were asked, as in the two previous questionnaires, to indicate
whether they thought it preferable for young people aged
16—18 to be educated in colleges or to attend schools which
contain younger pupils. Their responses to this item (given in
Table 8.9) were compared with their answers to an equivalent
item in the questionnaire completed during their second year
in the sixth form or at college. The figures in the table show
that while approximately two thirds of all the students opted
for a college system, this proportion was very much higher
for those who had actually attended a college at 16+. While
more than 80 per cent of college students were in support of
a college system, only half of those who had been in school
sixth forms thought that an all-through system was preferable.

The only group of students whose responses revealed a
significant change in their opinions over the intervening year
were those who had been in grammar schools, where there
was a tendency for those who thought a college system was
preferable while they were in the sixth form to change their
minds once they had left. The proportions involved were as
follows:

| | N = 247 | |
Students from grammar schools	*In second year sixth*	*After leaving the sixth form*
In favour of colleges	45%	34%
In favour of schools	34%	46%
Don't know	21%	18%

As on previous occasions students grasped the opportunity
provided by the questionnaire to reflect on the pros and cons
of attending a college as opposed to a school sixth form.

Table 8.9 (S3): Students in higher education or employment: preference for a school or college for the 16–19 age group (percentages)

| | Type of institution last attended | | | | | |
	Comprehensive School	Grammar School	Sixth-form College	Tertiary College	FE College	Total
Colleges	31	34	86	87	90	63
Schools	52	46	7	8	3	25
Don't know	16	18	6	2	5	10
Total = 100%	220	247	273	195	135	1070

Once again the students who had been in colleges expressed their appreciation of the adult atmosphere and the relaxed and friendly relationships with staff they felt these establishments engendered. (Many of them stressed how well they felt this type of background enabled them to adjust successfully to higher education, and this issue is discussed in the next section.) The following is a typical selection of the comments made on this topic by students in response to the third questionnaire. While there were a few comments in support of the school sixth form, they were not as numerous as those outlining reasons for preferring a college system. On the other hand, while many ex-sixth-formers were very critical of their experience, it was very rare to find anyone from a college background making equally adverse comments.

I've come to the conclusion that the standard of work we did at college and the teaching we received was particularly high. Much of the work I've encountered during my first year at university was a repeat of work done at college, frequently covered in more detail than it has been here. My A-level lecture notes have often come in useful to refer back to. I'm thankful I was able to attend ————— College, I met interesting people there who I probably would never have met otherwise. There's quite a lot of competition between students to do well in exams, which is advantageous since the students motivate themselves rather than having to be pushed into working by teachers. The staff–student relations at college were excellent, one wasn't afraid to approach teachers with problems, the atmosphere was friendly yet there was no lack of interest. In my particular year the classes were small. The largest class I attended had eight pupils though the numbers did increase for the year following us.

Teachers showed an interest in our intended careers and offered advice if they could. The careers officer was generally available to provide information and throw ideas at you. A measure of the co-operation between staff and students was demonstrated each

year by our open day for which there was no shortage
of students to run experiments and attempt to explain
them to visitors. Some students took home equipment
to make models and charts of viruses and such like for
use at open day. In summary, I'm extremely pleased
with the sixth-form education I received and I hope
the same will be available for my children. (Tertiary.)

I feel the education I received at the sixth-form college
has prepared me both for my university work and life.
We were treated as young adults and not children —
we shared responsibility in the running of the college.
Staff—student participation in reviews, plays, operas
and choirs was very pronounced and in my view typifies
the sixth-form college and the education it was designed
to give.

We were very lucky in having a beautiful purpose-built
building, away from students of other ages — I think
this is very important. Some people might say that the
building and facilities we have were too much but both
are looked after properly and are used to their full
potential. I feel that anybody who has the opportunity
to go to ————— Sixth-form College is very lucky —
both for academic work and the atmosphere and friendliness which you will find there. (Sixth-Form College.)

The most valuable experience for me at college was the
fact that I became involved with the Students' Union,
and the communication with lecturers arising from that
position was particularly useful. I also had a great deal
of communication with the students which enabled me
to be very active in the college.

The freedom and independence given to students at FE
college is by far the best way of preparing them for the
outside world, whether in higher education or employment. It promotes a sense of responsibility in the minds
of most individuals. The fact that I was a representative
on the academic board made me feel that it was bene-

ficial for us to have some say in our coursework, rather than have it dictated to us. (Tertiary.)

Having been educated in a grammar school which had a sixth form before leaving myself to attend a sixth-form college, I feel that I have at least some experience of both types of sixth form. At my previous grammar school, being only a small school, the sixth form was necessarily small and hence only a small range of subjects could be catered for. Also, as the sixth form was such a small part of the school, the equipment which could be provided for the special use of the sixth form i.e. only necessary for A-level subjects, tended to be inadequate. The sixth-form college however provides a greater range of subjects and also contains more specialised equipment. In my opinion, sixth-form colleges are far better than the old sixth-form system. (Sixth-Form College.)

Although it is my firm belief that a school needs its sixth-formers, I think great care should be taken when giving them responsibilities and authority. At my school we were allowed to take certain disciplinary action with the younger members of the school and on the whole I think they respected us. I do not think, though, that allocating menial tasks to sixth-formers does anything to increase their sense of responsibility. One of our many jobs was to run around with messages for staff, head-mistress and office, acting like some sort of internal postal service. Sixth-formers have, in my opinion, plenty of more important things to do and such jobs as these can be done equally well by 1st-, 2nd-, and 3rd-formers who have no pressure of public examinations to worry about. (Grammar.)

I think the sixth form provides a very solid backbone of life in a school, they provide a valuable service to staff and pupils alike. They are the intermediate society of a school and can achieve an easy relationship with lower school pupils and provide a useful intermediate voice.

I hope we will not see the end of sixth forms in schools for some time. (Comprehensive.)

I feel from my experience of sixth form at school that sixth-form colleges are a very good idea. If this cannot be brought about then another solution is colleges of technology. If I could turn the clock back I would have left my school when I was sixteen and gone to a local technical college to study A-levels and O-levels. I have found on going to a college of technology after I left the sixth form at school that I get all the attention, help and encouragement which was sadly lacking at —————— School. (Comprehensive.)

I remember being very disappointed with the sixth form at my school. Before it I was looking forward to doing my A-levels and being 'treated like an adult'. When I got there I found that nothing really had changed — all that had happened was that you wore a different coloured blazer. I think it is important that the sixth form at school *is* different and that people in the sixth form are treated in a different way especially if the sixth form is described as such. (Grammar.)

The sixth-form I attended had a distinctly enclosed atmosphere. In no way did it prepare me to cope with life either at college or in a job, had I decided to get one. Nobody in the VIth form was treated as a young adult with the privileges and the burdens that this term incorporates. Teachers were very much in control of the entire set-up. There was very little way anyone could voice any criticisms or suggestions of changes within the VIth form. A number of absurd regulations were imposed upon us, such as standard of dress and personal appearance. When questioned, such regulations were defended by staff who gave totally irrational explanations as to their purpose. We were given no say in any part of the running of the school save for items of and extremely trivial and superficial nature in the VIth form, such as repairing parties to fix hinges on broken doors etc. We were, however, obliged to do 'duties', which constituted nothing more than filling in on the 'dirty work' of the school, e.g. supervising dinner times, playground duty etc. (Comprehensive.)

iii. *Standard of teaching and facilities*

Students' responses to two items asking their views on the standard of teaching and facilities at their school or college are shown in Tables 8.10 and 8.11. In general students displayed a greater degree of satisfaction with the teaching they had received than with the equipment and facilities provided. Nearly half the students said they felt the standard of teaching had been particularly high in all or most of their subjects. There was a tendency for comprehensive schools to receive slightly less approbation in this respect than other types of institution. For example 17 per cent of ex-comprehensive sixth-formers said there had been no subjects in which the standard of teaching was particularly high, and 64 per cent said there were at least a few subjects in which it had been particularly poor, compared with 57 per cent or less of those who had attended other types of institution.

On the question of equipment, materials and facilities there was a clear difference between schools and colleges, facilities in the latter being more often cited as satisfactory. Over 40 per cent of the students who had attended comprehensive and grammar schools said there were no subjects in which the standard of facilities had been particularly high, and a quarter of ex-grammar school sixth-formers said it had been particularly low in all or most of their subjects.

Some students pointed out, however, that even though their school had certain facilities and items of equipment, they were not always used to their fullest extent.

When asked whether some subjects lacked equipment etc. I replied that some had, since the school already had a language centre installed in the lower-school building. It seemed ironic to me that, having used audio aids in my lower school years, to have no access to them whilst studying French at A-level. There seemed to be an idea that since one was in the academic half of the

Table 8.10 (S3): Were there any subjects or courses in which you felt the standard of teaching was particularly high? (percentages)

	Comprehensive School	Grammar School	Sixth-form College	Tertiary College	FE College	Total
Yes, in all subjects	8	11	10	7	8	9
Yes, in most subjects	31	39	39	43	37	38
Yes, in a few subjects	44	40	42	40	43	42
No	17	10	9	8	11	11

Were there any subjects or courses in which you felt the standard of teaching was particularly poor?

	Comprehensive School	Grammar School	Sixth-form College	Tertiary College	FE College	Total
Yes, in all subjects	1	–	–	1	–	–
Yes, in most subjects	4	4	3	3	2	3
Yes, in a few subjects	59	52	52	49	55	53
No	36	43	43	46	42	42
Total = 100%	220	247	273	195	135	1070

Table 8.11 (S3): Were there any subjects or courses in which you felt the standard of equipment materials or facilities was particularly high? (percentages)

	Comprehensive School	Grammar School	Sixth-form College	Tertiary College	FE College	Total
Yes, in all subjects	5	6	13	9	7	8
Yes, in most subjects	21	20	32	30	27	26
Yes, in a few subjects	32	26	30	32	37	31
No	41	47	25	28	28	34

Were there any subjects or courses in which you felt the standard of equipment materials or facilities were particularly low?

	Comprehensive School	Grammar School	Sixth-form College	Tertiary College	FE College	Total
Yes, in all subjects	4	7	3	2	2	4
Yes, in most subjects	7	18	8	5	4	9
Yes, in a few subjects	37	31	32	32	36	33
No	51	43	56	60	56	53
Total = 100%	220	247	273	195	135	1070

school one was expected to cope on one's own more
adequately without aids that would have made the
course generally more interesting and alive. (Comprehensive.)

After spending two terms at teacher-training college,
it has been made obvious to me that my previous school
neglected to use its teaching resources. The school had
an above average audio-visual aids department, with a
theatre, video, numerous record players and tape-
recorders, slide projectors, two film projectors and
several overhead projectors. During the whole of my
stay in the sixth form, these facilities were never used
in my course and from what I can gather, rarely in
other courses. The record is little better further down
the school. There seem to have been two major reasons
for this. First and foremost, examination pressure on
the teachers was such that nothing beyond dictating
notes within the syllabus was possible. Secondly, the
school had a very academic staff (qualifications-wise)
however, a large percentage of the staff had no teacher
training i.e. they had never received training in teaching
methods such as using audio-visual aids, and I am certain
that many of the teachers would have been incapable of
doing anything other than dictating notes. (Grammar.)

There were no significant differences between students
who had gone on to higher education and those who had
entered employment on either of these questions.

These findings do no more than give a very general indication of students' feelings and should not be used as hard
evidence of the standard of teaching and facilities in different
areas of 16+ education. They may, for example, conceal
significant differences between individual institutions, but
the numbers of students were too small to make further
investigation along these lines practicable. Nor was the
internal consistency of students' views investigated. Certainly
these figures give no cause for alarm as far as facilities are
concerned, and students' evaluation of the standard of
teaching they had enjoyed indicates a high degree of satisfaction.

iv. *Breadth and balance in the curriculum*

In view of the strength of feeling on the topic of general studies displayed in answers to the second questionnaire, it was decided to investigate students' opinions at this stage on the balance between the need to prepare for specialist examinations and to provide a more general education, and also to assess their view of the emphasis on preparation for higher education compared with employment. Students were therefore asked to state to what extent the statements listed in Table 8.12 applied to the school or college they had attended. Three quarters of the students felt that the statement 'there was an excessive concern with getting students through examinations' applied either moderately or strongly, and half that 'there was too much emphasis upon getting people into college or universities'. On both these issues there was a significant difference between types of institution. The ex-grammar school students were more inclined to endorse these statements, particularly the latter, than other groups.

> Students who decided to apply to university were encouraged to do so and not questioned as to why and consequently were not told of the other possibilities open to them. Whereas students who rejected the idea of full-time further education seemed to me to be thought of as failed academics and thus questioned about their decisions. (Grammar.)

On the other hand, less than a third of the students from FE and tertiary colleges felt that 'there was too much emphasis upon getting people into colleges and universities'. Responses to all the items in the table illustrate the comparatively academic nature of the grammar school sixth form and its emphasis upon preparation for degree courses. In addition to the two items already mentioned, grammar school sixth-formers were also the group most likely to agree that 'little attention was paid to people who wanted to enter work after school, rather than continue in higher education' and least likely to consider that the school 'attempted to prepare students for life in general, not just for particular jobs or university courses' or that 'the examination syllabus was not allowed to dominate my course to the exclusion of topics of a wider and general interest.

Because of the higher proportion of students in tertiary and FE colleges following vocational courses, it was not surprising that respondents who had attended these types of institution felt that there was less emphasis upon entry to courses in higher education and that more attention was paid to helping and advising students on entry to employment.

An analysis of the responses to these items by the students embarking on courses in higher education and those who subsequently went into full-time employment showed that there were significant differences between these groups on several of them. Students in employment were more likely to agree that 'there was an excessive concern with getting students through examinations' (79 per cent thought this applied moderately or strongly), 'there was too much emphasis upon getting people into college or university' (52 per cent) and 'little attention was paid to people who wanted to enter work after school or college rather than continue in higher education' (49 per cent).

Many students who intended to take a job on leaving the sixth form or college commented on the lack of attention paid to students in their position.

> I think that the school I attended concentrated too much on getting pupils through exams. They did not help you to understand what it was like to leave school and enter employment or give advice about finding a job. (Comprehensive.)

> I felt that not enough help was given when I and others like me were looking for employment. I realise the present condition of finding jobs made things difficult but I would have thought that this would warrant more attention to those looking for jobs. No advice was given as to where to write to as the careers staff were more concerned with people who were going on to college. In fact teachers only became interested after I had been offered employment and my interviewer had asked for references from the college. (Sixth-form College.)

Table 8.12: Extent to which statement apply to school or college attended

Percentage of students saying statement applies either moderately or strongly

	Compre-hensive School	Grammar School	Sixth-form College	Tertiary College	FE College	Total
There was an excessive concern with getting students through examinations	79	83	74	65	77	76
The course was made interesting and worthwhile by the inclusion of general/liberal studies and non-examination work	27	30	48	42	42	38
The course would have been more rewarding if there had been more opportunity to study topics outside the set examination syllabus	49	51	38	32	33	42
The school/college attempted to prepare students for life in general, not just jobs or university courses	25	22	53	47	46	38
The general studies and non-examination work was a waste of time	34	41	30	39	26	35
There was a fair balance between examination work and provision of a broad general education	22	21	38	33	27	28
There was too much emphasis upon getting people into college or universities	56	73	51	31	26	50
Little attention was paid to people who wanted to enter work after school, rather than continue in higher education	50	62	33	29	22	41
The examination syllabus was not allowed to dominate my course to the exclusion of topics of a wider and general interest	29	26	40	40	33	34
Total = 100%	220	247	273	195	135	1070

> I noticed when doing my A-levels that the clever 'star'
> pupils, who all ended up going to university were given
> *all* the attention and tuition, at times even the extra
> facilities. I think that this is very wrong, because if a
> student is trying but is not so bright they should be
> encouraged more so. Also I would like to point out
> that no careers advice was given to me at all. I did casual
> work for a while then when I decided to get a job with
> a career in mind, (this was about 5 months after leaving
> school) I was informed about the local (Y.E.) Careers
> Office. I had heard of it before, but thought it was for
> people under 18 and that they only suggested careers
> to you. My school never even told me about it, in fact
> I think they could have made a connection for me.
> Actually, this is where I got my present job, luckily!
> (Comprehensive.)

There were also significant differences between students
in higher education and those in employment in their attitudes towards the general studies courses they had followed,
the latter group feeling more strongly that 'the course was
made more interesting and worthwhile by the inclusion of
general studies and non-examination work' and less likely to
consider 'the general studies and non-examination work was
a waste of time'.

Institutional variations on the items concerned with
general studies showed that the students from sixth-form
colleges seemed to have more positive attitudes than those
from other types of institution. Nearly half the students who
had attended sixth-form colleges felt that 'the course was
made more interesting and worthwhile by the inclusion of
general/liberal studies and non-examination work', and more
students in this category were inclined to feel that 'there was
a fair balance between examination work and provision of a
broad general education'. In general, however, the comments
made on general studies were still critical of this aspect of the
course.

> Whether or not this is a particularly relevant point, I
> would like to say that with regards to non-examination

subjects like liberal and general studies my lecturer had trouble even making sure that we all turned up, whether or not it was interesting. Nobody was concerned because there was no examination at the end and so for many it was felt to be a waste of time. We were occasionally asked to collect material or do some extra work for the lecture which nobody wished to do simply because it was a waste of our own time. Unfortunately, the way we are geared to work at school/college at O- and A-level is simply to complete the relevant course and hopefully receive the right piece of paper at the end, so anything that doesn't fit into that category is virtually ignored. (Sixth-form college.)

Very pragmatic attitudes of this sort towards sixth-form study were widespread:

My own view is that the whole point of studying in the sixth form was to gain qualifications as these are the standards, rightly or wrongly, by which you are judged. (Grammar.)

The idea of being at a college is to take and pass exams — not to take part in irrelevant frivolities that benefit the student in no way whatsoever. (Tertiary.)

Some students recognized that as well as its lack of formal certification, it is the artificial position of general studies, and the difficulty of generating discussion in a vacuum, that result in the low opinion held of it by students.

The questionnaire poses several questions about general studies/non-examinable studies against syllabus studies. This was and still is at university a topic of many arguments. In the sixth form, on an intensive science course governed by the syllabus, there was dissatisfaction and contempt for the non-examinable studies which were compulsory. Some was due to lack of interest in the topics provided and this strengthened the feeling that these studies wasted time which could have been used in syllabus studies. These general studies failed to widen interests away from syllabus studies. But discussions of topics of a wider scope *did* occur in the social life of the sixth form and to a large extent within the examinable studies. The tutorials and practical periods were more open discussion times than any general studies lesson. These discussions always started by being related to the course but always gradually drifted into more topical discussions. Of course, these depend entirely on the teacher present but were of more significance and interest than the attempts at general studies. (Comprehensive.)

Many of us did not want to do any extra general studies work, I felt that the three A-level subjects I was doing gave me a great deal of work to do and I had no time left for other work. This was mainly due to the fact that I studied languages and so all my free lessons were spent in conversation classes with our French and Italian assistants. I probably learned more from the topics we discussed in the conversation classes than I would have from general studies classes. (Grammar.)

(It is worth noting that it was experiences such as these which led to the development of the general studies courses operated by a tertiary college described in Chapter 6.)

There were, however, significantly more suggestions made by students at this stage on what they would *like* to see included in a general studies syllabus than on the earlier questionnaire. They were unanimous in their view that this time should be spent in informing them about very practical, day-to-day issues such as those outlined in the comments which follow.

Non-examination subjects were simply a waste of time. The teachers did not take the classes seriously, which led to a total disinterest in them. Often they dealt with very abstract subjects. Surely it would be far more sensible to teach a subject which would be useful in later years such as short courses in law, economics, politics, insurance, or some practical subjects such as woodwork, cookery (for both sexes) and so on, and also to make these subjects compulsory. (Comprehensive.)

It is surprising how much education cushions you from the outside world of reality. At the school I went to, studies were very much concentrated on exam success. Teachers with an enlightened view would perhaps broaden lessons to encompass subjects of more general interest but, despite the existence of a very ineffective general studies course, little consideration was given to the matters of practical living. NOT ONCE did I receive any instruction on banking, cooking, insurance, tax matters or the daily requirements of living, working, eating and budgeting. Perhaps the school felt boys of our intelligence would know all these things for themselves. I'm glad however that I've had eight months spare between school and university. I have learnt many basic things which I would have been otherwise unaware of. Employment and its realities become a nasty shock as I found out after leaving school. (Grammar.)

My school gave me no information concerning such things as tax, national insurance and the rules concerning sick leave and holidays. Such information would have been very valuable to me now and even more so to those entering permanent employment. The potentially very useful general studies periods were totally wasted and overall the education given was far too academically orientated. (Grammar.)

The extra-curricular studies were not fully explained as to their intentions i.e. stretching people's minds, we therefore thought of them and treated them as a waste of time. I regret the fact we were never introduced to politics at any stage or the social services and at no stage in my schooling was I given any type of sex education (moral or otherwise). (Tertiary.)

The comments made by students illustrate all too clearly

the essential conflict between the need to pass examinations in specialist subjects and at the same time, learn something of the realities of daily life, particularly at work. On balance, students would appear to favour a greater concentration on the latter, but the present approach to general studies does not gain their interest or support. As far as it is possible to ascertain, general studies is used at present either to serve in a compensatory capacity, i.e. to overcome the effects of over-specialization by, for example, teaching English to science specialists, or as a means of filling up a student's timetable with a selection of recreational, artistic or sporting activities. Students are only too aware of the sharp distinction between the specialist and the general parts of the curriculum and, given the importance and emphasis placed upon academic qualifications, the fact that general studies is usually un-examined is for them proof of its unimportance.

To what extent either the current proposals to replace A-levels with N- and F- or TEC and BEC schemes for students on vocational courses will generate new thinking on general studies remains to be seen.

c. Preparation for higher education

A total of 700 students completed the questionnaire who were in some form of full-time higher education. The qualifications being studied for by the students in the HE sub-sample are shown in Table 8.13 according to the type of institution last attended.

They show that the majority were following degree courses. Only five per cent were studying for teaching certificates, and a similar proportion for HNDs. Under the 'other' category are included small numbers of students studying for the Diploma in Higher Education and qualifications in art, drama, journalism, archaeology, cartography and radiography.

A number of questions were included in the third questionnaire to investigate the extent to which students felt their sixth-form or college course had prepared them for the demands of higher education. In answer to an item asking them to what extent they had experienced difficulties in settling down to the academic life at college or university, 43

Table 8.13 (S3): Qualifications aimed at by students in S3 sub-sample in higher education (percentages)

	Comprehensive School	Grammar School	Sixth-form College	Tertiary College	FE College	Total
Degree	77	81	83	71	75	79
Teaching Certificate	9	5	5	4	3	5
HND	4	6	1	6	13	5
Other	10	7	12	19	9	11
Total = 100%	161	176	194	101	68	700

Type of institution last attended

per cent had no difficulty at all and 39 per cent reported slight difficulties. Responses to a similarly worded item asking about the social life showed that 70 per cent had no trouble at all and 20 per cent only slight problems. On neither of these items were there significant differences in the views of students from different types of sixth-form institution.

There were however a number of comments from students in higher education highlighting certain problems of adjustment, some of them suggesting that there were differences in the ways in which their sixth-form experience affected these.

Many students who had attended a college at 16+ used this opportunity to emphasize that they thought this had been a more appropriate preparation both academically and socially, for higher education than a school sixth form.

> I believe that my attendance at a college as opposed to a school sixth form has greatly helped the transition to a university. I think this is due to the more informal and adult environment provided at a college. I think this is only possible where the 16—18 year age group is separated from the younger groups. (Tertiary.)

> The more adult atmosphere of a sixth-form college is very helpful in preparing students for the social and academic life of college or university. I found that I could settle into organizing my study and leisure relatively easy, for we had been encouraged to do so at sixth-form college. (Sixth-form college.)

> If I had gone from school straight to a college of education, instead of going to a separate sixth-form college first, I don't think I would have been able to cope with the free time, work etc. and my experiences would have been very narrow. (Sixth-form college.)

> I personally feel that the transition from 6th form college to university was much easier than from a school to a university. The college was the in-between place where

we were prepared for university both academically and socially. (Sixth-form college.)

My sixth form gave me the confidence to communicate with others and enjoy new friendships and new freedom. I believe the step from a traditional sixth form to university would place a greater stress upon people who are shy and do not make friends easily. (Tertiary.)

Having attended a college to study A-levels and now attending a polytechnic, I find it much easier to mix with people than I perhaps would have if I had stayed on at school in the sixth form. At college, students are treated in a more adult manner, and have much better relations with lecturers. The atmosphere is altogether more informal which suited my personality. Also, having previously attended a single sex school, I think it was especially beneficial to attend a mixed college. (Tertiary.)

Some ex-sixth-formers, on the other hand, found it difficult to cope with the new-found freedom of university, and with the style of work now expected of them.

After a fairly strict timetable, compulsory attendance and other restrictions of the sixth form, it is difficult at first to adjust to the new-found freedom of university life and to discipline yourself to doing most of the work in your own time. (Grammar.)

My real criticism is that at school, we should have been given some briefing on the academic atmosphere at college. Many students who I have talked to feel the same way. We all began by attending every lecture, of course, but were quite baffled on what sort of work and how much was to be undertaken in our own time. At school, we had got used to being given set essays etc. but the school never talked about the type of work or change of responsibility we would have to cope with, on our own, at college or university. This is my main criticism. (Comprehensive.)

The comments made by students were not entirely one-sided in their support for a college-based system at 16+ as a preparation for HE, as the two following quotations illustrate, but positive views about school sixth forms of this sort were very much rarer.

> I feel that my sixth-form course at school prepared me for college life in many ways. For a start, I learnt how to talk to people in a relaxed, friendly manner at interviews and to convince them that I was the sort of person that would do well at their college. Consequently, I made a success of my first interview and was accepted at the first college of my choice. Similarly, the work towards examinations was well planned and prepared with ample private study time and facilities provided within the sixth-form complex and if I did not take full advantage of the opportunities open to me then it was no-one's fault but my own. The change from a small school to a large college can be overwhelming but during my time in sixth form I had learnt to make the first move towards making friends. Consequently I settled in quickly and painlessly and now enjoy a full social life and have many gratifying friendships. In the academic field, I had been prepared for organising myself to work to a planned schedule and I found that I adapted very quickly to a much more relaxed atmosphere that can mislead people into thinking that no real work is necessary. I found many of my friends found this transition bewildering and failed in the first term. On the whole, I feel myself to be coping well at college and with life in general and I am sure that preparation in the sixth form at school made this possible in many ways. (Comprehensive.)

> My sixth-form experience at —————— High School in some way prepared me for my present course of teacher training because of the contact with pupils lower down the school. We had contact which gave valuable experience by doing dinner duties once a week and by becoming a form counsellor to lower forms. Therefore daily

contact prepared me for dealing with and talking to younger people. (Comprehensive.)

At the same time there were also a few examples of ex-college students who were aware of their lack of academic readiness (but note that a feeling of social superiority sometimes compensates for this shortcoming!).

The lack of academic discipline in my sixth-form college left me extremely unprepared for the demand for personal academic discipline at university. As a result my work at university is suffering greatly as I still lack this discipline, and also lack what little supervision *was* provided at sixth-form college. (Sixth-form college.)

I have both worked and been to a college, I think I am more prepared for life than someone who has come straight from school. You can tell them, at the beginning of the year, they are still a bit wet behind the ears. These people are probably more capable of adjusting to the work, though. I still find it difficult to take coherent notes in lectures. At college a couple of lecturers started off by lecturing, but most simply dictated notes, which was fine for revision, but it was a bit of a shock to have to take notes, when the time came. (FE.)

The views of students on the effectiveness of their preparation for the demands of academic study in higher education are outlined in the following chapter.

d. Preparation for employment

Three hundred and seventeen students completed the questionnaire who had left the sixth form or college to enter employment. When asked to state whether they viewed their present post as a permanent one, only 183 (58 per cent) answered in the affirmative. Students with vocational qualifications were significantly more likely to see their present employment as permanent than those who had followed A-level courses.

The jobs held by the students in permanent employment

were classified according to the Hall-Jones scale, and it was found that the great majority fell into one of three classes:

Class 3 Inspectional, supervisory and other non-manual (higher grade), e.g. nurse, computer programmer, bank clerk (27 per cent).
Class 4 Inspectional, supervisory and other non-manual (lower grade), e.g. laboratory technician, secretary, trainee manager (33 per cent).
Class 5 Routine grades of non-manual work and skilled manual, e.g. shop assistant, typist, hairdresser, cook (35 per cent).

The students in permanent employment were asked to indicate the extent of their agreement with the statements listed in Table 8.14. In general, they reported that they were happy with their jobs, got on well with the people they worked with and did not regret leaving full-time education. Very few of them had found it difficult to settle down at work. There was, however, a significant difference in the responses to some of these items from those who had followed academic courses at 16+ to those who had undergone some form of vocational training. Those entering permanent employment after taking A- and O-level courses were much less likely to agree with the following statements:

'My school/college gave me good advice about the sort of job I should take'
'My course helped to prepare me for the sort of work I now do'
'My school/college gave me valuable assistance with job application'.

Differences between the views of students who had previously attended different types of institution on these items were not investigated as the numbers involved were rather small for any general conclusions to be drawn from them.

Of the 134 respondents who said their present employment was a temporary position, 80 per cent planned to stay in it for a year or less and then to enter some other occupa-

Table 8.14 (S3): Students in permanent employment (percentages): extent of agreement with statements N = 183

	Not at all	Slightly	To a Moderate Extent	To a Great Extent
I have found it difficult to settle down at work	69	21	8	1
My school/college gave me good advice about the sort of job I should take	42	31	20	6
My course helped to prepare me for the sort of work I now do	34	22	20	21
I have not found work very different from what I expected	16	35	27	19
I find it easy to get on with the people at work	1	3	19	75
My school/college gave me valuable assistance with job applications	41	27	15	15
I regret that I did not continue my education further	73	13	6	3
I find the work I do now more demanding than school/college work	27	19	30	23
People at work treat me more like an adult than the teachers at school/college did	17	24	26	31
I have to behave very differently now from the way I did at school/college	27	30	21	20
I am happy with the job I have at the moment	2	4	21	71

tion or to continue their education. Slightly more of this group planned to continue their education than to change their field of employment. A small proportion of the students in this category had already been offered a place in higher education for October 1977 and were deliberately taking a year off. But in spite of this, the proportion seeing their employment as temporary is surprisingly high. It suggests that many of the young people concerned viewed their current job as an immediate, short-term solution to the problem of earning a living, but not as their first step towards a career. Possibly the hard realities of the job market caused many of them to take jobs which did not match up to the plans and expectations they had formulated while in the sixth form. Disillusion with the types of jobs available to school leavers may have prompted them to see a return to full-time education as the only way of ultimately securing a worthwhile position. Students who had entered the job market after taking an A-level course were particularly likely to think in terms of changing their position in the near future, and they seem to have experienced a more problematic transition from school or college to work than other groups.

Reading the comments of the students in employment was a rather sobering experience, apart from those of the fortunate individuals who had undergone some form of vocational training and subsequently found appropriate employment.

> I found the course at college very useful in relation to my present occupation. However, I think of myself as lucky. A number of people who were at school with me have not been as lucky. On the basis of this I feel that pupils should be encouraged to think seriously about their careers during their time at school to ensure that they enrol on the right sort of course on entering college. (OND business studies student now working in local government.)

What criticisms there were of vocational courses were usually concerned with their lack of relevance to modern working conditions and their over-emphasis on outdated theory.

> Most of the lessons given at the college such as accounts, economics and food and beverage control have been invaluable in the day-to-day running of the coffee bar. On the other hand I feel that too much emphasis was placed on the preparation and serving of top class French cuisine, whereas the majority of people leaving catering

college tend to go in for the industrial side of catering. Therefore I think a lot more time should be spent on other types of food preparation and service. (OND hotel and catering student now manageress of a coffee bar.)

Although fewer than one per cent of the respondents to the questionnaire were unemployed at the time of its completion (Spring 1977), there was evidence that quite a lot of students, particularly those who had followed A-level courses, had either been unemployed for some time before finding a job, or had experienced considerable difficulty in securing an appropriate position.

I would just like to state that after leaving college I was on the dole for seven months and in all that time there wasn't one single job offered to me, that's how bad things are down in the West Country. My college had no interest whatsoever in anyone who wanted to go out into the world and work. Well, to me it's not right! In college you are channelled to further education, you are taught nothing of the realities of life in general. I may sound bitter and that's because I am. I am now doing a job *well* under my ability and intelligence but my only alternatives are the dole queue again or further education. (Ex-FE student who failed both A-levels taken, now working as a shop assistant.)

When I left college, I had two A-levels, and no idea what to do with them. I got a job with a diamond company doing clerical duties, because at the time I had nothing else to do. I stayed with them only about three months, because the work was so boring and gave me no opportunities to use my brain.

I have now been unemployed for nearly four months and still have no idea what I want to do. Before long I will no doubt be lucky enough to find another job of a similar nature, which may provide a temporary answer but not a solution. Basically, I suppose A-levels, unless for the purpose of further education or as a definite lead into a particular field, are little use in helping to choose a career.

I believe that if more time was spent throughout one's education on the interests of the individual, be they academic, physical or practical, at the end of it all one might have a better idea where to take one's qualifications. (Ex-FE student.)

At the interviews I got the impression that someone with A-levels, with respect to O-level standard, is too well-qualified and therefore someone who had just completed a fifth-form course was more adequate as he could be trained further according to their methods and paid less because of his age . . . Am I fair in saying A-levels are designed purely for college, polytechnic or university degrees? (Ex-comprehensive sixth-former with two A-levels, unemployed.)

Some students who originally intended to enter higher education reconsidered their decision in view of the implications this course of action had for their future employment prospects, and others who had actually embarked on a degree course left after less than a year because they doubted whether the qualification they were studying for would eventually be of use in getting a job.

At the end of my course at ———— I decided not to carry on with my plans to go to teacher training college for several reasons. One of the most important reasons was that I felt I would be spending three years' further study for a 'dead end' job owing to the rising number of unemployed teachers. After thinking about it seriously I decided not to apply, believing that in three years' time I could have a job with a more secure future than teaching.

Having had no luck getting a job before leaving college I came to accept the fact that I would have to be on the dole for a time — little did I know that I would be waiting ten months before having any job-hunting luck. The thing which annoyed me most was the fact that would-be employers would not accept anyone unless they have 'previous experience' in clerical work — how could I be expected to get experience when no-one would give me the chance in the first place! On the other hand, at other interviews I was told I was over-qualified (I have two A-levels and six Os). As you can guess I was left very confused.

As it happens all has turned out for the best. I have a good job with (I hope) a future in it — even though I have had to wait ten months to get it. I don't regret staying on until sixth form as I enjoyed my course there, and felt that I matured in my attitudes to life considerably during my two years there. However I feel that employers should be more considerate towards other young people, instead of giving views that tend to contradict one another, leaving the person totally be-mused, and sometimes wondering whether their qualifi-cations are a help or hindrance to them. (Ex-sixth-form college student, now a clerical officer with the DHSS.)

I did not do as well in my examinations as I had ex-pected to. Nonetheless I was offered and took a position to study at university. I am interested in law and this course I took at university was supposed to include law in its syllabus. However the syllabus turned out to be at least 80% social theory. I enquired as to what sort of qualification I would have at the end of three years. A degree, but not one I could apply successfully to the type of work I am interested in.

It is obvious that I left the university. I now work for a bank and I am in the process of gaining professsional qualifications through the bank. I am very much happier now and the course involves a balance between law and accountancy.

A previous question asked if too much emphasis was

placed on getting people to university. In my school this was true but the students did not know what sort of qualifications they would have at the end of three years and what jobs would be open to them. It is my belief the potential university students should be given some idea of what courses are professionally qualifying and what alternative there is in the world of commerce and industry. Many students from my year will end up on the dole queue because they have taken courses which cannot be applied to a job; even teaching is unsafe at the moment. Unemployment figures out today (26.4.77) show that more school leavers are unemployed. What is going to happen to our country if we allow more and more of our youth to drift blindly or obtain useless university degrees?

I saw that my degree would be of no practical use to me but what of those who haven't? I'm very lucky to be working at the moment and I do not regret leaving university. (Ex-comprehensive school sixth-former with three A-levels, now a bank clerk.)

This apprehension about ultimate employment prospects was shared by some of the first-year undergraduates in the sample.

Not enough information was given on what we could do once we completed our degree. We were channelled into university without being given any positive alternatives. Most of the people I know have no idea of what they intend to do once they leave university, and find this disturbing. Some of them are even thinking of leaving because they cannot see themselves gaining anything from continuing their course. (Ex-sixth-form college student reading geography.)

Throughout my later school life I wished to eventually study medicine, but like many other A-level students, I failed to obtain the necessary grades. At the moment I am studying biology which, unlike medicine (and dentistry, law and a few other subjects) is purely an academic subject and is not aimed at a particular occupation. In fact it is very likely, with the job situation as it is, that my eventual job will be completely unrelated to my present course. Thus, like many other students, I am beginning to wonder if it would not have been better to have left academic life after A-level. The obvious question is why didn't I? The reason is that all sixth forms are geared to act as a stepping stone to higher education so that all pupils that eventually pass their A-levels find themselves on the conveyor belt to higher qualifications.

The problem is both the attitude and the structure of sixth-form education, and how it relates to jobs. I would like to stamp out the impression that only second-rate pupils seek employment after A-levels, and that a degree is an essential qualification for later life. On the second count I would like to be more constructive. For those pupils hoping to go into higher education I would like to see another system operating on the same lines as UCCA — whereby students are informed of available jobs in their desired field, and can be sponsored through higher education by their eventual employers. This would involve much closer co-operation between university, employers and sixth forms but I see no reason why it should not be viable — the armed forces operate such a scheme.

Did students have any other constructive suggestions for improving this rather sorry situation? More advice and attention for people planning to take jobs was the commonest plea. We have already seen that half the students going into employment agreed that there was 'too much emphasis upon getting people into colleges or university', and there were innumerable comments to the following effect:

I found that at my school everyone was encouraged to try and get to university, so much so that people who did not want to were treated as second-rate students.

I do not think that the careers officer helped to a great degree with finding employment for people wishing to leave college to get a full-time job, but they were very interested in getting you a place at a university or polytechnic.

My college was very biased towards continuing education as against leaving to get a job. Leaving to get a job was almost looked upon as a failure on the part of the student.

I think the present system is overgeared towards pushing people into university. I particularly found this when I decided not to go to university — many teachers tried to persuade me to change my mind. I think the problem with going to university is that you are still not guaranteed a career when you have obtained a degree.

I felt a lot more emphasis should be placed on studying with a view to employment at school. I also felt that careers advice was not very helpful to people leaving the sixth form for full-time employment, whereas people continuing their education are given a great deal of help and advice. I think there should be more assistance and advice available to people entering employment.

The only other innovations suggested by students as a possible improvement in the transition to employment were more links between school and local industry and work experience.

I think that school students should be given a much better idea of different types of work, rates of pay, applying for jobs etc. General studies lessons could be used visiting factories, offices, building sites etc. to give pupils a good impression of working conditions and the type of jobs which they will be doing immediately after leaving school. (Ex-grammar school sixth-former.)

I feel that there should be a stronger link between students and the industrial environment. Sixth-form curriculums tend to neglect this aspect of the real world and do not help enough to prepare young people for future careers in industry. Sixth-form colleges should try and arrange more visits to local industries and more talks and discussions with local industrial representatives from the shopfloor, management and trades unions. Maybe industrial relations could be introduced as an examination subject if it has not already been done so.

As part of a general studies programme, I feel that it would be a good idea to educate students on matters they could meet in everyday life when they leave school, like filling in income tax forms, insurance, social security etc. (Ex-comprehensive school sixth-former.)

I feel that sixth-form staff should have a general knowledge of different careers. Careers are never discussed, and most pupils enter courses or employment with narrow minds. The only job I've personally come into contact with is the teaching profession. Teachers are the only adults we actually see working. It is the only career pupils come into real contact with; this is probably why so many students opt to go to teacher training. Perhaps if students could go to places of work — offices, workshops, science labs, hospitals, factories — they would have a better idea of what they were going to do. (Ex-comprehensive school sixth-former.)

In common with the findings of a previous research report which investigated this area[19], it was found that many of the students who were working for a year before entering higher education found this an extremely beneficial experience whether the job had any relevance to their intended course or not, and that for some of them this experience had a significant effect on their plans.

The taking of a job during this year has had far more far-reaching effects than I ever imagined. Since I stayed on till November 1976 to take my entrance exams to Cambridge, I had to find a job to occupy myself in the time from January to October 1977. Quite fortuitously I found a job in a hospital as a lab technician, and I immediately found it such tremendously enjoyable work that I decided after a short while that I was far better suited in an atmosphere of using my knowledge to help other people, rather than of pursuing knowledge purely for its own sake. I was therefore almost happy when I failed to gain entrance to Cambridge, for it left my future occupation entirely open; within a few weeks I had been accepted for medical school where I commence in October 1977.

The immediate effect I felt of leaving school and going to work was that I had so much more free time. So I commenced several new hobbies that the excessive pressure of school had hitherto thwarted. I regret now that I previously let my academic work hold so great a place in my life, and do not intend to let this mistake repeat itself when I go to college.

Another thing that struck me was the entirely different atmosphere at work. Although I am working among very intelligent people, a fair number of them don't know many things learned at school — the knowledge is easily accessible but (quite unlike the impression we were given at school) there is really no need in the real world to carry around in your head a multitude of facts (something that persistent exams had made me think almost as the be-all and end-all of success in the real world). (Ex-comprehensive school sixth-former.)

In my case, I took a year off between leaving school and going to university. At first I was reluctant to do so but after nine months, I feel so much more mature and confident, and less fixed in my ideas, that I recommend all prospective university students to do likewise.

Not enough emphasis was laid on this 'year off', at

schòol. Mainly, it was just a breathless rush to *get* to a
university, *get* a degree, and *then* start work, without
experiencing actual working life before. Many more
people should be given information and encouragement
to work before dashing off to higher education. This is
my strongest complaint about the sixth form. (Ex-
comprehensive school sixth-former working abroad in a
school for the mentally handicapped.)

To what conclusions do these experiences of students
entering the job market after two years in post-compulsory
education point? First, it is clear that A-level is still commonly regarded as an entry requirement for higher education and
not as a useful qualification in its own right. Whereas schools
and colleges have considerable knowledge and expertise to
draw on when it comes to filling in UCCA forms etc. and
advising students on appropriate courses in higher education,
they are, because of the educational process teachers themselves have undergone, not in a position to offer equal
assistance to those who wish to enter employment. For this
reason, students feel they are being pressurized into applying
to higher education and that undue attention is being paid to
those who follow this course of action.

While openings in the job market for which A-level is the
most relevant and appropriate qualification have always been
limited, this situation is now exacerbated by the general
shortage of vacancies for school leavers. Difficulties encountered in finding a suitable position led some students to
question the benefits of staying on after 16. While many
agreed that they had enjoyed their time in the sixth form or
at college, they were aware that their immediate job prospects
were not much better and, in some cases, worse than if they
had left at 16.

The following remarks were made by an ex-tertiary college
student who passed A-levels in English and history.

I now work as a bonus clerk for my local council. I cannot think of anything further from my expectations. I
actually feel very disillusioned with my college education. It seems to have been a waste of time unless I had

gone on to higher education. Even though I did enjoy my time at college, I do feel there leaves something to be desired in the careers help available at college.

This student regarded herself as being in temporary employment, and talked of entering an occupation 'suited to my qualifications (at the time none of them are needed) and also one in which I was more of an individual and which I enjoyed'. But one wonders how many of the young people in this position would manage to find employment more appropriate to their qualifications and talents in the near future, or indeed how many of the substantial proportion planning to re-enter full-time education would eventually do so.

While a much larger-scale study would be necessary to determine the relative success of students following different courses at 16-plus in their transition to work, the comments made here do suggest that OND, City and Guilds, secretarial students etc. felt more settled in employment and had fewer problems in finding work which was relevant to the course they had followed.

These findings are certainly replicated by a recent OECD study[20] of young people in a number of European countries, which stated:

It may also be noted that those who have received no more than a general education at any level face problems in obtaining employment even during a period of high economic growth. The great majority are obliged to take low paid jobs with poor promotion prospects. By contrast, those who have acquired a vocational qualification, either through the educational system or apprenticeship, secure employment relatively easily — employment which is, as a rule, satisfying, even though the remuneration paid to skilled manual workers and technicians may be felt to be insufficient . . .

The links between school and work are virtually non-existent for young people who have not acquired a usable occupational skill at school. This category in-

cludes those who do not go beyond compulsory schooling, those who drop out of upper secondary education
or complete the upper secondary cycle but have not
followed vocationally oriented courses. It also includes
many of those who drop out of higher education and in
many cases those who take liberal arts, social science or
even pure science degrees which do not have a direct
correspondence to the needs of industry or the public
services. For all these categories the search for the first
job may be difficult. They may have to take jobs which
are far from corresponding to their qualification.

This does not mean that everyone at the age of 16 should
be encouraged to take a vocational course if they are definite-
ly not aiming at higher education, but it does point to the
need for informed decisions to be made at that stage and for
possible alternatives to A-level to be discussed with *all* fifth-
formers. Any lack of co-operation or co-ordination at this
vital stage between schools and FE can only work against the
best interests of students. It is unfortunate that, under secondary regulations, there are so few alternatives to A-level — in
fact, for most fifth-formers with the necessary ability staying
on *is equated* with A-level. At the moment, for anyone who
has reached a certain level of attainment, staying on to take
A-levels is always regarded as a good thing. FE is only considered as a possible solution for students who cannot be
persuaded to continue along the academic path, either
because they are determined upon a particular career for
which secondary regulations cannot cater or because they
have outgrown the school ethos. We must avoid a situation
where FE is regarded as second best — a haven for misfits —
and encourage 16-year-olds to evaluate objectively the
different courses of action open to them, and most important, the implications this decision will have for their ultimate employment, whether they intend to start work at 17,
18 or 21+. Most students were, after all, staying on after the
age of 16 in order to improve their career prospects or to
obtain qualifications which would enable them to enter their
chosen career. Judged on this criterion, the education system
is failing many young people whose present problems might

have been alleviated by fuller and more effective guidance at 16. While closer links with local industry and the introduction of work experience schemes might enable students to gain a picture of the world of work and encourage them to think realistically about the opportunities available to them, the present dual system of schools and further education may not be in their best interests.

Chapter 9

Study Skills

---

a. Introduction

The emphasis placed on the development of students' academic and intellectual qualities by the heads and principals of the institutions involved in the study has already been discussed in the section dealing with the aims of 16—19 education in Chapter 12. This was seen by them to be the second most important general aim, after the development of social responsibility and awareness.

The ability to study on one's own and to assume responsibility for one's own work schedule is an integral part of this process, and several heads specifically mentioned this as one of the most valuable educational experiences they provided for this age group.

> The opportunity of developing habits of independent study. We consider it essential to be able to strike the right balance between work and leisure before leaving school.

> To work in an adult environment and to give them practice in working on their own. To enable them to have experience in apportioning their time for study.

> The encouragement of independent private study as a continuing life-long process.

The need for students intending to go on to higher education to acquire the necessary study skills while in the sixth form cannot be overemphasized. Their ability to cope with the style of work demanded at degree or equivalent level will be dependent on their having done so. 'To equip students with study skills, work habits and general attitudes necessary for success in higher education' was one of the aims of 16—19 education generally endorsed by the heads of institutions.

But the third quotation above raises an interesting point — that the ability to study is not only necessary for aspiring undergraduates. It can be argued that such skills are increasingly required in employment and in adult life generally. The current rate of change in industry means that only a minority can be trained in skills which they will continue to use throughout their working life. Retraining is likely to be a common experience for those now entering the job market. In addition, the success of the Open University, with its concentration on self-directed learning, suggests there will be an expansion in this type of adult education in the future.

Most institutions are now allocating a certain amount of private study time to all their students, including many 'new sixth-formers' and those on vocational courses, and encouraging them to use this time purposefully. There is a feeling in some quarters that too much teaching can be counterproductive. The principal of a tertiary college expressed his thoughts on this matter thus:

> We will, I hope, take a long cool look at our student contact time. Not for economy reasons, but for educational ones. Do we not tend to overteach? (OND — 27 hours; A-level subject — 5¼ hours each; O-level subject — 4½ hours e.g.). Do we need to spend this amount of time to get the students through examinations? What other objectives do we have? Can we consider more directed private study to exploit the growing resources of the library and use the good private study facilities available? Have we yet given sufficient time in helping students learn how to learn? And why can we not consider the day-release classes too in this context —

does all their day have to be spent with a lecturer in a class situation? There is considerable interest today in 'continuing education' and if a pattern of recurrent spells of education for many people is to emerge in the future, then we must train our youngsters to be adaptable — and to know how to study (on their own!)

It appears therefore that the development of study skills is an important priority of 16—19 education as far as the institutions responsible for this age group are concerned. But how far are they achieving their aims in this respect, and to what extent are students aware that they have acquired such skills?

b. Problems encountered by students

Information collected from students during the course of the study suggested that they often found themselves unable to cope with the demands of private study and that problems related to this had been a major source of difficulty during their course. It was also evident that very few institutions make conscious efforts to prepare students to cope with this aspect of their education. Only rarely did schools and colleges actually teach their students how to study, and there was a widespread assumption that they would acquire the necessary skills of their own accord.

It will be recalled that students who responded to the second questionnaire at the end of two years in 16+ education were asked to complete a number of sentences including the following: 'The least satisfactory part of my course has been . . .'; and 'The greatest difficulty I encountered on my course was . . .' When the completed questionnaires were examined, it was found that certain themes were recurring in the answers to these items. Among these frequently recurring topics were those concerned with the difficulties, both intellectual and practical, which students had encountered in studying on their own.

A detailed analysis of these difficulties illustrated by quotations from the students' responses, is contained in a report entitled *16—19: Study Problems*. Its main findings are summarized here but readers with a particular interest in this area are referred to this report.[21]

Approximately 60 per cent of students said either that problems connected with private study had been the least satisfactory part of their course or the source of their greatest difficulty or that, if they were starting their course again, they would make some change in their study habits or techniques. A sub-sample of one in three of these students was drawn at random, and their responses to these items analysed in greater detail.

The problems encountered by these students could be classified into five main groups. The proportions mentioning each one are given in brackets. (Because some students mentioned more than one problem, the percentages total more than 100.)

1. Problems of self-discipline and organization (30 per cent)
2. Coping with the amount of work required (30 per cent)
3. Problems of adjustment (15 per cent)
4. Coping with poor facilities (15 per cent)
5. Other difficulties (15 per cent).

i. *Problems of self-discipline and organization*

The greatest single problem encountered in this category was that of overcoming a lack of self-discipline and getting down to work on their own initiative. Many students made comments of the following type. (Students were equally likely to raise study problems in answer to the items on the least satisfactory part of their course or the greatest difficulty they had encountered. No distinction has therefore been made between them, and all the quotations given are from students' responses to either of these two questions.)

> I have not settled down to my work as well as I should have done, mainly because I have got into the habit of using my free time as recreational periods rather than study periods.

> Making myself work (initially impossible) to the extent I knew I was capable of doing. Self-discipline where work concerned.

Organizing and planning a sensible work schedule was another source of difficulty.

> Organizing my time properly and using private study periods constructively. But I would not have it any other way — I think learning to organize one's work properly is an invaluable experience.

> Trying to organize my work timetable. I found it difficult to make the adjustment from the set O-level timetable for homework to arranging it myself. This does not however mean that I believe sixth forms should have homework timetables as I believe that one has to organize oneself at some time. I do feel though we should be given advice on how to organize it and cope with it when entering the sixth form.

A small number of students said they felt they would have coped better if they had been under more pressure from their teachers, although it is doubtful whether the majority would subscribe to this view. Most young people seem to appreciate the opportunities for a new, more friendly and relaxed relationship with staff that the sixth-form or college atmosphere provides.

There were two other factors mentioned by students which had contributed to their problems in the area of self-discipline and motivation. These were overcoming pressure from friends and the temptation to relax and finding the atmosphere in their school or college not conducive to work.

> Trying to make people understand that some nights I must stay in and work. Some of my friends who have never had to study do not seem to understand the work that is involved.

> Trying to impress upon myself the need to work. The atmosphere of the college being as it is, it is easy to become involved in after-school activities and forget about work.

ii. *Coping with the amount of work*

An equivalent number of students said that they had had difficulty in keeping up with the volume of work necessary. While many comments simply complained about the amount of work expected and the pressures involved, there were several specific points.

The first of these was the difficulty of finding and maintaining the correct balance between academic work and social activities.

> Keeping outside interests and at the same time keeping up with homework. Lack of organization and strong interests in politics/church/drama meant a losing battle in keeping up to date with homework and little actual recreation or leisure either.

> Not being able to develop any hobbies or out-of-college activities, due to the time spent doing college work.

Other students felt they were inundated with homework and had relatively little time in which to do it. A shortage of free periods, particularly on the part of students on vocational courses, only exacerbated the problem.

> The lack of time at school needed to write good essays. My free time came in short periods suitable to answer mathematical problems and the like, thus most work was done at home which was difficult in my case.

> The mass of work which has to be done. I personally only get one free period each week and this has contributed to the fact that I am finding the work load very large.

iii. *Problems of adjustment*

Approximately 15 per cent of the students said they had found it difficult to adjust to the standard and method of work expected on their present course. Many of them specifically mentioned the contrast between the approach required for O-level and A-level.

Adapting to the different style of work from the 5th form to the 6th form. From following a very broad course of 10 subjects up to O-level without much chance to organize my own work or have private study periods, I found some difficulty in making the transition to the sixth-form style of working.

Those who embarked on A-level courses with CSE qualifications found the adjustment especially hard.

I studied CSE in my lower years. I therefore found it a little difficult to catch up with those who had studied O-level subjects, when starting my A-levels. This may be due to the fact that O-levels go into more depth than do CSE subjects. I think this is a disadvantage to those who studied CSE and wish to go on to A-levels.

One of the most important issues to emerge from this study is the lack of guidance and tuition students are given in making this changeover. There were some explicit comments to this effect, and from some students a plea for courses in study skills to be offered.

Pupils ought to have the difference in type of work expected of them at A-level from O-level explained more clearly. Too many are entering into 6th and 7th years unprepared.

My initial failure to adjust from 5th to 6th form conditions of work. The course seems to assume the change just happens and consequently does not cater for the slower developers.

Students who enter the sixth-form are still not adequately prepared for the type of work which is expected of them. They need more help in planning their work, including background knowledge and private study.

For at least some of the earlier part of the course it would be better, instead of simply giving students 'study periods' to give classes on 'how to study'. This is done in some American universities and the results are supposed to be encouraging.

iv. *Coping with poor facilities*

The only other problem which was mentioned by a significant proportion of the students was that of coping with the often inadequate facilities for private study provided by their school or college.

> The lack of facilities for private study. The common room is in an open-plan building and when some students want to talk and others want to work it makes concentration extremely difficult and leads to fraying tempers.

> There is also difficulty in finding study areas within the school, although a room has been provided for 6/2, this is still not adequate when there are over 60 students in 6/2.

These conditions led students to resent any restrictions on their movements during the day. Many felt that they could study more effectively at home and that regulations requiring them to be on the school premises all day were an infringement of their adult status.

> The fact that if we have free periods in the morning we are unable to remain at home to study. If we are considered adults we should be capable of deciding where we can best work. Also if people choose not to work hard it is they who suffer the consequences and they should not be pressurized.

Although no systematic analysis was undertaken, it appeared that problems caused by lack of facilities were not encountered by students in FE institutions as often as those in the schools sector. This was not because FE establishments had libraries and private study rooms of sufficient size and number to accommodate all their full-time students but that under FE regulations, students are not required to register every morning and are often allowed to leave the premises when they have no timetabled lessons.

c. **Other findings related to study problems**
Because of the number of respondents who mentioned study problems in the open-ended sections of the pilot version of the second questionnaire, it was decided to include a number of precoded items in the final version investigating the amount of assistance students had received from staff with particular study techniques and also their rating of the effectiveness of this assistance. This section will discuss the responses to these precoded items.

Students were asked to rate the effectiveness of the help they were given with each of the following aspects of their course:

a. Making one's own notes from what a teacher or lecturer says
b. Getting down to work in private study periods
c. Applying background reading in any piece of set work
d. Discussion and analysis of facts rather than simply memorizing and repeating them
e. Planning one's own work schedule
f. Adjusting to the difference in standards and scope between fifth-form and sixth-form or college work.

These were coded on a five-point scale, where a score of one represented 'not at all effective or no help received' and five, 'very effective'. Students could choose not to rate any item which was not really applicable to their course. The responses to each of these items by students in different types of institution are presented in Table 9.1.

These figures show that over 75 per cent of students had received *some* help from their teachers with the aspects of study included in these questions, although there were significant variations between their views of the effectiveness of this help.

Of the various aspects of study investigated, students were most satisfied with the help they had been given with dis-

Table 9.1 (S2): Students' ratings of help given with various aspects of study (percentages)

(1 = not at all effective/no help received, 5 = very effective)

Making one's own notes from what a teacher or lecturer says

	Compre-hensive School	Grammar School	Sixth-form College	Tertiary College	FE College	Total
1	20	22	12	14	13	17
2	20	18	18	18	16	18
3	26	24	29	26	26	26
4	15	14	20	20	22	18
5	10	10	13	11	14	12
Not applicable	8	10	6	11	7	8
Mean rating	2.7	2.7	3.1	3.0	3.1	2.9

Getting down to work in private study periods

1	21	30	17	26	22	23
2	23	23	22	23	20	22
3	25	22	25	25	25	24
4	18	16	21	16	16	18
5	11	7	14	8	9	10
Not applicable	—	1	—	3	6	2
Mean rating	2.7	2.5	2.9	2.6	2.7	2.7

Applying background reading in any piece of set work

1	12	13	8	10	13	11
2	22	24	17	29	20	22
3	28	31	27	31	26	28
4	21	18	29	15	19	21
5	13	10	16	10	15	13
Not applicable	2	3	3	4	6	4
Mean rating	3.0	2.9	3.3	2.9	3.0	3.0

Discussion and analysis of facts rather than simply memorizing and repeating them

1	7	6	4	5	6	6
2	13	13	7	10	11	11
3	24	21	20	24	19	21
4	28	28	31	27	27	28
5	25	29	36	30	31	30
Not applicable	2	2	2	3	3	2
Mean rating	3.5	3.6	3.9	3.7	3.7	3.7

Table 9.1: *continued* **(S2)**

Planning one's own work schedule

	Compre-hensive School	Grammar School	Sixth-form College	Tertiary College	FE College	Total
1	23	26	16	19	23	22
2	24	23	18	22	21	22
3	25	25	32	26	20	26
4	15	16	19	18	18	17
5	8	6	11	8	8	8
Not applicable	3	3	2	5	8	4
Mean rating	2.6	2.5	2.9	2.7	2.6	2.7

Adjusting to the difference in standards and scope between fifth-form and sixth-form or college work

	Compre-hensive School	Grammar School	Sixth-form College	Tertiary College	FE College	Total
1	21	23	13	14	18	18
2	22	23	15	18	18	19
3	28	25	27	27	27	27
4	17	19	25	23	16	20
5	9	7	17	12	13	12
Not applicable	1	1	1	4	5	2
Mean rating	2.7	2.7	3.2	3.0	2.9	2.9
Total = 100%	439	549	563	296	464	2311

cussion and analysis of facts. Only six per cent said they had received no help at all with this, and nearly a third rated the help they had received as very effective. This would suggest that most of the teachers in the institutions involved were conducting their classes in a way which encouraged discussion amongst students and that this was appreciated by them.

The aspects with which students were least likely to have been helped were planning their own work schedule and getting down to work in private study periods. This substantiates the findings from the open-ended items, where it was shown that this type of difficulty was most likely to be mentioned by students. On the other hand, getting down to work in private study periods is a problem with which it is very difficult for staff to give direct assistance.

There were some variations in the ratings between different types of institution, but in general these were not as great as the variation in ratings for different aspects of the course. There appears to be a slight but consistent tendency for students in sixth-form colleges to express greater satisfaction with the help they had received than those in other types of institution. On each of the aspects considered fewer sixth-form college students said they had received no help at all or that they had found the help totally ineffective than any other group. In general the college-based students showed a slightly greater degree of satisfaction than those in school sixth forms. In particular, they were more likely than those in all-through schools to have received help in making the adjustment from fifth- to sixth-form work.

Many advocates of the separate college system have claimed that by concentrating on the 16—19 age group they are able to acquire an expertise in the problems and needs of young people and to provide more effective guidance than would be possible in an all-through school. Because colleges take in students with very varied backgrounds, they must make a conscious effort to accustom them to their new environment and help them settle in as quickly as possible. A break at 16 has positive benefits in that it requires students, and their teachers, to reconsider their new status and its implications. Attention is therefore focused on many issues like study skills which could be glossed over in an all-through school. It is also likely that sixth-form and tertiary colleges, particularly those which are purpose-built, will be able to make more satisfactory physical provision for private study than schools.

In addition to these items, the questionnaire also included a section in which students were asked to indicate to what extent a number of statements about sixth-form or college life applied to them. The following statements were among these: 'I still have difficulty in organizing my own work'; 'During my course I have learned to organize my own work and to study independently'. The distribution of answers to these items for students in each type of institution is presented in Table 9.2.

These figures indicate that approximately a third of students were still having moderately- to strongly-felt difficulties in organizing their own work, and that there was little variation between institutions in the percentage of students

Table 9.2(S2): 'I still have difficulty in organizing my own work' (percentages of students giving each response)

	Comprehensive School	Grammar School	Sixth-form College	Tertiary College	FE College	Total
1. Does not apply at all	29	30	25	33	35	30
2. Applies only slightly	37	35	37	30	33	35
3. Applies moderately	26	23	24	25	21	24
4. Applies very strongly	8	10	12	10	8	10
Mean rating	2.1	2.1	2.2	2.1	2.0	2.1

'During my course I have learned to organize my own work and to study independently'

	Comprehensive School	Grammar School	Sixth-form College	Tertiary College	FE College	Total
1. Does not apply at all	7	6	4	6	7	6
2. Applies only slightly	16	16	14	19	18	16
3. Applies moderately	39	41	39	44	35	39
4. Applies very strongly	37	37	42	29	39	38
Mean rating	3.1	3.1	3.2	3.0	3.1	3.1
Total = 100%	439	549	563	296	464	2311

Study Skills 277

falling into this category. Fewer students in colleges of further education said they were still having difficulties compared with other institutions, but this probably reflects the greater proportion in this group of students following courses with a significant practical component, e.g. City and Guilds and secretarial courses, where these problems would be less likely to occur.

The second statement, 'During my course I have learned to organize my own work and to study independently' was agreed with, moderately or strongly, by 77 per cent of the sample with little institutional variation. This finding somewhat tempers the impression gained from the students' comments. It should be noted that in spite of the problems described, the majority of students do feel by the end of their course that they have acquired some of the essential skills. There were, in fact, a number of replies to the first of the open-ended items on the questionnaire which indicated that some students regarded this as the most important benefit of their sixth-form or college experience. The following examples are typical:

The most valuable thing I have gained from being at school or college this year is . . .

> Knowledge in the three subjects I chose to study at A-level and an ability to concentrate for longer periods and to work on my own without being pushed.

> To be able to discipline myself to work on my own at a steady rate without being coerced by teachers.

> The ability to work and study on my own as well as with teachers and to be able to discuss with teachers on a person-to-person basis rather than a teacher-to-pupil basis.

d. Preparation for academic study in higher education
Because of the frequency with which problems connected with private study had been raised in responses to the second questionnaire, it was decided to investigate to what extent the students who went on to higher education felt they had

been helped by their school or college in mastering the sort of study techniques required of them at this level.

Students in higher education were asked how effective their school or college had been in preparing them for each of the aspects of study listed in Table 9.3, rating each one on a scale from 1 to 5, where 1 represented 'not at all effective' and 5, 'very effective'. The mean values for students entering higher education from each type of post-16 institution are given in the table. On the following items college students rated the help they had received as significantly more effective than those who had been in school sixth forms:

a. 'Making notes from lectures'
b. 'Preparing papers for seminars or discussion groups'
c. 'Background reading for a piece of set work'
e. 'Discussion and analysis of information, rather than memorizing and repeating facts'
f. 'Developing one's own ideas rather than relying on those learned from text books and lectures'
g. 'Planning one's own work schedule'.

Many students who had attended school sixth forms commented on their problems in adjusting to the demands of study in higher education, particularly with reference to items e. and f. above. Criticisms of A-level examinations and the type of teaching associated with them were implicit in many of their remarks.

> The main difficulty I have found is the transition from what is expected at A-level to what is expected at college. At A-level you were more or less 'spoonfed' with facts which you memorized — sometimes without any real comprehension or analysis, now at college I have been expected virtually straight away to be able to analyse, criticize and discuss facts and I have great difficulty in making my mind question facts, ask why they are there, rather than simply memorizing them as I have been used to. (Grammar.)

> My school sixth form tended to 'spoon-feed' me too

Table 9.3 (S3): Students in higher education: effectiveness of help received in coping with different aspects of study

1 = *Not at all effective*   5 = *very effective*

Mean ratings

	Comprehensive School	Grammar School	Sixth-form College	Tertiary College	FE College	Total
a. Making notes from lectures	2.8	2.9	3.3	3.3	3.1	3.1
b. Preparing papers for seminars or discussion groups	2.1	2.2	2.4	2.1	2.4	2.2
c. Background reading for a piece of set work	2.9	2.9	3.1	3.0	3.0	3.0
d. Getting down to work in one's own time	3.4	3.5	3.7	3.6	3.7	3.6
e. Discussion and analysis of information, rather than memorizing and repeating facts	3.0	3.0	3.4	3.2	3.5	3.2
f. Developing one's own ideas rather than relying on those learned from text books and lectures	2.7	2.8	3.1	2.9	3.3	2.9
g. Planning one's own work schedule	3.0	3.2	3.4	3.3	3.5	3.3
h. Adjustment to the pressure and amount of work	2.9	3.2	3.3	3.2	3.3	3.2
i. Getting used to the higher standard of work now expected	3.1	3.2	3.4	3.4	3.5	3.3
j. Completion of work on time	3.5	3.7	3.5	3.4	3.4	3.5
Total = 100%	161	176	194	101	68	700

much — whenever we moved on to a new topic we did not have to prepare it first on our own — rather, the teacher would first 'teach' it to us and only *then* leave us to work around the topic on our own. But one teacher did make a positive effort to reverse the situation — he let us find out about the topic first and then discuss it with us — as often happens at university. Although at school it was easier and more convenient to be 'spoon-fed' in the long-term it did not really help us to cope with studying at university and also in a future career, where we will have to research a subject on our own thoroughly. (Grammar.)

My A-level courses at school were run on a too traditional basis, with none or not enough emphasis on organizing one's own work or developing one's own ideas. All the emphasis was placed on taking notes in lessons and learning them and writing essays with the use of a limited supply of textbooks. We were never encouraged to question what we were taught or put forward alternative ideas from those which the teacher told us. I think students from traditional schools such as mine suffer in higher education because they have not been prepared for working on their own and developing their own ideas. (Grammar.)

One student from a tertiary college went as far as to suggest that the inability of his contemporaries to discuss topics was adversely affecting the quality of his academic experience.

I am at a polytechnic and the social life is greatly inferior to that of the college. The same applies to the academic life although this is partly due to the fact that the majority of students are grammar school science-based — they have missed the personality-developing aspects of college and are seemingly incapable of discussion. Class sizes at polytechnic are far higher than at college, and the fact that standards were higher at college does lead to some disenchantment and disillusion. (Tertiary.)

e. Teacher's views on the teaching of study skills

These findings concerning students' problems were sub-sequently discussed with teachers from institutions taking part in the project. The views expressed at these meetings are also discussed at greater length than is possible here in *16—19: Study Problems*[21], but a brief summary follows.

Most teachers recognized that the problems described were encountered by the students in their own school or college but there seemed to be considerable variation in both the extent to which institutions took steps to combat these and the strategies they adopted. In general, the teachers fell into two groups — those who thought it essential to initiate specific courses in study skills for sixth-formers and those who felt that subject specialists can adequately cover study skills as an integral part of their class teaching. Implicit in the latter view is the belief that study skills are subject specific; that the skills required by an English student will be so different from those required by a mathematician that no course could be designed which would cater for both. The advocates of a centrally-organized course felt that the assumption that subject teachers deal with this is erroneous and that, in fact, very few students receive tuition in study skills in this way.

There was a tendency for teachers in all-through schools to feel that study skills are primarily the responsibility of subject teachers, and for those in 16—19 colleges to favour a more centrally organized approach. The only examples of study skills courses in operation which the project team encountered were all taking place in sixth-form, tertiary or FE colleges. One example of such a course run by a sixth-form college will suffice to illustrate the sort of positive steps that an institution can take in order to alleviate some of the problems described in this chapter. All first-year students at this college are required to follow a course in study skills consisting of one 45-minute period per week. The course followed by students planning to spend one year in the college (i.e. those mainly on O-level and CSE courses) lasts for 18 weeks and deals with the following topics:

Weeks 1 and 2	Introduction and questionnaire
Weeks 3 and 4	Organizing time — weekly and daily time-tables

Week 5   Motivation and concentration — the
                    development of techniques
Weeks 6 and 7   Tackling books — use of contents, index,
                    summaries etc.
Weeks 8 and 9   Making notes — from books and in lessons
Week 10 and 11   Writing essays
Weeks 12 and 13   Coping with examinations — revision
                    techniques
Weeks 14 and 15   Faster and better reading — comprehension
                    and reading speeds
Week 16   Words . . . words . . . words. Language and
                    spelling
Weeks 17 and 18   Library skills.

Two-year students are required to take a similar, more con-
densed course which covers approximately the same ground
over eight weeks. The principal, vice-principals and senior
tutors of the college all teach on these courses.

Several other approaches were encountered. For example,
some colleges favour an intensive one- or two-week induction
course for new entrants which serves as a general introduction to the college as well as providing some tuition in study
techniques. One of the tertiary colleges operates a study skills
centre which is open to any student who has problems in
presenting written work or has not yet acquired self-discipline
in study. The centre is open daily and manned by staff drawn
from all departments of the college. Other colleges distribute
booklets to new students intended as guides to study techniques, and follow these up by means of tutor group meetings. In view of the fact that college students rated the help
they had received as more effective than the school sixth-
formers, it would appear that this type of strategy is on the
whole more successful than leaving the matter in the hands of
subject teachers. Some college lecturers were particularly
doubtful about the concept of subject-specific skills.

> At our college the different departments say there are
> distinctly different techniques for each subject and
> therefore it's organised departmentally. I go round
> sitting in on these courses and I find them doing almost

exactly the same thing in every department. So I think there's a lot of myth about this. Obviously science and maths will have specific subject skills but I think there's a whole range of study techniques which go right across the board. Nothing I've seen in going round these introductory courses has made me think otherwise. (Director of curriculum, sixth-form college.)

At the moment it is not possible to state with any certainty which approach to the teaching of study skills is the most effective. The purpose of this chapter has been to illustrate that students are encountering difficulties that could be alleviated, and that, while many institutions are already aware of this and actively engaged in tackling the problems, others feel that their present arrangements are satisfactory.

It is felt that one of the most urgent research topics to arise from the present project is the need to consider in greater detail the provision made for teaching study skills in different institutions, and to carry out some sort of evaluation of these in order to provide those involved in 16–19 education with information on what might be the most effective policies for their own institution.

Chapter 10

11–16 Schools

In chapter four consideration was given to the effect different types of 16-plus provision might have on the attitudes of fifth-formers towards staying on in full-time education. The reorganization of a local education system into separate institutions for those up to the minimum leaving age and those beyond it holds a number of other implications for the resulting 11–16 schools, and these are explored more fully in this chapter.

a. Background

Many of the earliest views expressed on 11 (or 12)–16 comprehensive schools appeared in the wake of the Department of Education and Science's *Circular 10/65*, which had requested all LEAs to draw up plans for reorganizing their secondary education system along comprehensive lines, one of the six possible schemes outlined being that of 11–16 comprehensive schools combined with sixth-form colleges for pupils over 16. Although the idea of separate institutions for 16-plus education had been in existence for a number of years, at the time of the Circular there were in this country very few working examples from which experience could be drawn or firm evidence collected — a fact which was acknowledged both in the Circular and in succeeding publications from various sources. It was not until the early 1970s that reports began to appear on how such systems were working in practice. (See, for example, Benn[22], Benn and Simon[23] King[16].)

In its brief discussion on a sixth-form college system *Circular 10/65* stated:

> A sixth-form college may involve disadvantages for the lower schools; there are few obvious arguments in favour of comprehensive schools with an age range of 11 to 16. Children in this age group may lose from a lack of contact with senior pupils of 16 to 18. There is a danger that the concentration of scarce specialist teachers in the sixth-form college will drain too much talent away from the schools. Some teachers may find unattractive the prospect of teaching the whole ability range in a school offering no opportunities for advanced work, and many teachers express a preference for work in schools catering for the whole secondary age range.

Taylor[24], writing in the same year, also drew attention to the potential difficulties of staffing an 11—16 school through being unable to offer sixth-form work. The National Union of Teachers[25] linked potential staffing difficulties to a divergence in salary levels which they predicted would develop between 11—16 schools and sixth-form colleges. The Headmasters' Association[26] took the view that separate institutions for pre-16 and post-16 education would lead to a stratification of the teaching profession 'into 11—16 staff (mainly non-graduates) and 16—19 tutors (mainly graduates)'. King[16] in his study did in fact find that graduates comprised a minority of the staff in 12—16 schools and a majority in sixth-form colleges. He also reported that whereas non-graduates tended to hold head of year- and head of house-type appointments in the schools, there was a tendency for head of department posts to be held by graduates. Difficulties in attracting academically well-qualified staff were reported by some of the head teachers in Benn's small survey of 11/12—16 comprehensives[22]. One head, however, did not consider that such teachers were necessarily the most suitable for an all-ability, younger age-group, and reported receiving applications from excellent candidates. Edmonds[27], writing about Scunthorpe, stated that after two years of working it was clearly possible to attract and maintain able staff in 11—16 schools.

The absence of sixth-formers, which was seen in *Circular 10/65* as a potential disadvantage to the pupils in 11—16 schools, was also similarly viewed by Taylor, the NUT and the HMA, the latter stating: 'The effect of a sixth form as an inspiration to younger pupils would be forfeited.' The value which a sixth form brings to a school was also emphasized by Murphy[28]:

> 'The society of the school is a kaleidoscope of courses for individuals and this is an invaluable feature. Whatever path a pupil chooses to follow he can see others ahead of him along the way.'

In contrast, however, the absence of sixth-formers is also seen to bring certain advantages, especially to the fifth-formers, who are able to assume the role and responsibilities of senior pupils in their final year of compulsory schooling. This new opportunity for them was acknowledged in *Circular 10/65* and by the NUT and the HMA. The NUT, however, questioned whether the relationship between fifth-formers and the younger pupils, in terms of responsibility and understanding, could develop to the same extent as it does between sixth-formers and the same pupils. One of the head teachers in Benn's survey saw an advantage in the absence of sixth-formers in that it removed an overemphasis on academic studies which 'becomes the only criterion by which the rest of the pupils are judged'. Another head teacher attributed the absence of serious behaviour problems among fifth-formers to their added responsibilities and also to the tendency of staff to treat them more as young adults. On the same subject of discipline, Edmonds reported no deterioration in the 11—16 schools in Scunthorpe. It has been suggested that the removal of the 16—19 students facilitates the assertion of an appropriate discipline in a school. In 1959 the Crowther Committee[29] had stated:

> 'The presence of quite young boys and girls involves a paternalism in discipline which often spreads upwards to those who do not need it.' (para 603.)

Concern about the curriculum in 11–16 comprehensive schools was also evident in the publications of the NUT and the HMA. In addition to the related problems of staffing and the absence of stimulating sixth-form work, practical difficulties were anticipated in correlating syllabuses between schools feeding the same 16-plus institution and also in sustaining continuity between pre-16 and post-16 courses. Stephens[30] stressed that the fifth year is not necessarily the end of an educational stage for all pupils, some being only part-way through O-levels or CSE, and feared that separate 16-plus institutions would cause this flexibility to be lost. The opportunity for pupils to bypass O-levels and proceed straight to A-levels is also seen as a potential casualty of such systems. One of the head teachers in Benn's survey gave 'the virtual inability for a pupil to bypass O-level and aim directly at A-level' as one of the disadvantages of 11–16 schools.

The smaller size of 11–16 schools is one of their most often claimed advantages. Apart from their economical convenience of fitting into existing school premises, the more personal atmosphere of a smaller institution is considered a valuable gain for both staff and pupils. The smaller size can, however, result in fewer courses being offered. Benn and Simon, for example, reported that the 11–16 schools in their survey offered on average half as many O-level subjects as the 11–18 schools, but this was not supported by King[16], who found that the academic provision of the 12–16 schools in his survey, in terms of curricular and examination opportunities, compared favourably with any available standards, as did the academic performance of their pupils.

The lack of pressure to build up sixth-form numbers is seen as an advantage of 11–16 schools as it can lead to more impartial guidance to post-16 courses, and in the case of schools with very small sixth forms, which can make a heavy drain on staff time and resources, the removal of the 16-plus students is considered beneficial by enabling the school to concentrate more fully on the needs of the 11–16 age-group. A further advantage of short-course schools was suggested by King[16] in that equality of provision between neighbourhood schools is more easily achieved with this type of school than with all-through 11–18 schools where the financing of the whole school is related to its proportion of older pupils.

b. The survey of teachers and fifth-form pupils

i. *Method*

The subsidiary study which was undertaken to investigate some of the issues surrounding 11—16 schools has already been outlined in Chapter 4. The remainder of this chapter is concerned with the second and third purposes of the study as described in Chapter 4, namely,

(2)   to determine the effects of the presence or lack of a sixth form within a school on the attitudes and experiences of pupils in the fifth form;

(3)   to investigate in general the views of senior staff in 11—16 schools on the advantages and disadvantages of this form of secondary provision.

A summary of the method adopted for the investigation is given below, but for a more complete account the reader is recommended to turn back to Chapter 4.

Pupils' questionnaire

Questionnaires were administered to a random sample of fifth-year pupils in both 11—16 and 11—18 schools towards the end of their final year of compulsory schooling. The types of schools involved were all-through and 11—16 comprehensives, grammar schools and secondary modern schools. The all-through comprehensives and the grammar schools had been involved in the main study of the project, and the 11—16 comprehensives were those feeding the sixth-form colleges and tertiary colleges in the main study. Seven secondary modern schools were included in this study to provide a more complete picture of a fifth-year population. Two of the secondary modern schools had sixth-forms; the remainder were 11—16 schools. In all, the subsidiary study involved 417 fifth-formers in 40 different schools (Table 10.1).

Teachers' questionnaires

The head teachers and up to three senior members of staff in each of the 11—16 comprehensive schools were asked to complete a questionnaire dealing with some of the issues surrounding 11—16 schools. The head teachers were additionally asked for information about their fifth-form leavers, the previous history of their schools and about staffing. The findings from these questionnaires relevant to this chapter are discussed in the next section.

The head teachers of the seven secondary modern schools were also asked to complete a questionnaire. This dealt with background information on their schools and their fifth-formers. Issues arising from these are discussed in the final section of this chapter.

A total of 51 completed questionnaires were received from staff in the 14 short-course comprehensive schools taking part in this subsidiary survey. The composition of this staff sample is shown in Table 10.2.

ii. *The merits of 11—16 schools*

All the teachers were presented with a list of possible advantages of not having a sixth form, and were asked to rate them on a scale ranging from 'very much an advantage' to 'not really an advantage'. The responses are shown in Table 10.3.

From the results it is clear that almost all the teachers saw the opportunities created for fifth-formers to take on responsibilities (item a) as an advantage of the 11—16 school, with three quarters of the teachers placing it in the two higher categories on the scale (categories 1 and 2). The curriculum and teaching methods were not seen to gain, by a large minority of the teachers (two fifths), but this viewpoint was balanced by an equal number who felt that a considerable or moderate advantage was to be gained in these areas. This divergence of views reflects the variety of opinion which was apparent among the teachers in the sample. The absence of the administrative work associated with a sixth form was the item considered least advantageous, with a mean rating of 3.0. Just over two-fifths of the teachers did not see any benefit from this, and, of those who did, half rated it only a slight advantage. The lack of pressure to build up a sixth form was generally considered an advantage, although this view was not shared by approximately a quarter of the teachers. There was, however, a tendency for those teachers

Table 10.1: Fifth-year pupil survey

School with Sixth Forms	Number of Schools	Number of Pupils
Comprehensive	13	152
Grammar	6	38
Secondary modern	2	31
Total	21	221

Schools without Sixth Forms

Comprehensives feeding Sixth-form colleges	9	58
Comprehensives feeding tertiary colleges	5	55
Secondary modern	5	83
Total	19	196

Table 10.2: Survey of teachers in 11–16 schools

Type of School	Number of Head Teachers	Number of Senior Teachers	All Teachers
11–16 comprehensives feeding sixth-form colleges N = 9	9	24	33
11–16 comprehensives feeding tertiary colleges N = 5	5	13	18
Total	14	37	51

Table 10.3 (T5): The advantages of not having a sixth-form

	Very Much an Advantage	A Moderate Advantage	A Slight Advantage	Not Really an Advantage	Unable to Say	Total
a. It creates opportunities for 15-year-olds to assume the responsibilities and status of senior pupils	20	19	10	2		51
b. Teaching methods and curriculum are not dictated by the needs of advanced and academic work in the sixth form	8	13	4	21	4	50
c. There is no pressure to build up sixth-form numbers, so pupils can be given impartial guidance on vocational and educational choice at 16-plus	14	10	7	14	3	48
d. The social and disciplinary system can be adjusted more closely to the needs of the 11—16 age range	20	13	7	10	1	51
e. Staff time and other resources need not be concentrated upon needs of small numbers of sixth-formers	21	11	7	11	1	51
f. Staff are free of the administrative burdens associated with a sixth form	8	5	14	23		50

in the sample who had previously taught in grammar, direct-grant or comprehensive schools with a large sixth form (N = 27) to see this as a greater advantage than did the other teachers, but this difference did not prove to be statistically significant. The opportunity to cater more specifically for the 11–16 age-group in terms of their social and disciplinary needs (item d) was the second most highly valued item in this part of the questionnaire, and here there was a significant difference ($p<.05$) between the teachers with experience of large sixth forms, who indicated a greater awareness of this benefit, and the other teachers. The distribution of the former group showed a dichotomy between those who rated this item in the two higher categories and those who saw no advantage, whereas approximately a third of the second group of teachers opted for the third category (a slight advantage). The absence of the demands of a small sixth form on staff time and resources was generally considered an advantage by all the teachers, two thirds of them giving this item the two higher ratings.

iii. *The disadvantages of 11–16 schools*

The teachers were also asked to rate in the same way as before seven suggested advantages of 11–18 schools. Their responses to the question 'To what extent is an 11–18 school at an advantage when compared with an 11–16 school?', in respect of each item, are shown in Table 10.4.

The results show that as far as two of the items were concerned — the contribution made by sixth-formers to the general running of a school (item a) and the benefit to staff morale of sixth-form teaching (item d) — half the teachers considered the all-through school to be very much at an advantage. In each case this view was supported by a number of other teachers who considered the advantage to be a moderate one, making total proportions for these two points of view of approximately four fifths for item a and three-quarters for item d. Perhaps not unsurprisingly, the teachers who had worked in schools with large sixth forms voiced even stronger views on item a than the other teachers ($p<.05$). Similar total proportions for the first two categories were achieved for three other items (b., c. and f.) but in these cases

Table 10.4 (T5): The advantages of an 11–18 school

	Very Much an Advantage	A Moderate Advantage	A Slight Advantage	Not Really an Advantage	Unable to Say	Totals
a. Sixth-formers make a useful contribution to the daily running of a school	26	17	6	2		51
b. Sixth-formers set an example of behaviour to younger pupils	16	21	7	6	1	51
c. The presence of a sixth form demonstrates to younger pupils the attraction of continuing education after 16 years	18	23	5	5		51
d. Opportunities for sixth-form teaching benefit staff morale	25	12	9	4	1	51
e. Presence of sixth-form studies raises academic standards throughout the school	17	14	11	5	4	51
f. Sixth-form activities benefit the social and recreational life of a school generally	16	23	10	1	1	51
g. Sixth-formers contribute to the development of good relations between school and surrounding community	11	16	10	9	5	51

it was the second category which attracted the highest number of responses. Nevertheless, this reflects that in the opinion of a large majority of the teachers, the 11−18 school is clearly at an advantage over the 11−16 school in having sixth-formers, rather than fifth-formers, as leaders and to act as a reference group for the younger children. Although more evenly distributed between the first three categories, the teachers' responses to items e. and g. show that a majority also valued the beneficial effect of a sixth form on academic standards and the contribution sixth-formers make to the promotion of good relationships between the school and local community.

As arguments for and against 11−16 schools cannot be divorced from those about the transfer of all 16-plus education to separate institutions, the same teachers were also asked for their opinions on various aspects of separate 16-plus provision.

iv. *Views on separate 16-plus provision*

Their responses to the question 'To what extent have each of the following appeared in practice to be an advantage of separate educational provision at 16-plus?' (Table 10.5) show that the teachers considered colleges to be at a distinct advantage over schools by being able to offer a wider range of courses and by having greater resources with which to support these. Over 80 per cent of the sample placed these two aspects in the very much/moderate categories (with the largest single response in each case being in the former).

None of the other proposed advantages attracted such agreement among the teachers, although approximately two thirds valued fairly highly the more adult atmosphere of a college. No clear picture emerged of the advantage to be gained by a possible increase in staying-on rates among disenchanted pupils in a college system, the teachers' ratings being fairly evenly distributed among the four main categories.

The claim that colleges are able to provide a better preparation for a young person's immediate future, whether this is in employment or in higher education, also brought a mixed response from the teachers. Very few (10 per cent)

Table 10.5 (T5): The advantages of separate 16-plus provision

	Very Much an Advantage	A Moderate Advantage	A Slight Advantage	Not Really an Advantage	Unable to Say	Totals
a. Pupils who have become disaffected with school are more likely to continue their education after 16 at a college	10	14	14	9	4	51
b. Colleges offer a wider range of courses and subjects than would be possible in an 11–18 school	30	15	2	2	2	51
c. Colleges offer fuller specialised resources and equipment than would be possible in an 11–18 school	29	12	7	1	2	51
d. Colleges provide a social atmosphere and regime more appropriate for young people over 16 years of age than that found in school sixth forms	14	20	6	7	4	51
e. Colleges are more able than sixth forms to prepare young people for the personal and intellectual demands of higher education	5	12	7	18	9	51
f. Colleges are more able than sixth forms to prepare young people who want to enter employment at 17 or 18 years	15	9	5	15	7	51
g. Colleges provide more effectively for the less academic or non-traditional type of student	16	8	7	12	8	51

considered colleges to have a great advantage over sixth forms
where higher education is concerned, although almost a
quarter of the sample did rate the advantage as moderate.
However, the largest single response for this item was in the
negative category and when this is added to the numbers
who were undecided it reveals that a slender majority of
teachers had reservations over the benefit of a college education in this respect. Where preparation for employment is
concerned, appreciably more teachers (30 per cent) rated the
colleges' advantage highly, and overall there was a small
majority favouring them. A college's provision for the non-
traditional type of 16-plus student brought a very similar
response from the teachers, just over half of them seeing
some advantage. Over this issue, however, there was a difference of opinion ($p < .01$) between the teachers who were
in schools feeding tertiary colleges and those who were in
schools feeding sixth-form colleges. The tertiary college
group of teachers almost unanimously rated the advantage
as very much or moderate, whereas half the sixth-form
college group rated it as slight or not a real advantage at all,
with a further quarter being unable to say. This is perhaps
not surprising in view of the greater range of vocationally
biased courses available at a tertiary college and no doubt
reflects the greater similarity in the type of course available
in 11–18 schools and sixth-form colleges.

When asked to rate in a similar way some suggested disadvantages of separate 16-plus provision, the teachers generally
agreed that they did represent disadvantages, but they did
not on the whole rate them as highly as they had the advantages. In only three of the 14 items was the largest single
response in the 'very much' or 'moderate' categories (Table
10.6). The greatest disadvantages were seen to be the loss of
an established relationship between school and parents, the
difficulties of communicating information about individual
pupils across the 16-plus threshold, the loss of the sheltered
atmosphere of a school and the temptation for students in
colleges to spend too much time on leisure or social pursuits.
In each of these there was a majority of teachers who considered the disadvantage to be either very much or moderate.
In contrast more than half did not see any real disadvantage

Table 10.6 (T5): The disadvantages of separate 16-plus provision

	Very Much a Disadvantage	A Moderate Disadvantage	A Slight Disadvantage	Not Really a Disadvantage	Unable to Say	Totals
a. College has not the time to develop a full understanding of each pupil's personal and educational needs	11	12	15	5	7	50
b. Relationships built up between school and parents over the years are wasted if pupils have to make a move at 16 years	18	12	12	9		51
c. Transition to a new institution at 16-plus raises problems of educational record keeping and communication of information on individuals not experienced in 11–18 schools	6	21	13	10	1	51
d. Expertise in dealing with particular pupils and getting the best out of them is lost when they transfer to college	6	14	15	10	6	51
e. Some pupils require the sheltered atmosphere of a school community	12	14	17	7	1	51
f. It is difficult for pupils to know what college is like before they decide to go there	5	12	13	19	1	50
g. Entrants to college are expected to adjust to new surroundings and new courses at the same time	4	12	16	19		51

Table 10.6 *(Continued)* (T5)

	Very Much a Disadvantage	A Moderate Disadvantage	A Slight Disadvantage	Not Really a Disadvantage	Unable to Say	Totals
h. Students are obliged to make a great number of social contacts and relationships when they enter college	1	4	14	32		51
i. The time a student actually spends at college may be as short as a year and it will rarely be more than two years	9	5	14	23		51
j. Classes at college are larger than in schools	2	10	8	14	16	50
k. At college students have no opportunity to assume responsibility for younger pupils, e.g. as prefects	7	10	9	21	4	51
l. Discipline at college seems too relaxed for the good of some students	8	9	17	9	8	51
m. It is easy for some students to spend too much time on leisure and social activities at college	10	21	12	3	5	51
n. The community atmosphere of a school is lost at college	7	12	14	9	9	51

at all in students' having to make new social contacts and relationships on entering a 16-plus college, and the same view was expressed by just under half in respect of the relatively short length of a student's college career.

Although most of the teachers saw some disadvantage in the absence of an opportunity to take responsibility for younger pupils — a third feeling fairly strongly about this — the largest single response came again from those who did not see this as any real drawback. Two aspects of pastoral care — getting to know students' personal and educational needs and the skill of getting the maximum out of each of them — were generally seen to suffer in a college system, although most responses were in the slight/moderate disadvantage categories. That students may not know what they are letting themselves in for when they decide to go to college attracted a small number of responses (10 per cent) in the 'very much a disadvantage' category, but again the largest group of teachers saw this as no real disadvantage. A very similar response pattern was given to the item concerning the various adjustments a student has to make when moving on to a college. The more relaxed discipline of a college and its lack of the type of community atmosphere found in a school were viewed varyingly by the teachers. Relatively large numbers felt unable to express an opinion, but the largest single response in each case was that the disadvantage was slight. Also attracting a large number of 'unable to say' responses was the question concerning the possible disadvantage of the larger classes to be found in a sixth-form or tertiary college. Apparently not all the teachers agreed with the premise that classes are larger, as the following remark suggests: 'Classes are considerably smaller in colleges than in comprehensive schools.' (Teacher in an 11—16 school feeding a sixth-form college.) Of those who appeared to accept the statement that classes are larger, no clear picture of opinion emerged, almost equal numbers assessing it ether as a moderate disadvantage or none at all.

v. *Staffing an 11—16 school*

The head teachers of the 14 11—16 comprehensive schools involved in the fifth-year survey were asked in their question-

naire how often the absence of sixth-form teaching opportunities had created any difficulties in recruiting staff in the
past few years. The 13 responses were distributed over the
four alternative answers as follows:

Often 1   Occasionally 7   Rarely 3   Never 2

Those answering 'often' or 'occasionally' were also asked to
describe the form the difficulties tended to take. Their
responses, which are reproduced below, show that these
difficulties mainly took the form of low numbers of graduate
applicants for vacant posts, which in the case of 'shortage'
subjects exacerbated an already difficult situation. As with
the head teachers in Benn's survey, the view was expressed
that graduates, however, are not always the best teachers.

> Young graduate teachers who have turned down an
> appointment because on second thoughts, they wished
> to be involved in sixth-form teaching.

> Graduate staff at interviews always ask about the
> future possibilities of sixth-form teaching. Some write
> and ask, others have obviously applied simultaneously
> to schools with sixth forms and prefer to take offers
> with those schools. There is no problem with non-
> graduate staff many of whom are better teachers than
> graduates.

> There is often a disappointing response to advertise-
> ments from graduates. Languages are a particular cause
> for concern — Hons. graduates do not wish to teach
> pupils of low ability. Even in senior posts where women
> are most suitable the response has been disappointing
> (e.g. senior mistress posts before the Sex Discrimination
> Act.)

> Good candidates did not wish to take posts without
> sixth-form work, believing that work with a limited age
> range would reduce their chances of returning later to
> A-level work.

Number of applications smaller than received by a neighbouring 11—18 school. Withdrawal after consideration of implications of restricted age range. Further difficulty — staff transferring to 11—18 schools in area after experiencing loss of sixth-form teaching.

Language appointments.

Teachers of science, mathematics, modern languages for instance look for VI form work — either withdraw application (after thought) or do not apply.

1) Presence of a sixth form increases the overall points available enabling one to offer higher scale posts, and hopefully thus attract a superior quality of teacher. This influence is very likely to be important in subject areas such as modern languages and mathematics in which there are teacher shortages. This observation is based upon the small number of applicants for teaching posts in the above mentioned subjects in the recent past at this school.

2) The necessity of involving teachers in subjects other than their specialisms is educationally disadvantageous and creates difficulty in staffing all subject areas in the curriculum in a satisfactory manner. The extent of this problem very likely could be reduced in some degree if one had a sixth form.

vi. *Pupils' experiences of fifth-form life*

Pupils in the 11—16 and 11—18 schools were presented with 'some remarks that people in the fifth form might make about life at school', and were asked to indicate the extent to which they felt they applied to their own personal experience (Table 10.7).

Although over some of the issues the views of the two groups of fifth-formers generally coincided, there were some significant differences between them. The vast majority of both groups, for example, considered they should have more freedom and privileges, as the following freely given comments illustrate:

Table 10.7 (P5): Pupils' experiences of fifth-form life (percentages)

11–16 schools N = 196   11–18 schools N = 221

	Applies Strongly		Applies Moderately		Applies Slightly		Does not Apply at All		Level of Significant Difference (chi-square)
	11–16 Schools	11–18 Schools	11–16 Schools	11–18 Schools	11–16 Schools	11–18 Schools	11–16 Schools	11–18 Schools	11–18 Schools
a. Pupils in the fifth form of this school are allowed to help in the daily running of the school	10	3	40	16	37	47	13	34	.01
b. Fifth-formers in this school are not really respected by pupils in lower forms	22	27	32	27	35	33	11	13	ns
c. Fifth-formers in this school have few special privileges or facilities which younger pupils don't get as well	31	25	25	40	32	27	11	9	ns
d. There are not enough opportunities for fifth-formers to carry out special duties and responsibilities in this school	15	30	29	32	29	25	27	13	.01
e. There is plenty of freedom for people in the fifth form of this school	10	5	37	26	33	42	19	28	.01
f. Life as a fifth-former is made more pleasant because we have some special privileges and facilities	24	7	31	21	33	44	12	27	.01
g. People in the fifth form are not treated any differently from younger pupils in the school	11	20	21	24	36	35	32	21	.05
h. Once people are in the fifth form they should be given more freedom than we get at presnt	38	47	29	31	22	13	11	9	ns

There aren't enough privileges given to fifth-form pupils and their life is of no considerable difference to that of any other year. The only difference to be found is in the sixth-form centre. I feel this is wrong as for some it will be their last year and so they should gain some privileges and respect from the teachers. (11–18 comprehensive school pupil.)

I think that more freedom should be given to pupils as they go up through the school. When in the fifth year you get a little more freedom but not as much as I and many others would like to have. (11–16 comprehensive school pupil.)

However, the fifth-formers in the 11–16 schools indicated that they currently enjoyed some extra privileges in their position as head of the school which were not shared by their counterparts in the all-through school ($p<.01$). More of the former stated that life had been made more pleasant because of these, with a quarter stating that this applied strongly to them. Similarly, the fifth-formers in the 11–16 schools, while joining in the general plea for greater freedom, also indicated that they currently enjoyed more than the 11–18 schools fifth-formers ($p<.01$). Not unexpectedly the 11–16 fifth-formers considered themselves to be more involved in the running of their schools and to have more responsibilities and duties. Half of them said the statement referring to helping in the daily running of the school applied strongly or moderately to them, against only a fifth of the pupils in the 11–18 schools. ($p<.01$). Pupils in the latter group showed a greater dissatisfaction with the opportunities open to them for carrying out duties ($p<.01$). The 11–16 fifth-formers also tended to consider themselves to be treated differently from the rest of the school ($p<.05$). Almost a third of them disagreed with the statement that they were not treated any differently.

Despite the likelihood that they enjoy more freedom and have more privileges and responsibilities, the pupils in the 11–16 schools did not consider themselves to be any more respected by the pupils in lower forms than did the fifth-formers in the 11—18 schools. Almost four fifths of each group agreed to some extent with the statement that they were not really respected, and over half in each case said the statement applied strongly or moderately. This is perhaps somewhat surprising in the case of the fifth-formers in the 11—16 schools, who had demonstrated that certain aspects of their fifth-form life differed significantly from that in the 11—18 schools. It presents some support for the earlier view-point of the NUT[25] that the narrower age gap between fifth-formers and the rest of an 11—16 school does not allow them to build up the same relationship with the younger pupils as 17—18 year old sixth-formers can. The responses of the 11—16 school fifth-formers in this survey may be reflecting the relatively recent establishment of their schools in their present form, although by the time the survey was carried out the majority of the schools would have been in their fourth or fifth year of reorganization. It could be maintained that this is sufficient time for a school to become adjusted to a differently aged leader group. This low esteem in which both groups of fifth-formers felt themselves to be held by the younger pupils reflects a major difference between them and sixth-formers — the fact that their numbers included the early-leaving, disenchanted pupils whose negative behaviour and attitudes must be apparent to the rest of the school and colour their views of fifth-formers as a whole. Awareness of this greater heterogeneity among fifth-formers was reflected in the comments of a pupil in an 11—18 school, who acknowledged the difficulty in striking the right balance between too much discipline and not enough:

> In my opinion there is too big a jump and too many privileges for sixth-formers. Pupils in the fifth form are still treated like any other member of the lower school. However this can be somewhat justified, in that some people in our form for instance would just abuse and take advantage of the freedom without responding like adults. (11—18 comprehensive school fifth-former.)

In conclusion, the pupils' responses to this part of the survey show, not unexpectedly, that there is a difference between fifth-form life in an 11—16 school and that in an 11—18 school, with pupils in the former generally enjoying greater freedom and more privileges and responsibilities. Despite this — and again not surprisingly — very few in either group demonstrated their satisfaction with their current situation. Their assessment of their image as seen through the eyes of the younger pupils, however, underlines the great assortment of personalities and attitudes in a typical fifth-year group, which unquestionably must present difficulties in deciding on what is an appropriate régime for them.

c. Secondary modern schools

i. *Their position and role*

Although the number of secondary modern schools is steadily declining as comprehensive schooling expands, in certain areas of the country such schools still represent the only form of secondary education available to large numbers of pupils. A brief consideration of their role is therefore merited, particularly in relation to the post-compulsory student.

The traditional role of secondary modern schools has been as providers for those pupils who at the age of 11 do not demonstrate a particular aptitude for a highly academic education. After a five-year general secondary education many of their pupils have traditionally left school to take up employment — which might or might not involve further training — or to follow a full-time vocationally based course at the local college of further education. There has always been in the secondary modern schools, however, a small number of 'late-developing' or 11-plus 'borderline', academically inclined pupils who from the age of 11 show an increasing aptitude and for whom a continued academic education beyond 16 is more appropriate. This has resulted in some secondary modern schools providing GCE A-level courses, although this development has depended on the extent of the demand and the alternative arrangements available locally. The sixth forms of local grammar schools, for instance, are generally willing to absorb secondary modern school pupils who wish to take two or more A-levels. Alternatively, these pupils may decide to transfer to a local college of further education. In addition, some secondary modern schools develop as 11–18 schools by providing for the 'new' sixth-former who wishes to improve his or her general academic qualifications — generally in one year — before entering employment or embarking on a further course of education.

Secondary modern schools at the present time, therefore, include those which provide a five-year secondary school course only — requiring those pupils who wish to remain in full-time education beyond 16 to move on to another institution — and those which make their own provision for their 16-plus students. Although major differences (by definition) exist between the balance of courses available throughout secondary modern schools and comprehensives, the two types of institution nevertheless share similar interests where their 16-plus students are concerned. Short-course comprehensives and 11–16 secondary modern schools, for example, are equally concerned that their 16-year-olds are well prepared for and suitably guided into the various paths they may follow after 16, and that maximum continuity with their next stage is achieved where this is particularly important. In those cases where they retain their 16-plus students, both comprehensives and secondary moderns are faced with the challenge of providing courses and opportunities which adequately meet the requirements of the clients.

The small sample (seven) of secondary modern schools included in the fifth-year survey is not claimed to be representative of all secondary modern schools. As the focus of the main project was on full-time educational provision for the 16–19 age group, those secondary modern schools which had relatively large numbers of pupils entering full-time post-compulsory education were obviously of greater current interest. The opportunity was also taken to obtain the views of the seven head teachers on certain aspects of 16–19 education, and these are reported in the following paragraphs. As mentioned in Chapter 4, the seven schools were selected as a result of a request by the research team for their LEAs to nominate suitable schools.

Two of the schools provided post-compulsory education for their pupils, although only one offered GCE A-level work.

The main work at the sixth-form level involved O/AO levels and CSE, both new and retakes. Neither school currently offered the Certificate of Extended Education (CEE). The school offering A-level work reported that some of the work was done in co-operation with the local college of further education and the local grammar school. Both CSE and O-level work done at the sixth-form level involved attending fifth-form classes. Both schools reported that a few (between one and four per cent) of their pupils had transferred to the local grammar school sixth form in the previous year and that 10 and 20 per cent respectively had transferred to the local FE colleges to follow A-level, O/AO level, OND and City and Guilds courses. The proportion of their fifth-formers remaining at school was approximately 20 per cent. In the fifth-form, pupils were entered for O-levels and CSE. One of the schools had 20 pupils that year who were taking four or more O-levels. The other school had relatively less O-level work; in the year of the inquiry nine pupils were involved, each taking one subject only. The majority of the pupils in both schools were taking five or more CSEs. Both schools made special provision for their sixth-formers in terms of separate teaching areas and common rooms. The sixth-formers in both schools became prefects and were given duties to perform. One school stated that they gave a choice of certain items in the school uniform at the sixth-form level. Overall the two schools reported that approximately 40 per cent of their fifth-formers remained in full-time education after the minimum leaving age.

The five 11–16 secondary modern schools also reported that their students were encouraged to enter the sixth form of a local grammar school if this was considered appropriate. In the year prior to the survey between one and three per cent of their fifth-formers had transferred to other school sixth forms. The proportions usually entering full-time FE courses ranged from 10 to 35 per cent. At the fifth-form level four of the schools entered some of their pupils for O-levels as well as CSE. As with the two 11–18 schools, most of the pupils were taking five or more CSEs. The courses taken by the pupils who went on to FE colleges included A-levels, O/AO levels, OND and City and Guilds.

ii. *Head teachers' views*

The head teachers seemed generally satisfied with the opportunities which were open to their pupils for post-compulsory education. One said he was 'extremely satisfied', and another drew attention to the variety and number of courses available at the local FE college and at evening institutes. The head of a school in a rural area outlined the problems of distance and transport which can be encountered: 'Transport and distance are obvious problems in a rural area, ——————14 miles, ——————20 miles, ——————Grammar school = 8 miles + .'

The head of one of the 11—18 secondary modern schools reported a difficulty in arranging for pupils to follow combined O- and A-level courses, other than at the local FE college. Such pupils evidently were not catered for by their own school despite its being an 11—18 and offering A-level courses. Link courses with the local college were valued by the same head through their mixture of a school base and time spent in an adult atmosphere. Another head stated his satisfaction with the transferring of A-level pupils to the local grammar school, but expressed concern about the pupils who went on to the local FE college, whose results in the past had not been totally satisfactory. He added that discussions were being held over this.

Following the questions asked of the head teachers about the full-time courses their leavers followed in FE colleges were two open-ended questions asking how the heads felt these pupils benefited, or were handicapped, by a change of institution at 16. Their responses, although obtained in an unstructured way, were generally in line with the views expressed by the heads and teachers in the teacher survey reported earlier. All the six secondary modern head teachers who answered this section, for example, mentioned the adult atmosphere of a college as a benefit to the 16-plus students: 'The environment at colleges of FE is in many ways more suitable for pupils in the post-16 age group; the school which, has concern primarily for the 11—16 age range cannot provide a sufficiently adult "self-determining" atmosphere.' (Head of an 11—16 secondary modern school.) In line with the other teachers, there were those who were aware of the potential hazards of this more relaxed atmosphere: 'Appreciate "adult" atmosphere in most cases — for a minority this is ultimately their undoing.' (Head of an 11–16 secondary modern school.)

The wide range of courses available in the institutions to which their pupils transferred was also seen as a benefit, as was the opportunity to mix socially with students from a wider background. Perhaps particularly applying to secondary modern pupils was the benefit as seen by one of the heads of the pupils encountering students of higher ability: 'After being very near the top of their groups, academically, there is a greater challenge in a more competitive situation.'

One also cited as a benefit the fact that in colleges the students do not have to spend time on monitoring duties. This can be equated with the question concerning the absence of opportunities for students in 16-plus colleges to take responsibilities for younger pupils in the other teacher survey, where the largest single response was that this represented no real disadvantage. The following comments perhaps summarize the general views expressed by the secondary modern head teachers on the benefits of a break at 16:

> Only a small minority transfer to the sixth form of a local grammar school, so all comments are made with this factor in mind. 1. Already spent five years in one school — familiarity suitable for some. 2. At 16+ they are young men and women but at school still get treated as schoolchildren. Tech. college more adult approach. 3. Peer group actively more stimulating and relevant at 16+. Meeting wider spectrum of individuals. 4. Not expected to carry out 'monitoring duties' — more time for study.

The issues raised voluntarily by the heads on the subject of the possible disadvantages of a break at 16 were also generally in line with the views expressed by the other teachers, e.g.:

> Less confident pupils need a more watchful situation. More guidance needed in subject discipline and overall

curriculum. Pupils' strengths and weaknesses are known by school staff and pupils respond to staff whom they know i.e. school staff (11–18 head.)

Some may be affected adversely for a short period on losing the close family atmosphere of the school, but this would not have a lasting effect and the percentage would be small anyway. (11–18 head.)

Knowledge of the pupils' capabilities and personal character is largely lost by a transfer at 16. Also the greater responsibility given to the student for his own progress. (11–16 head.)

A small minority prefer the formal structure of the school and find the relaxed atmosphere of the tech. college not conducive to good results. (11–16 head.)

One head summed up his views of the disadvantages of changing institutions at 16-plus in one word, 'none', and another expressed concern over the duplication of courses in schools and FE and was of the opinion that if the courses were all in schools more pupils (five to 10 per cent) would be inclined to stay on.

In response to an invitation to make any suggestions for improving the present situation, one of the heads said he felt a concentrated effort was needed to publicize the range of courses which were available to the 16-plus student, and that staff should be appointed specifically for this.

Fifth-formers in secondary modern schools

The secondary modern pupils' responses to the fifth-year questionnaire were included in the general analyses of the fifth-year survey reported in Chapter 4 and earlier in this chapter. Of the 114 secondary modern school pupils taking part in the survey, 83 were in the five 11–16 secondary modern schools and 31 were in the two 11–18 schools. The 83 11–16 secondary modern pupils comprised 42 per cent of all the pupils in 11–16 schools in the survey, and a separate analysis was carried out to discover whether their experiences

in the 11—16 comprehensive schools (Table 10.8). In effect,
there were very few differences between the two groups. The
secondary modern fifth-formers appeared to be slightly less
vociferous in their appeal for more freedom, and seemed to
consider themselves slightly better respected by the younger
pupils. These were slight differences, however, and did not
have any statistical significance. There was a significant
difference, nevertheless, in the extent to which they considered themselves to be involved in the daily running of their
school. The secondary modern pupils' ratings were overall
lower than those of the 11—16 comprehensive school fifth-
formers ($p < .01$), indicating that they saw themselves as
taking less part than did the comprehensive-school pupils. A
quarter of the secondary modern pupils said the statement
that they were allowed to help in the running of the school
did not apply to them. It may be that the short course
comprehensive schools are more conscious of their role as
11—16 schools because of their relatively recent establishment and are taking more positive steps to nurture the fifth
formers as a leader group. Half of the 11—16 comprehensives
had had a sixth form prior to reorganization, and the loss of
it could be expected to have caused a reconsideration of the
role to be played by the fifth-formers and the taking of
positive steps to achieve whatever changes were considered
desirable.

This small study of secondary modern schools has served
to illustrate the position such schools find themselves in with
regard to their 16-year-olds who wish to continue with full-
time education. Those schools which make their own provision are nevertheless dependent, as are the 11—16 schools,
on both the co-operation of the neighbouring grammar
schools and the local college of further education in order
that all the students' requirements are met. As in other
11—18 schools, efforts are made in 11—18 secondary modern
schools to treat their post-compulsory students differently
from the rest of the school by providing special areas for
their academic and social needs and by giving them special
responsibilities and privileges. Both the schools in the survey
followed the practice of timetabling the sixth-formers in with

Table 10.8: Mean ratings of fifth-formers' experiences of fifth-form life

11–16 comprehensive schools v 11–16 secondary modern schools

(1 = applies strongly   2 = applies moderately   3 = applies slightly   4 = does not apply at all)

	11–16 Comprehensive School Pupils (N = 113)		11–16 Secondary Modern School Pupils (N = 83)		Level of Significant Difference
	mean	S.D.	mean	S.D.	
a. Pupils in the fifth form of this school are allowed to help in the daily running of the school	2.40	.78	2.67	.97	.01
b. Fifth-formers in this school are not really respected by pupils in lower forms	2.22	.91	2.49	.99	ns
c. Fifth-formers in this school have few special privileges or facilities which younger pupils don't get as well	2.17	.98	2.27	1.11	ns
d. There are not enough opportunities for fifth formers to carry out duties and responsibilities in this school	2.60	1.08	2.72	1.00	ns
e. There is plenty of freedom for people in the fifth form of this school	2.60	.96	2.60	.88	ns
f. Life as a fifth-former is made more pleasant because we have special privileges and facilities	2.34	.96	2.30	1.03	ns
g. People in the fifth form are not treated any differently from younger pupils in the school	2.88	1.05	2.81	1.01	ns
h. Once people are in the fifth form they should be given more freedom that we get at present	1.91	.98	2.24	1.06	ns

fifth forms where courses other than GCE A-levels were involved, and it is clear that not all secondary modern schools with sixth forms offer A-level work. All seven schools demonstrated that their fifth forms normally include appreciable numbers of students (between 10 and 40 per cent of all their fifth-formers) who wish to avail themselves of further full-time education, and their head teachers generally expressed satisfaction with the provision that was made for them locally, although problems of guidance and travel were reported. The latter features perhaps underline the particular positions in which the secondary modern schools find themselves when compared with schools in totally comprehensive areas, whether these are all-through 11—18 schools or 11—16 schools combined with 16-plus colleges, which is that the secondary moderns' problems over placing their 16-plus students on appropriate courses are not problems shared by all the schools in their LEA area and such opportunities as do exist for their students are spread over a number of institutions, which at the least causes some inconvenience to the students, their teachers and the institutions.

Chapter 11

Summary and Conclusions

a. Outline of the project

The research project, funded by the NFER, began in 1974 with the aim of surveying and evaluating the different institutional forms of full-time education available to students aged 16—19 in the maintained sector, i.e. comprehensive school sixth forms, grammar school sixth forms, sixth-form colleges, colleges of further education, tertiary colleges.

It was decided at the beginning of the project to focus on the consumers of the education system and to evaluate these alternatives in terms of their impact on students. The effect of attending a particular type of institution on students' expectations and experiences, their degree of preparation for higher education or employment and their academic performance were the major criteria adopted.

The research activities focused on a study of a sample of 4,448 students aged 16-plus in 45 different institutions of the types outlined above. The majority were on courses leading to A-level examinations, but those studying for O-levels, Ordinary National Diplomas, secretarial qualifications, City and Guilds craft certificates and other non-advanced FE qualifications were also included.

Questionnaires were administered to this sample during their first term of full-time post-compulsory education in autumn 1974. A second questionnaire was administered to those on two-year courses during their final term, and information was collected on their examination results and destinations. A sub-sample of this group was asked to complete a third questionnaire during their first year of employment or higher education.

A number of subsidiary studies were carried out.

1. A study of the aims and objectives of 16—19 education as perceived by the heads and principals of the institutions in the main sample was undertaken.
2. Differences in the background and motivation of students on one- and two-year courses were investigated and the examination results of the one-year group were analysed[9].
3. Questionnaires were administered to a sample of fifth-formers in schools with sixth forms and without them in order to ascertain the differences between their experiences of life in the fifth form and their plans for the future.
4. Heads and senior staff in a number of schools without sixth forms were asked for their views on the advantages and disadvantages of this type of provision and of the effects of a break at 16.
5. Data were collected from a number of schools and colleges, including those in the main sample, on the courses and subjects offered, numbers of students, facilities, staff, rules and regulations etc.
6. A critical review of the literature on 16—19 education was carried out[2].

b. Summary of major findings

i. *Aims of 16—19 education*

There was broad agreement among the heads and principals of the institutions in the sample about the most important aims of 16—19 education. These were:

1. The development of social responsibility and awareness.
2. The development of mental, intellectual or academic capacities.
3. Preparation or qualification for career or vocational roles.
4. Development of personal qualities, particularly maturity and confidence.

There was, however, a noticeable difference between
schools and colleges in what the heads saw as the most
valuable educational experiences provided by their establishment for students in this age group. While the schools stressed
the benefits of contact with younger pupils and leadership
opportunities, the colleges most often mentioned the provision of an adult (or near adult) environment.

ii. *Staying on at 16*
An investigation of the reason given by students for staying on at 16 showed that they fell into three main groups:
those wishing to improve their career prospects generally,
those wishing to qualify for the particular career they had
already decided on and those wishing to go on to higher
education. There were relatively few students for whom
practical considerations of this sort were less important than
a wish to further their education for its own sake. However,
an interest in a particular subject often played an important
part in the decisions made by students when choosing their
course.

Students felt the main disadvantage in staying on at 16
was being short of money. They did not like being financially
dependent on their parents, and some who had part-time jobs
said they found the money earned failed to improve their
position to any real extent. A number of comments was
made in support of grants for everyone over the school-
leaving age staying in full-time education.

The reasons given by students for entering their sixth form
or college were varied. Most of those in grammar and comprehensive schools were happy to stay on in the sixth form
of the school they already attended, and few had considered
going elsewhere. Most students in sixth-form and tertiary
colleges had previously attended schools without sixth forms
and therefore had no choice but to transfer to the college at
16. The colleges of further education were found to contain
large numbers of students who had not been able to follow
the course they wanted at school and had come to the college
for this reason. This was particularly likely in the case of
students studying subjects such as catering, hairdressing, business studies and engineering, which schools are not able to

offer.

There was, however, a number of students in the FE colleges who could have stayed on in the sixth form but, having grown to dislike school, left in search of a more adult atmosphere. Many of those taking A-levels in colleges of further education fell into this category. It was found that the opportunities available in FE were not widely publicized in schools, and many students were not made aware of the alternatives that exist to the sixth form. The findings suggest that students are sometimes persuaded into staying on at school when they would have been better advised to go to a college of FE and train for a specific job.

Despite these differences, students in all types of schools and colleges expected to be treated like adults, and this was the aspect of college or sixth-form life which they hoped would be most different from the fifth form.

iii. *Experiences in the sixth form or at college*

Although students expressed the hope that they would be treated like adults and be subject to fewer rules concerning their appearance, attendance etc., there was considerable difference between the extent to which institutions granted them these privileges. All the sections of the questionnaires which dealt with this issue showed that college students were consistently more satisfied than the school sixth-formers. Because the colleges cater only for students over the age of 16 they are able to provide a more adult atmosphere as well as to offer their students a wider range of courses and subjects to choose from. Two thirds of students felt, by the end of their course, that a college system was preferable to an all-through school for 16—18 year olds. Only a fifth of students felt it was better to stay on at the same school at 16, mainly because it was a familiar environment where one already knew the teachers and other pupils. The opportunity to act as prefects and to be responsible for younger pupils was not seen as an important advantage of the school sixth form. Some students in this position said they felt the duties they had to carry out were trivial and afforded them no real responsibilities.

The grammar schools came in for much more criticism

than the comprehensive schools over their treatment of sixth-formers. Many students in grammar schools said they had been misled about the nature of the sixth form and that they had, in fact, found themselves required to comply with the same rules and regulations as much younger pupils in the school. The comprehensive schools appeared to vary more in this respect. While some were almost indistinguishable from the grammar schools in their régimes, others allowed their sixth-formers considerable freedom, sometimes providing them with a separate sixth-form block with common room and other facilities. The sixth-form colleges, especially those which were purpose-built, seem in general to have provided the fullest facilities. The colleges of further education and tertiary colleges did not seem to be quite so well-endowed with common rooms, private study rooms and libraries, but it must be remembered these institutions had also to cater for large numbers of part-time students.

Although the majority of students said they had learned to organize their own work and to study independently, it was obvious that coping with private study had been a major problem for them. Few institutions appear to make more than minor efforts to teach their sixth-formers how to study or give them a clear indication of how they are expected to make use of their free periods. Most students had learned to discipline themselves and to overcome distractions, both at school or college and at home, but in many cases this had proved very difficult. Very few institutions had study facilities that were felt to be entirely adequate, and students in schools and colleges which did not allow them to study at home when they had no lessons were critical of this regulation.

General studies was an issue that students felt strongly about, and a significant proportion felt that this had been the least satisfactory part of their course. 'A complete waste of time' was a phrase used many times to describe their feelings about it. It was rare to find anyone who thought it had been worthwhile even though some institutions, particularly the colleges, offered their students a considerable range of general studies courses to choose from. It was not until after they had left that students realized there were gaps in their knowledge which general studies could have been used to fill.

For example a number of comments was made on the third questionnaire calling for more information to be given on income tax, tenancy agreements, mortgages, bank accounts and other practical matters which students now had to cope with whether they were in employment or in higher education.

iv. *Entry to and preparation for higher education or employment*

Whether they eventually went on to some form of higher education at 18-plus or entered employment few students appeared to be completely satisfied with the careers guidance they had received. A feeling among students that they were pressed into applying for university, regardless of whether this was relevant to their career plans, was widespread. Some students in higher education felt they had no real sense of purpose in being there nor any clear idea of where it might lead them. The minority who had taken six months or a year off before taking up a place recommended that all students be encouraged to do this because it provided a breathing space in which to sort out their motives and priorities.

Students who did not intend to apply for places in higher education reported a tendency for teachers to regard them as second-class sixth-formers and very much resented this. On the whole, advice from teachers about filling in UCCA forms and on courses at different universities, polytechnics and colleges was much more detailed and helpful than advice about getting a job. There were some exceptions to this. Students on vocational courses in colleges of further education who were less likely to want to carry on in full-time education received more helpful advice from the lecturers about employment. Once again, students in all three kinds of college were more satisfied with both the higher education and careers advice they had received than those in school sixth forms. This may reflect the tendency for large institutions to be able to employ full-time specialist staff more often than a small school.

Of the students in the sample who went on to higher education, few reported that they had encountered any particular difficulty in settling down either to the academic or the

social life. However, a number who had previously attended a
college felt that this was a better preparation for higher
education than a school. Having been used to a more informal,
relaxed atmosphere, they considered themselves more socially
confident and also felt that there was less contrast between
the style of work now expected of them, e.g. lectures, seminars, tutorials, and that practised in the college they had
previously attended. While some grammar school sixth-formers
complained of being 'spoon-fed', the ex-college students said
they had been encouraged by their teachers to discuss and
question the material in the syllabus.

Of the students who took a full-time job, those who had
undergone some form of vocational training appeared to have
fewer problems in finding relevant employment than those
who had taken an A-level course. People entering the job
market with A-level qualifications were very disappointed
at the lack of suitable vacancies, and often had to take jobs
which they felt were far below their capabilities. Many of
them were convinced that their employment prospects were
no better, and in some cases actually worse, than if they had
left school at 16. A significant proportion in this category
regarded their current job as temporary and hoped eventually
either to obtain more demanding employment or to go back
into education.

As a result of our research, we suspect that too many
people are encouraged to embark on A-level work at 16 without a clear idea of what implications this course of action has
for their future. It is probably not true to say that A-levels
are a waste of time for those who do not intend to go on to
university, polytechnic etc. There is, however, a clear need
for information on the alternatives to A-level, especially the
vocational courses offered by colleges of further education,
to be made available to all students of 16 who are considering
staying on, and for students to think very carefully about
what might suit them best.

v. *The effects of a break at 16*
The kind of provision available to students over the age
of 16 does not appear to play a large part in the decision of
fifth-formers whether or not to continue in full-time educa-

tion. Senior staff in 11—16 schools felt that on balance more pupils were in full-time education as the result of the opportunity to enter a college but that the percentage whose decision was affected either way was small.

There appeared to be some difference between the experiences of fifth-formers in schools with and without sixth forms, those in the latter enjoying at least some of the responsibilities and privileges normally associated with the sixth form. Fifth-form pupils in 11—16 schools agreed more strongly than those in 11—18 schools that 'Pupils in the fifth form of this school are allowed to help in the daily running of the school' and 'Life as a fifth-former is made more pleasant because we have some special privileges and responsibilities'.

The teachers in 11—16 schools felt that the opportunity created for fifth-year pupils to take on this role was the most important advantage of the 11—16 school. They did, however, also feel that there were respects in which they suffered in comparison with an 11—18 school, the most important being that the opportunity to teach sixth-formers benefits staff morale, and that sixth-formers make a useful contribution to the daily running of the school.

The main advantages of a college system of 16-plus as perceived by staff in 11—16 schools were the wider range of courses and subjects than could be offered by a school and the greater resources and facilities with which to support them. Teachers in schools feeding tertiary colleges also felt that the colleges were in a better position to cater for the less academic or non-traditional type of student.

The disadvantages of separate provision at 16-plus were not as highly rated by the teachers as the advantages. They saw the loss of established relationships between school and parents, the problems of communicating information about pupils to the colleges and the need of some pupils for the sheltered atmosphere of a school as the main disadvantages. The heads of the 11—16 schools reported 'occasional' difficulties in recruiting staff, particularly graduates, because they were not able to offer sixth-form teaching.

vi. *A-level examinations*
The proportion of students withdrawing from A-level

courses varied from 15 per cent in the grammar schools to 31 per cent in the comprehensive schools. Students who had three or fewer O-levels at the beginning of the course were more likely to withdraw than those who were better qualified.

Although there were differences between the various types of institution in their overall pass rates at A-level (the grammar school sixth-formers performed best in this respect and the FE students least well), these were found to be closely related to the ability of the students entering different types of institution. Using the number of O-level passes as a rough measure of ability, in no particular type of institution did students perform significantly better or worse at A-level than their O-level results would predict. There was, however, some evidence to suggest that students in tertiary colleges with six or fewer O-levels do better at A-level than similarly qualified students in other types of institution.

c. **Conclusions**

Much of what has been written in recent years about 16–19 education has taken as its central theme the merits and drawbacks of introducing a break at 16 and catering for students over that age in a separate institution. This has been the issue of concern to many local authorities. Some have been faced with this choice as part of reorganization from selective to comprehensive secondary education. However, economic stringencies and the prospect of falling school rolls have led others which have been operating a comprehensive system for some years to review their provision at 16-plus. This has most often occurred where authorities introduced a system based on all-through schools, but not exclusively so. It is possible to cite examples of areas where sixth-form centres and sixth-form colleges have undergone further reorganization, usually to amalgamate with an FE establishment to form a tertiary college. Whatever their current arrangements it seems probable that 16–19 provision will remain an area of concern and one which will be kept under review by educational administrators and planners for some time to come.

The research described in this report was not concerned with the economic issues which authorities will doubtless bear in mind but the nature of the educational experience offered to students by different types of institution.

At the beginning of their course, students' expectations and motivations were broadly similar. In spite of differences in the degree of choice they had exercised at 16 and their reasons for choosing a particular type of institution, most were staying on in the belief that extended education would enhance their career opportunities.

There appear, however, to be significant differences in students' opinions of their experiences in 16-plus education. The attitudes of college students were more positive than those of school sixth-formers on many of the issues on which their opinions were elicited. This does not mean that there was evidence of severe dissatisfaction among the school sixth-formers. Although some students in grammar schools were vocal in their criticisms of the traditional sixth form, with its emphasis on school ritual, leadership roles and academic study, comprehensive schools much less often evoked critical responses of this kind.

The data collected on the aims of 16—19 education showed that while there was general agreement about them, there was much greater disparity among heads and principals in their views on the most valuable educational experience provided by their institutions. In other words, the means are different but not the intended ends. The contrast between the emphasis on the 'provision of an adult or near-adult atmosphere' of the colleges and that on the 'benefits of contact with younger pupils and leadership opportunities' of the schools may be the key to the variation in student feeling. At the beginning of their course more students opted for 'adult atmosphere' as the most important expected difference between fifth- and sixth-form life than any other. Two years later the colleges' adult atmosphere was also the most important reason students gave for preferring a college, yet 'contact with and responsibility for younger pupils' was not seen as the most important characteristic of the school sixth form by the minority who stated a preference for this type of education.

While schools and colleges therefore may not see their functions as being distinctly different, the contrasting ways in which they set about their educational task can have far-reaching effects on their customers. It appears that the nature of the educational experience offered by colleges is more often attuned to the mood of today's 16—19-year-olds than school sixth forms and particularly those operated along traditional lines.

The establishment of separate colleges for students over the school leaving age seems to have much to recommend it. Not only do students prefer them, but the colleges also appear to be developing expertise, perhaps because of their greater resources, in various areas specifically concerning 16—19, e.g. careers advice and tuition in study skills.

The research also shows that many of the doubts and reservations expressed about the effects of a break at 16 are without foundation. It has been claimed that students, especially those from working-class families with no tradition of extended education, will be deterred from staying on if to do so entails transfer to a college. We could find no evidence to support this. While students whose fathers are in manual occupations are under-represented in post-compulsory education in general, they are not particularly under-represented in the 16—19 colleges. Nor was there any indication that the types of institution catering for 16-plus students in their area are of primary concern to fifth-formers faced with the decision whether or not to further their full-time education. The essential role played by the sixth-former in the running of the school has also been one of the major justifications of the integral sixth form. The evidence presented in Chapter 10 suggests that both pupils and teachers feel that fifth-formers can assume some, if not all, of these responsibilities in an 11—16 school. Indeed, this structure allows all students, not just the proportion who stay on, the opportunity to assume the leadership roles traditionally associated with the sixth form. In general, teachers in schools without sixth forms were more aware of the advantages of the colleges, particularly their ability to offer a wider range of courses and more specialized resources and equipment, than of the resulting disadvantages of the 11—16 schools.

While this would seem to argue for an increase in the number of sixth-form colleges and tertiary colleges, there is clearly much that teachers in all-through schools could do to alleviate some of the dissatisfactions expressed by their sixth-form students. Where possible it would seem sensible to develop a separate sixth-form block within which the sixth form can function more or less independently from the rest of the school. Facilities similar to those found in a Student Union in higher education could be provided, and a more relaxed attitude taken towards individual choice in matters of dress etc. We encountered no compelling reasons for subjecting sixth-formers to the same rules and regulations as those that govern the day-to-day life of the younger pupil.

Perhaps greater efforts should also be made towards establishing a more adult relationship between teacher and sixth-form student, although some students reported that having known, and having been known by, the same teachers for the previous six years made it difficult to develop a new kind of relationship. In general, any measure which would strengthen the identity of sixth-formers as adults is likely to engender a positive response from them.

Should a local authority decide to establish a 16-plus college, it is then drawn into the next stage of the debate, which is whether the college should operate under secondary or further education regulations.

Much of the data presented in this report show that, as far as their students' attitudes are concerned, the sixth-form colleges have been a successful venture. However, the sixth-form college curriculum is limited to those courses which can be offered in secondary establishments, and they are hampered in the extent to which they can provide the full range of courses at 16-plus because of the regulations under which they operate. This gives cause for concern on two counts. First, A-level is not the most suitable target for all students who embark on A-level courses but so many continue to do so because, under secondary regulations, there are no alternatives for the able student. Secondly, as almost all sixth-form colleges now operate an open-access policy they are having to cater for an ever-growing number of 'new sixth-formers'. Academic courses, particularly O-level, have proved unsuitable for many of these young people. While some sixth-form colleges and schools appreciate this and are searching for an alternative, experimenting with CEE or the City and Guilds Foundation Courses or courses of their own devising, O-level is still widely used as the major component of the curriculum for the non-A-level sixth-former. Whatever efforts the sixth-form colleges make, this system perpetuates the division at 16-plus between academic and vocational work, the former being undertaken by the sixth-form college and the latter by the FE college. There are no doubt some people who would claim that the element of choice of institution is a valuable feature of the system, but this argument would carry more weight if the evidence did not suggest that this choice is, in many instances, circumscribed.

Many fifth-formers are not fully informed about the opportunities in FE, and some schools encourage all their pupils to stay on in the sixth form, regardless of the relevance of the courses offered to students' aptitudes and vocational interests. In such circumstances only the very determined transfer to FE, either because of a high degree of vocational commitment or a high degree of dissatisfaction with school. A more satisfactory arrangement for dealing with a range of institutions catering for 16-plus students is operated by a number of local authorities, who produce booklets which outline the courses available in each one. These are then distributed to all fifth-formers, who make a choice among the alternatives presented and go through a formal application procedure.

However, with the increasing diversity of students remaining in full-time education, such a simple dichotomy of academic versus vocational loses credibility. Students can no longer be so easily categorized. Education must reflect the changing needs of society, and we can no longer afford a situation where a large sector of post-secondary education continues to be dominated by university matriculation requirements.

While the sixth-form colleges have shown that a break at 16 can work successfully, it is the tertiary colleges which point the way to a future where the two sectors are fused together and post-compulsory education is seen as a cohesive whole. This does not represent an FE takeover, as some critics of the tertiary system would seem to suggest, but a synthesis of the best of both systems incorporating the further education sector's flexibility, responsiveness to industry, technical and vocational experience and the secondary sector's expertise in academic teaching and emphasis on pastoral care.

References

1. SCHOOLS COUNCIL (1970). *Sixth Form Pupils and Teachers*. Schools Council Sixth Form Survey, 1.
2. DEAN, J. and CHOPPIN, B. (1977). *Educational Provision 16—19*. Slough: NFER.
3. KING, R. (1976). *School and College: Studies of Post-sixteen Education*. London: Routledge & Kegan Paul.
4. CLEEVE, D. (1976). 'Sixth form centre', *Contact*, 5, 3 (ILEA).
5. NAS/UWT (1977). *Educational Provision for Pupils aged Sixteen to Eighteen Plus*. See paragraph 7 — 'The consortium solution to sixth form provision'.
6. WILCOCK, R. (1977). 'Co-operation or separation', *TES*, 4th November.
7. DEPARTMENT OF EDUCATION AND SCIENCE (1963). *Higher Education* (The Robbins Report). London: HMSO.
8. SCHOOLS COUNCIL (1970). *16—19: Growth and Response. 1. Curricular Bases*. Schools Council Working Paper 45. London: Evans/Methuen Educational.
9. VINCENT, D. and DEAN, J. (1977). *One-Year Courses in Colleges and Sixth Forms*. Slough: NFER.
10. ORR, L. and DEAN, J. (1975). 'Alternatives to the traditional sixth form: a preliminary report', *Educ. Res.*, 17, 3.
11. HEADMASTERS' ASSOCIATION (1974). *Compendium of Sixth Form and Tertiary Colleges*. London: HMA. See also: STANDING CONFERENCE OF PRINCIPALS OF SIXTH FORM AND TERTIARY COLLEGES (1978). *Compendium of Sixth Form and Tertiary Colleges*. Huddersfield: Greenhead College.
12. TIMES EDUCATIONAL SUPPLEMENT (1977). 'Which way for the sixth former?', *TES*, 15th July, pp. 8—9.
13. EDUCATION (1977). 'How many pupils make a viable sixth form?', *Education*, 2nd December.
14. See BENN, C. (1971). 'School style and staying on', *New Society*, 24th June.

15. EGGLESTON, S.J. (1967). 'Some environme... correlates of ...tended secondary education in England', *Comparative Ed...* ι, 3, 2.
16. KING, R.A. (1974). 'Short-course neighbourhood comprehensive schools — an LEA case study', *Educ. Rev.*, 26, 2. See also: KING, R.A. (1974). 'Social class, educational attainment and provision — an LEA case study', *Policy and Politics*, 3.
17. DEPARTMENT OF EDUCATION AND SCIENCE (1976). '16 and 18 year olds: attitudes to education', *Reports on Education*, 86.
18. WATSON, J. (1973). *Liberal Studies in Further Education: an informal Survey*. Slough: NFER.
19. ORR, L. (1974). *A Year Between School and University*. Slough: NFER.
20. OECD (1977). *Entry of Young People into Working Life*. Paris: OECD.
21. DEAN, J. (1978). *16—19: Study Problems*. Research in Progress series, 2. Slough: NFER.
22. BENN, C. (1971). 'Short course comprehensives', *Comprehensive Education*, 18.
23. BENN, C. and SIMON, B. (1970). *Half Way There*. Maidenhead: McGraw-Hill.
24. TAYLOR, E. (1965). 'Some thoughts on the sixth-form college idea', *Conference*, 2.
25. NATIONAL UNION OF TEACHERS (1966). *Secondary Reorganisation: Sixth Form Colleges*. London: NUT.
26. HEADMASTERS' ASSOCIATION (1968). *The Sixth Form of the Future*. London: HMA.
27. EDMONDS, J.V. (1972). In: DAVID, T. (Ed) *The Sixth Form College in Practice*. London: Councils and Education Press.
28. MURPHY, J. (1972). 'The sixth form in a comprehensive school', *Secondary Education*, 3, 1.
29. CENTRAL ADVISORY COUNCIL FOR EDUCATION (1959). *15 to 18* (The Crowther Report). London: HMSO.
30. STEPHENS, W.E.D. (1969). 'The case against tertiaries', *Education*, 134, 8.